# Old House
# Measured and Scaled Detail Drawings
# for Builders and Carpenters

## An Early Twentieth-Century Pictorial Sourcebook
with 183 Detailed Plates

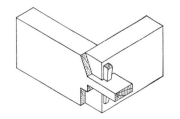

### William A. Radford

with a New Introduction by
John J. Mojonnier, Jr.

## Dover Publications, Inc., New York

Published in Canada by General Publishing Company, Ltd.,
30 Lesmill Road, Don Mills, Toronto, Ontario.
Published in the United Kingdom by Constable and Company,
Ltd., 10 Orange Street, London WC2H 7EG.

This Dover edition, first published in 1983, is an unabridged
and unaltered republication of the work originally published by
The Radford Architectural Company, Chicago, Ill., in 1911, under
the title *Radford's Portfolio of Details of Building Construction*.
A new Introduction has been written especially for the Dover
edition by John J. Mojonnier, Jr.

Manufactured in the United States of America
Dover Publications, Inc., 180 Varick Street, New York, N.Y.
10014

**Library of Congress Cataloging in Publication Data**

Radford, William A., 1865–
  Old house measured and scaled detail drawings for builders
and carpenters.

  Reprint. Originally published: Radford's portfolio of detail of
building construction : Chicago : Radford Architectural Co., 1911.
    1. Building—Details—Drawings.  I. Title.
TH2031.R3  1983    690'.8              82-17712
ISBN 0-486-24438-5

# INTRODUCTION TO THE DOVER EDITION

Written in Chicago when Frank Lloyd Wright and his Prairie School contemporaries were perfecting America's first modern architecture, Radford's *Details of Building Construction* was prepared to acquaint small-town carpenters and architects with details of the new Rectilinear style, known variously as Prairie, Craftsman, Mission or Arts and Crafts.

In the Preface, editor William C. Radford quotes a letter received by his firm:

> We carpenters in small country towns usually have to be the architect, contractor, foreman, and carpenter, all rolled up into one. We are the "whole cheese;" but when we wish to do something extra nice or up-to-date, we find ourselves up against it. My greatest trouble is with inside finish, generally. Can you refer me to some book giving inside details?

Drawing upon the wealth of architectural information available in Chicago, Radford prepared such a book, including every conceivable architectural feature in the form of measured or scaled drawings. Various sections dealt with such characteristic period features as beamed ceilings, wainscoting, window seats, fireplaces, inglenooks, sideboards, stair railings, furniture and a full range of other details. Also included were details from Colonial Revival architecture and many utilitarian designs for commercial and agricultural buildings.

At the time of publication in 1911, the Radford Architectural Company advertised itself as the "Largest Architectural Establishment in the World." The firm was founded and run by William C. Radford, who was born in 1865 in Oshkosh, Wisconsin, one of eight children of William and Elizabeth Radford. Educated in the Oshkosh public-school system, he went on to join Radford Brothers, a family lumber business specializing in millwork. During Radford's youth, Oshkosh was a center of millwork production in the Midwest, and there can be little doubt that he was exposed to all aspects of interior finish and construction.

In 1890 Radford married Helen Manuel of Wichita, Kansas, and became Secretary-Treasurer of the Radford Sash and Door Company. Sometime between 1890 and 1899 he moved to the Chicago area, and settled in Riverside, a picturesque suburb in a parklike setting planned by Calvert Vaux and Frederick Law Olmsted, located several miles from Wright's Oak Park. Active in local affairs, he served as a Riverside village trustee in 1900 and village president in 1901–02.

In 1902 he founded the Radford Architectural Company, establishing himself as president and treasurer. With offices in Riverside, Chicago and

LEFT: William C. Radford (1865–1943). BELOW: Interior, The Radford Architectural Company, Chicago, ca. 1909.

Seven-room house of cement stucco construction
from *Radford's Cement Houses and How to Build Them.*

Brick veneer and stucco residence
from *Radford's Mechanical Drawing.*

New York, he published one of his first plan books, *The Radford American Homes—100 House Plans,* in 1903 with the assistance of two architect-draftsmen, C. W. Ashby and W. H. Schroeder. Most designs were Rectilinear versions of the popular Queen Anne style, and were competent, though not outstanding, examples.

In the midst of an expanding America, Radford foresaw the need for inexpensive, accurate, systematic and standardized plans and books for builders. From 1902 to 1926 his firm of "licensed architects of the highest professional standing, assisted by a staff of expert draftsmen" produced complete plans and specifications for more than 1000 different kinds of buildings, and published more than 40 technical books and three monthly trade journals.

Although the primary activity of the firm was the preparation and sale of standardized plans and specifications, equal emphasis was given to the publication of technical books. Between 1903 and 1908, efforts were devoted to publishing two multivolume compendia, *Radford's Cyclopedia of Construction* (12 volumes) and *Radford's Cyclopedia of Cement Construction* (five volumes), as well as the journal *American Carpenter and Builder.*

Between 1908 and 1921, the firm concentrated on publications devoted to specific topics of interest to the building trades and smaller architectural offices. Titles included *Practical Plans for Barns* (1908), *Artistic Bungalows* (1908), *Portfolio of Plans* (1909), *Cement Houses* (1909), *Framing* (1909), *Stores and Flat Buildings* (1909), *Garages* (1910), *Cement and How to Use It* (1910), *Details of Building Construction* (1911), *Mechanical Drawing* (1912), *Architectural Drawing* (1912), *Estimating and Contracting* (1913), *Our Farm and Building Book* (1914) and *Architectural Details for Every Type of Building* (1921).

In 1926 Radford retired and moved to his Seven Springs Ranch in Cupertino, California, where he died in 1943.

The firm's work contributed significantly to the journeyman architect and building-trade literature of the period, and could be considered a forerunner to such publications as Ramsey and Sleeper's *Architectural Graphic Standards,* found in every architect's office today.

Of special interest to students and scholars of the Prairie School is the correlation between the output of the Radford Architectural Company at its height (1908–14) and the flowering of Prairie School architecture in the Midwest and elsewhere.

Although Radford's designs for exterior facades and interior planning lack the sophistication of Wright and his contemporaries, we find in *Details of Building Construction* a very keen understanding of Prairie School interior detailing and treatment. This kind of detailing created much of the sense of interior spaciousness that became the hallmark of the Prairie period. It was advocated and used not only by Wright in the Midwest, but by Gustav Stickley in the East and the Greene brothers in the West as an essential part of the new American architecture. Radford's emphasis exemplified the degree of broad appeal the style had achieved by 1911.

Commenting on the relationship between wall treatment and the character of a house, Gustav Stickley wrote in his book *Craftsman Homes:*

Two-flat building
from *Radford's Mechanical Drawing.*

Six-room cement stucco residence
from *Radford's Architectural Drawing.*

Brick-and-stone bank building
from *Radford's Portfolio of Plans.*

Residence of seven rooms
from *Radford's Architectural Drawing.*

Five-room bungalow
from *Radford's Cement Houses and How to Build Them.*

Cement garage with man's room and service pit
from *Radford's Portfolio of Plans.*

Nine-room house with fireplace inglenook
from *Radford's Portfolio of Plans.*

A Christian Science church, seating capacity 200,
from *Radford's Portfolio of Plans.*

When the walls are rightly treated, it is amazing how little furniture and how few ornaments and pictures are required to make a room seem comfortable and home-like. The treatment of wall spaces in itself may seem but a detail, yet it is the keynote not only of the whole character of the house, but of the people who live in it.

In this volume, Radford provided excellent examples for living rooms and libraries (plates 7–9), dining rooms (plates 11–15, 96–98 and 115), bedrooms (plate 18), numerous built-ins (including plates 96, 99–101, 107–121 and 153), gates and fences (plate 37) and Mission furniture (plates 136–146).

In view of the fact that the Prairie School era was short-lived (1900–16), and period documentation was limited, it is hoped that this republication of Radford's *Details of Building Construction* will provide architects, homeowners, craftspeople, students and those interested in restoration with authentic information from an original and creative period of American architecture.

JOHN J. MOJONNIER, JR.
*Chairman*
Oak Park Landmarks Commission
Oak Park, Illinois

# Old House
## Measured and Scaled Detail Drawings
## for Builders and Carpenters

# TABLE OF CONTENTS

# PREFACE

RADFORD'S PORTFOLIO OF DETAILS OF BUILDING CONSTRUCTION is offered with the expectation and hope that it will be of great practical utility to carpenters, builders, mill-workers, and architects. The aim has been to make it a complete manual of modern building practice as applied to carpentry construction and the use of mill-work, all points being made clear and understandable by means of the working drawing—the language of the blue print and the universal language of the building trades.

The Portfolio is a collection of full-page plates, accurately drawn by skilled draftsmen and reproduced to exact scale, showing clearly the details of modern building construction and finish. Brief explanatory text accompanies each plate, calling attention to some of the points illustrated. The drawings themselves, however, are of first importance and should be carefully studied. More helpful ideas and exact information is contained in a single one of these plates of details than could be crowded into a whole chapter of ordinary descriptive text.

Details are given showing the framing and construction of residences of every type—frame houses, brick houses, brick veneer houses, stucco or cement plaster houses, concrete block houses, etc. Also every popular and attractive style of interior trim is fully detailed. Special ideas are presented for the appropriate interior finish for every room or part of the house. These ideas are worked out complete, the drawings showing both the arrangement of the room and all the interior trim, including built-in features, fully detailed.

This is the day of "built-in" space and labor-saving features in the home. Carpenters and builders are called on continually to plan and build buffets and sideboards for the dining room; kitchen cabinets, cases, and cupboards for the kitchen and pantry; wardrobes and linen closets for the chambers; and window seats, fireplaces with decorative mantels, and built-in bookcases for the living room and library. These drawings have been prepared to show exactly how this kind of work is done. Many practical ideas are embodied in them; and new and attractive designs are presented from which the carpenter, the architect, or the builder can draw for all or any of these.

In every case complete details are presented, all accurately drawn to scale so that the millwork can be gotten out directly from the Portfolio, if need be, without any redrawing.

Many valuable details are also included in this collection, of special interest to the country carpenter and builder. These include barn framing details of all kinds, ice-house and cold storage construction, silo building, etc. There are also numerous suggestions and helps for doing the many pieces of work that the carpenter and the "handy man about the house" are called upon to do. Working details, drawn to scale, completely solve practically every building problem imaginable.

The practical utility of detail plates of this kind will probably be best appreciated by those who draw plans or who are called upon to make their own designs for building work. The drawings in this Portfolio, have been prepared to meet especially the needs of such workmen.

The following letter which was received about two years ago by the editor of this work, and which is typical of many similar letters received both before and since that time from practical builders, caused us to set actively about in the preparation of RADFORD'S PORTFOLIO OF DETAILS OF BUILDING CONSTRUCTION, to meet this long-felt want:

"Will you kindly give details of inside finish for window-seat as per enclosed plan?

"We carpenters in small country towns usually have to be the architect, contractor, foreman, and carpenter, all rolled into one. We are the 'whole cheese;' but when we wish to do something extra nice or up-to-date, we find ourselves up against it. My greatest trouble is with inside finish, generally. Can you refer me to some book giving inside details?"

There being no book, so far as we knew, along this line, the present work was undertaken. Its scope has been vastly broadened, however, so as to include not only the interior finish and special built-in features which are so much in demand at the present time, but also general carpentry construction, the timber framing of houses, barns, and miscellaneous buildings, brick and masonry construction, and architectural details of all kinds useful to carpenters and builders in general. Also, in addition to these, a great mass of information and details has been added for the country carpenter and the "handy man about the house." There are working drawings for numerous pieces of handcraft furniture of a kind that everyone likes to build in his home shop.

Especial attention is called to the Index of RADFORD'S PORTFOLIO OF DETAILS. This index has been made very complete, all the various features detailed on any of the plates being listed and cross-indexed so that they may be very quickly found, without the necessity of searching through the entire work. Since all the plates are completely indexed for ready reference, their full value is available for use by the busy man.

# PART I. DETAILS OF CONSTRUCTION AND FINISH

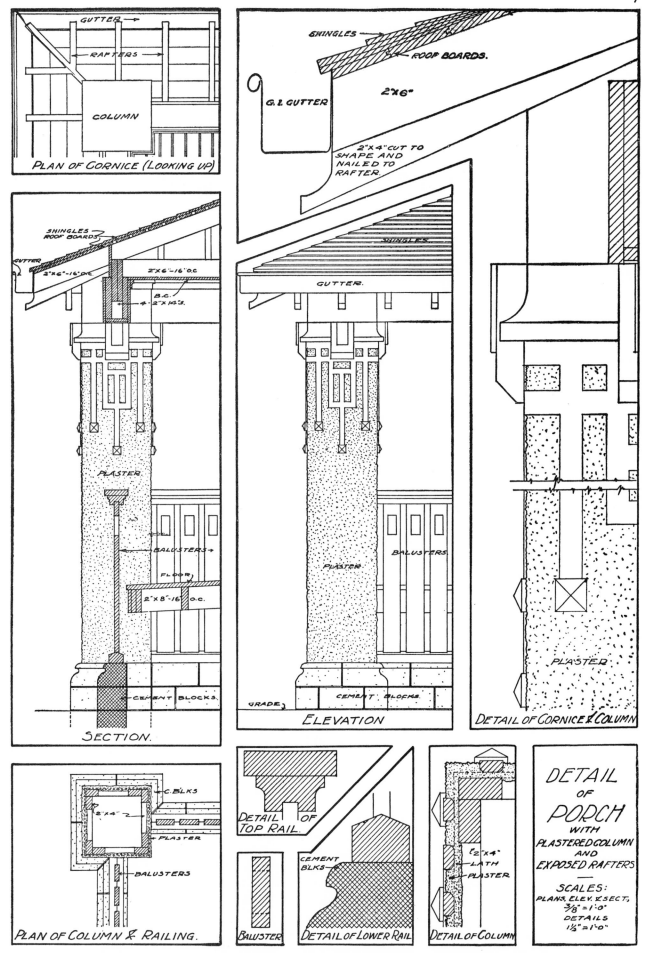

**PLATE 1—PORCH WITH PLASTER COLUMNS, MODERN STYLE**

Popular decorative details and approved construction for use with cement stucco houses. The columns are built up with two-by-fours and the ornamental bands are nailed to the lath before any plastering is done. Attention is called to the method of constructing the porch railing which extends down to the block course in front of the edge of the porch floor; thus serving the purpose of both rail and lattice. The roof is the ordinary exposed rafter style with the addition of a shaped piece nailed to the bottom of each rafter to give extra depth.

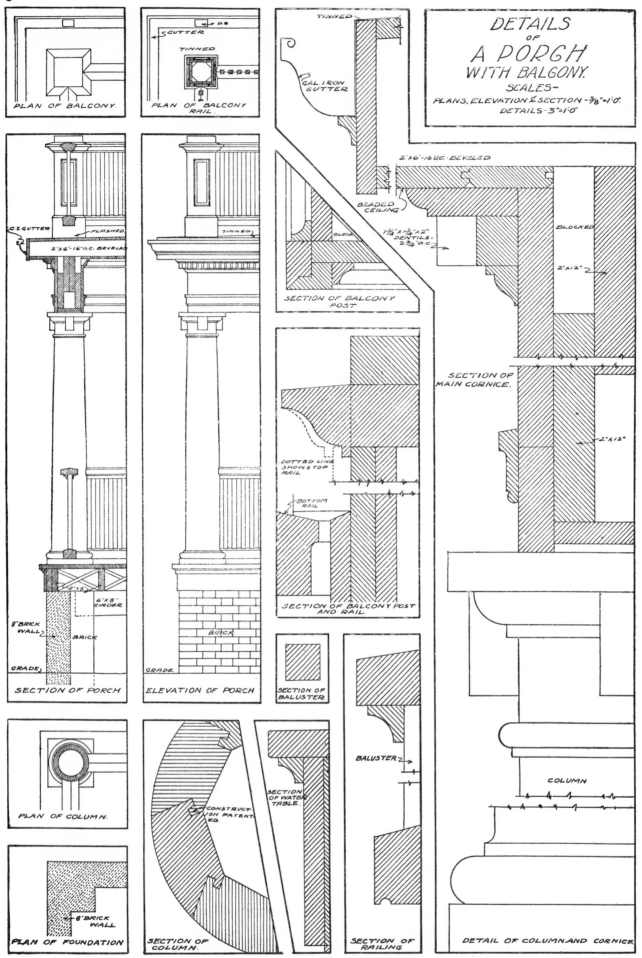

PLAN OF BALCONY.

PLAN OF BALCONY RAIL.

TINNED

GAL. IRON GUTTER

DETAILS
OF
A PORCH
WITH BALGONY.
SCALES—
PLANS, ELEVATION & SECTION - ⅜"=1'0".
DETAILS - 3"=1'0"

2"×6"-16'0.C.-BEVELED

BEADED CEILING

BLOCK

1¾"×1½"×2" DENTILS - 2¾" O.C.

BLOCKED

SECTION OF BALCONY POST

2"×12"

C.I. GUTTER          FLASHED
2"×6"-16"O.C. BEVELED

TINNED

SECTION OF MAIN CORNICE.

2"×12"

DOTTED LINE SHOWS TOP RAIL

BOTTOM RAIL

SECTION OF BALCONY POST AND RAIL.

2"×8"
6"×8" GIRDER.
8" BRICK WALL
BRICK
GRADE

BRICK
GRADE

SECTION OF PORCH

ELEVATION OF PORCH

SECTION OF BALUSTER

BALUSTER

COLUMN

PLAN OF COLUMN.

CONSTRUCTION PATENTED

SECTION OF WATER TABLE.

8" BRICK WALL

PLAN OF FOUNDATION

SECTION OF COLUMN.

SECTION OF RAILING.

DETAIL OF COLUMN AND CORNICE.

## PLATE 2—COLONIAL PORCH WITH BALCONY ABOVE

Complete constructive details for this popular design, appropriate for both new and remodeling work. Such a porch should never be made less than 8 feet in width, and a width of 10 or 12 feet will be found still better. It should be noticed that the soffit of the cornice equals in width the neck of the column and is centered exactly over the column. Attention is called especially to these two points as they are frequently disregarded with disastrous results architecturally.

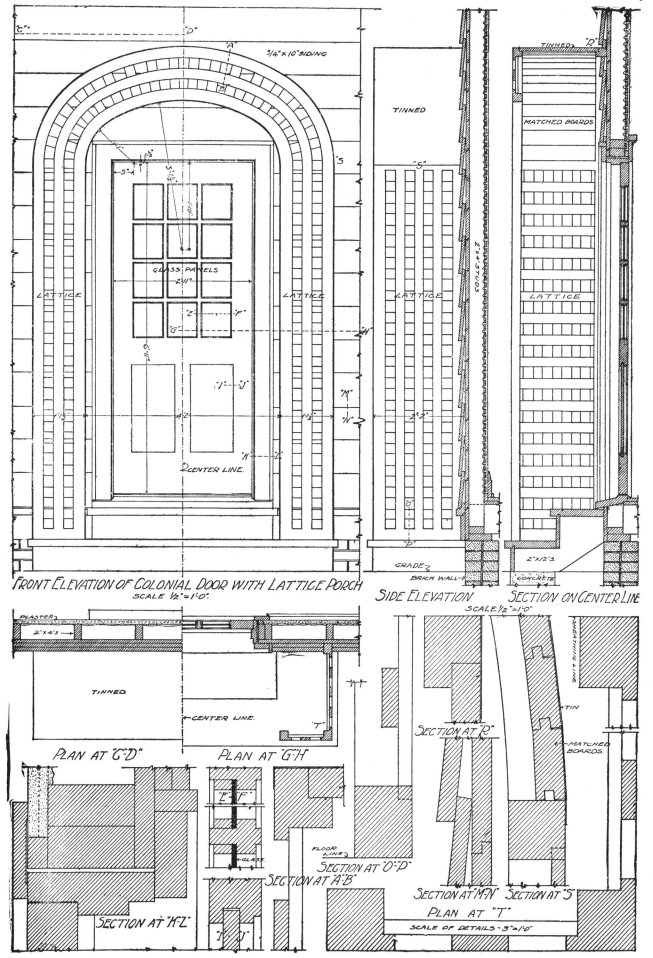

FRONT ELEVATION OF COLONIAL DOOR WITH LATTICE PORCH
SCALE ½"=1'0"

SIDE ELEVATION

SECTION ON CENTER LINE
SCALE ½"=1'0"

PLAN AT "C-D"

PLAN AT "G-H"

SECTION AT "R"

SECTION AT "O-P"

SECTION AT "A-B"

SECTION AT "K-L"

SECTION AT "M-N"  SECTION AT "S"

PLAN AT "T"

SCALE OF DETAILS - 3"=1'0"

## PLATE 3—DETAILS OF COLONIAL DOOR WITH LATTICE HOOD

The lattice hood is an attractive feature for the side entrance of Colonial frame houses. Such a porch when painted green, resting against the white body of the house, is unusually picturesque.

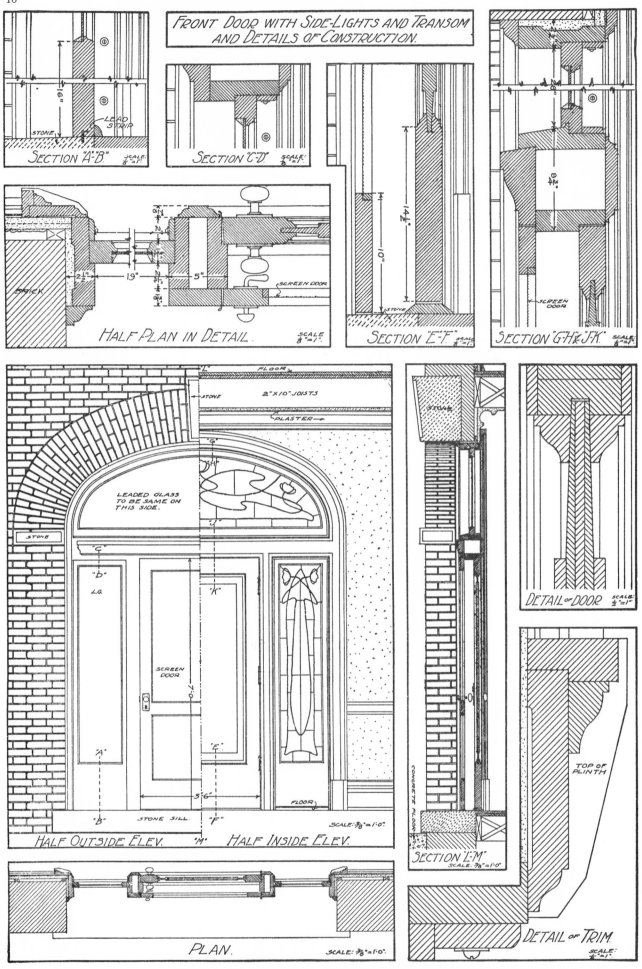

FRONT DOOR WITH SIDE-LIGHTS AND TRANSOM AND DETAILS OF CONSTRUCTION.

SECTION "A"-"B"    SCALE: 3/8"=1"

SECTION "C"-"D"    SCALE: 3/8"=1"

SECTION "E"-"F"    SCALE: 3/8"=1"

SECTION "G-H" & "J-K"    SCALE: 3/8"=1"

HALF PLAN IN DETAIL    SCALE: 3/8"=1"

LEADED GLASS TO BE SAME ON THIS SIDE.

HALF OUTSIDE ELEV.    HALF INSIDE ELEV.    SCALE: 5/8"=1'-0"

PLAN.    SCALE: 3/8"=1'-0".

DETAIL OF DOOR    SCALE: 3/8"=1"

SECTION "L-M"    SCALE: 3/8"=1'-0"

DETAIL OF TRIM    SCALE: 3/8"=1"

## PLATE 4—ELABORATE ENTRANCE DOOR IN COLONIAL BRICK HOUSE

The art glass side lights are stationary and the transom is hinged at the bottom and is provided with two chains at the top so as to open without the use of a transom lift. The door itself is shown without glass, although it might well be glazed in a design to match the side lights and transom. This is a broad, dignified entrance suitable for a fine residence of Colonial design.

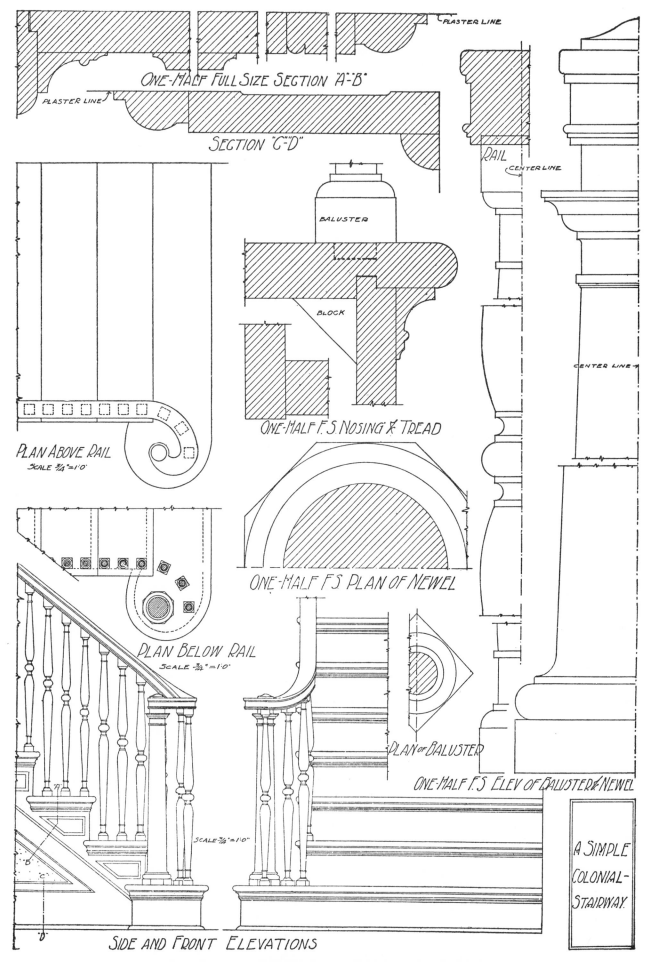

ONE-HALF FULL SIZE SECTION "A"-"B"

PLASTER LINE

SECTION "C"-"D"

PLASTER LINE

RAIL

CENTER LINE

BALUSTER

BLOCK

PLAN ABOVE RAIL
SCALE ¾"=1'0'

ONE-HALF F.S. NOSING & TREAD

CENTER LINE

ONE-HALF FS PLAN OF NEWEL

PLAN BELOW RAIL
SCALE ¾"=1'0"

PLAN OF BALUSTER

ONE-HALF F.S ELEV OF BALUSTER & NEWEL

SCALE ¾"=1'0"

SIDE AND FRONT ELEVATIONS

A SIMPLE COLONIAL STAIRWAY.

## PLATE 5—A SIMPLE COLONIAL STAIRWAY

A design of dignity and attractiveness appropriate for a Colonial house having a central hall. It is suggested that the stair treads and the hand rail and all doors should be finished in mahogany and the balance of the woodwork in white enamel. Details show design and thorough construction.

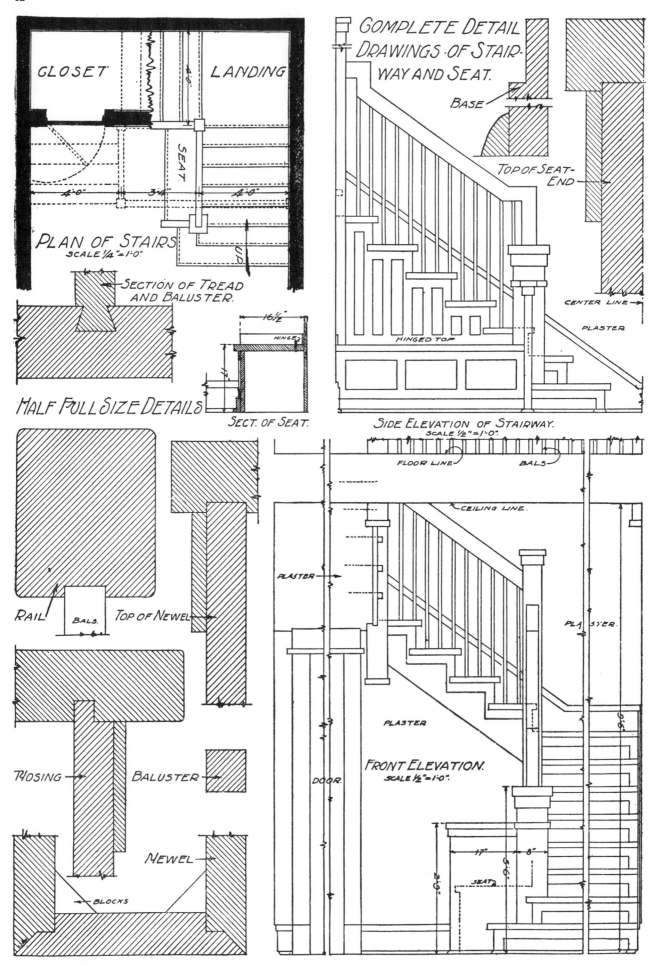

CLOSET　LANDING

SEAT

PLAN OF STAIRS
SCALE 1/4"=1'0".

SECTION OF TREAD
AND BALUSTER.

HALF FULL SIZE DETAILS

16 1/2

HINGE

SECT. OF SEAT.

COMPLETE DETAIL
DRAWINGS OF STAIR-
WAY AND SEAT.

BASE

TOP OF SEAT-
END

CENTER LINE

PLASTER

HINGED TOP

SIDE ELEVATION OF STAIRWAY.
SCALE 1/2"=1'0".

RAIL　BALS.　TOP OF NEWEL

NOSING　BALUSTER

NEWEL

BLOCKS

FLOOR LINE　BALS

CEILING LINE.

PLASTER

PILASTER.

PLASTER

FRONT ELEVATION.
SCALE 1/2"=1'0".

DOOR.

17"　8"

2'-6"

SEAT

## PLATE 6—STAIR HALL IN THE MODERN STRAIGHT-LINE STYLE

Floor plan and complete details for a platform stair with coat closet and built-in seat, designed in the "plain, square" style without mouldings.

A popular finish to be done in oak, stained dark brown. This is an appropriate stairway treatment for small houses.

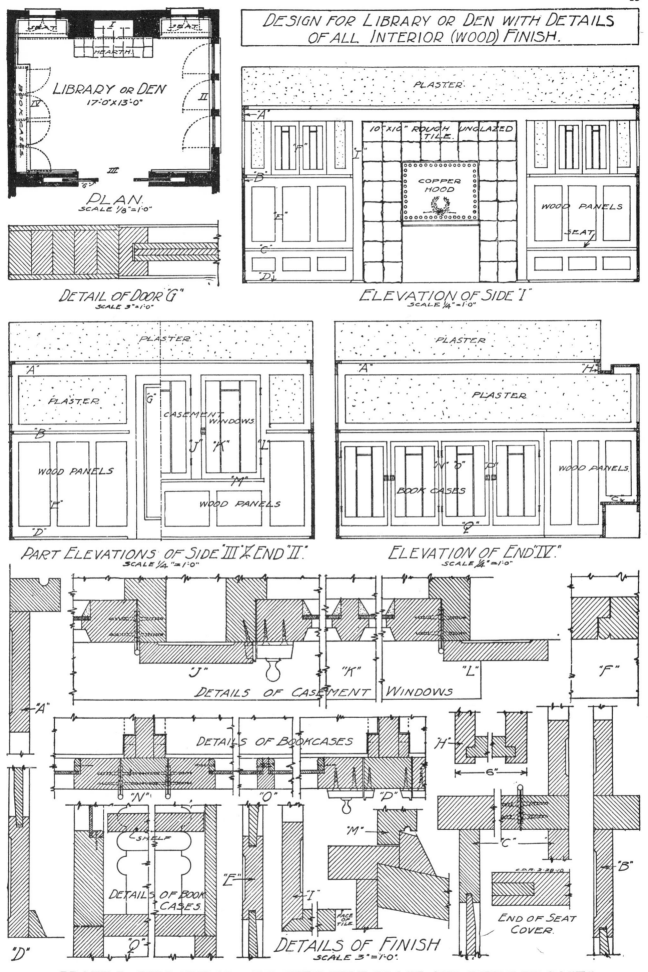

DESIGN FOR LIBRARY OR DEN WITH DETAILS OF ALL INTERIOR (WOOD) FINISH.

LIBRARY OR DEN
17'-0" X 13'-0"

PLAN.
SCALE 1/8"=1'-0"

DETAIL OF DOOR "G"
SCALE 3"=1'-0"

PLASTER

10"X10" ROUGH UNGLAZED TILE.

COPPER HOOD

WOOD PANELS

SEAT

ELEVATION OF SIDE "I"
SCALE 1/4"=1'-0"

PLASTER

PLASTER

WOOD PANELS

CASEMENT WINDOWS

WOOD PANELS

PART ELEVATIONS OF SIDE "III" & END "II".
SCALE 1/4"=1'-0"

PLASTER

PLASTER

BOOK CASES

WOOD PANELS

ELEVATION OF END "IV."
SCALE 1/4"=1'-0"

DETAILS OF CASEMENT WINDOWS

DETAILS OF BOOKCASES

DETAILS OF BOOK CASES

DETAILS OF FINISH
SCALE 3"=1'-0"

END OF SEAT COVER.

## PLATE 7—LIBRARY OR DEN WITH FIRE PLACE AND BUILT-IN CASES

Floor plan showing the arrangement of this room together with details of all interior wood finish, including paneled wainscoting. Designs and details for bookcases with leaded glass doors and for built-in seats. Cozy built-in features of this kind are now much in demand.

14

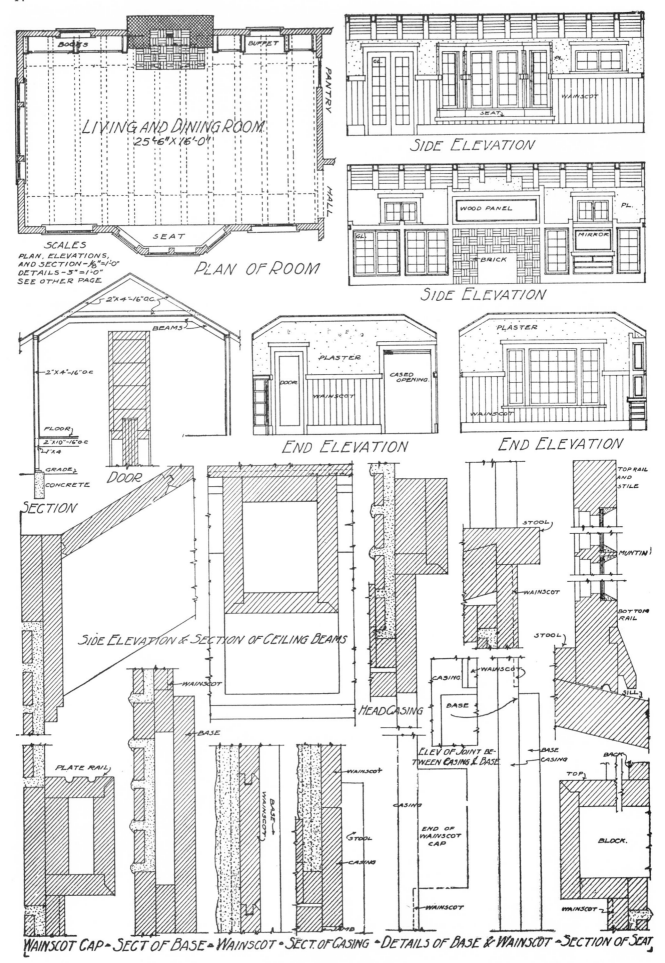

BOOKS

BUFFET

PANTRY

HALL

LIVING AND DINING ROOM
25'-6" X 16'-0"

SEAT

SCALES
PLAN, ELEVATIONS,
AND SECTION—⅛"=1'-0"
DETAILS—3"=1'-0"
SEE OTHER PAGE

PLAN OF ROOM

SIDE ELEVATION

GL.          PL.
SEAT
WAINSCOT

SIDE ELEVATION

WOOD PANEL     PL.
GL.          MIRROR
BRICK

2"X4"—16"O.C.
BEAMS

2"X4"—16"O.C.

FLOOR
2"X10"—16"O.C.
2"X4

GRADE
CONCRETE

DOOR

SECTION

END ELEVATION

PLASTER
DOOR     CASED OPENING
WAINSCOT

END ELEVATION

PLASTER
WAINSCOT

SIDE ELEVATION & SECTION OF CEILING BEAMS

HEAD CASING

WAINSCOT

TOP RAIL AND STILE

STOOL

MUNTIN

WAINSCOT

BOTTOM RAIL

STOOL

SILL

PLATE RAIL

BASE

WAINSCOT
BASE
WAINSCOT

WAINSCOT

STOOL
CASING

CASING     WAINSCOT
BASE

ELEV OF JOINT BE-
TWEEN CASING & BASE

CASING

BASE
CASING

END OF
WAINSCOT
CAP

TOP     BACK

BLOCK.

WAINSCOT

WAINSCOT

WAINSCOT CAP · SECT OF BASE · WAINSCOT · SECT. OF CASING · DETAILS OF BASE & WAINSCOT · SECTION OF SEAT

## PLATE 8—COMBINED LIVING AND DINING ROOM FOR BUNGALOW

Floor plan, elevations and details of interior trim of a large room, lighted on three sides and ornamented with a great amount of woodwork. Note novel beam ceiling arrangement. Details of buffet, mantel and fireplace, and built-in bookcase are shown in Plate 9.

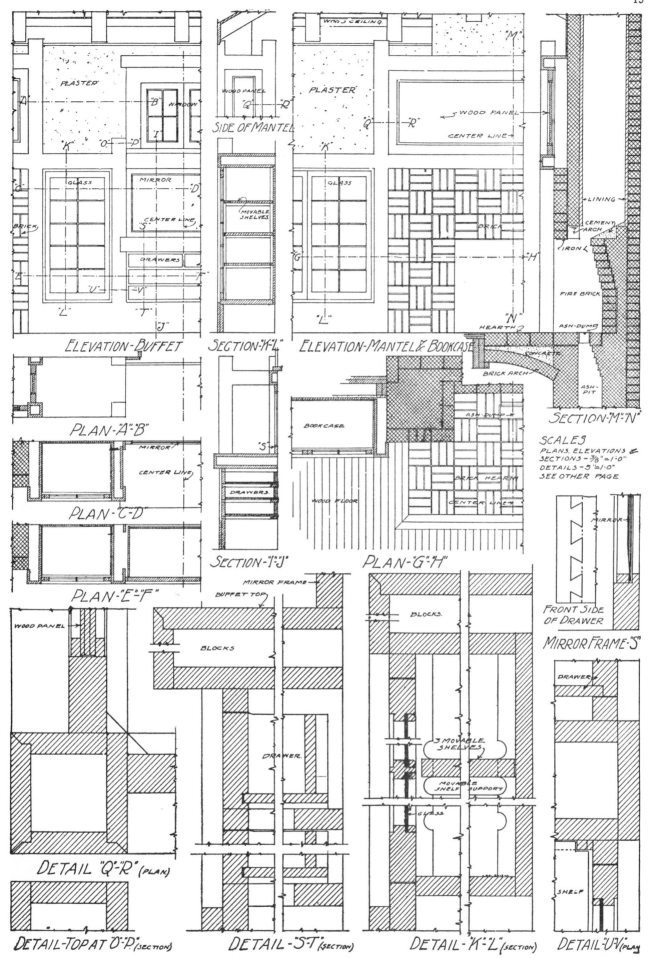

PLASTER

"B" WINDOW

"K"
"O" "P"

GLASS
MIRROR
"D"

CENTER LINE

BRICK
"S"

DRAWERS

"E"
"U" "V" "F"
"L" "T"
"J"

ELEVATION-BUFFET

SIDE OF MANTEL

WOOD PANEL
"Q" "R"

MOVABLE SHELVES

SECTION-"K"-"L"

WOOD CEILING

PLASTER

"M"

WOOD PANEL

CENTER LINE

"Q" "R"

"K"

GLASS

BRICK

"H"

"G"

"L"

HEARTH "N"

ELEVATION-MANTEL & BOOKCASE

LINING

CEMENT ARCH

IRON

FIRE BRICK

ASH-DUMP

SECTION-"M"-"N"

PLAN-"A"-"B"

MIRROR

CENTER LINE

PLAN-"C"-"D"

PLAN-"E"-"F"

SECTION-"I"-"J"

"S"

DRAWERS.

BOOKCASE

ASH-DUMP

BRICK HEARTH

WOOD FLOOR

CENTER LINE

PLAN-"G"-"H"

BRICK ARCH

CONCRETE

ASH-PIT

SCALES
PLANS, ELEVATIONS &
SECTIONS — 3/8" = 1'-0"
DETAILS — 3" = 1'-0"
SEE OTHER PAGE

MIRROR

FRONT SIDE
OF DRAWER

MIRROR FRAME-"S"

WOOD PANEL

DETAIL "Q"-"R" (PLAN)

MIRROR FRAME

BUFFET TOP

BLOCKS

DRAWER.

BLOCKS.

3 MOVABLE SHELVES

MOVABLE SHELF SUPPORT

GLASS

DRAWER

SHELF

DETAIL-TOP AT "O"-"P" (SECTION)

DETAIL-"S"-"T" (SECTION)

DETAIL-"K"-"L" (SECTION)

DETAIL-"U"-"V" (PLAN)

## PLATE 9—COMBINED LIVING AND DINING ROOM FOR BUNGALOW

Details of fireplace with wood mantel; also details of built-in bookcase, and buffet indicated in
the floor plan and side elevation, Plate 8.

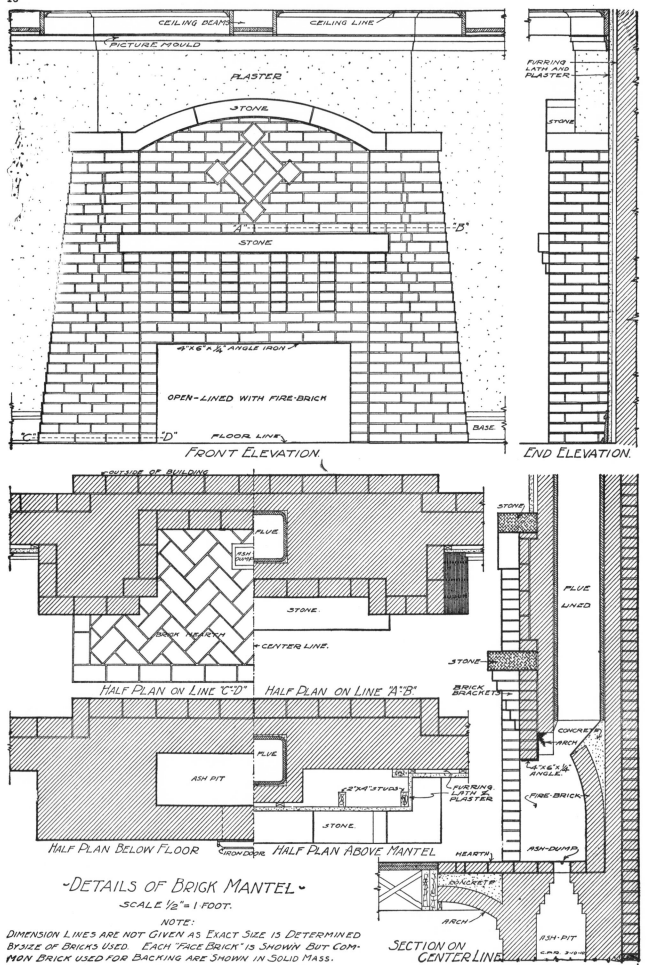

CEILING BEAMS — CEILING LINE
PICTURE MOULD
PLASTER
STONE
"A" — — "B"
STONE
4"x6"x¼" ANGLE IRON
OPEN-LINED WITH FIRE-BRICK
"C" — "D" FLOOR LINE
BASE.

FRONT ELEVATION.

FURRING
LATH AND
PLASTER
STONE

END ELEVATION.

OUTSIDE OF BUILDING
FLUE.
ASH
DUMP
STONE.
BRICK HEARTH
CENTER LINE.
HALF PLAN ON LINE "C"-"D"  HALF PLAN ON LINE "A"-"B".

STONE
STONE
BRICK
BRACKETS

FLUE
ASH PIT
FLUE
2"X4" STUDS
FURRING
LATH &
PLASTER
STONE.

HALF PLAN BELOW FLOOR  IRON DOOR  HALF PLAN ABOVE MANTEL

CONCRETE
ARCH
4"x6"x¼"
ANGLE.
FIRE-BRICK
HEARTH
ASH-DUMP
CONCRETE
ARCH
ASH-PIT
SECTION ON
CENTER LINE

~DETAILS OF BRICK MANTEL~
SCALE ½"=1 FOOT.

NOTE:
DIMENSION LINES ARE NOT GIVEN AS EXACT SIZE IS DETERMINED
BY SIZE OF BRICKS USED.  EACH "FACE BRICK" IS SHOWN BUT COM-
MON BRICK USED FOR BACKING ARE SHOWN IN SOLID MASS.

## PLATE 10—BRICK MANTEL DESIGN AND FIRE PLACE CONSTRUCTION

Rough texture brick varying in color from dark red to purplish and greenish red with white mortar joints. Stone trimmings white. This fireplace is appropriate for a large living room or hall. The construction and arrangement are best to prevent smoking and at the same time to give out the maximum amount of heat into the room. Iron damper to be placed in throat if desired.

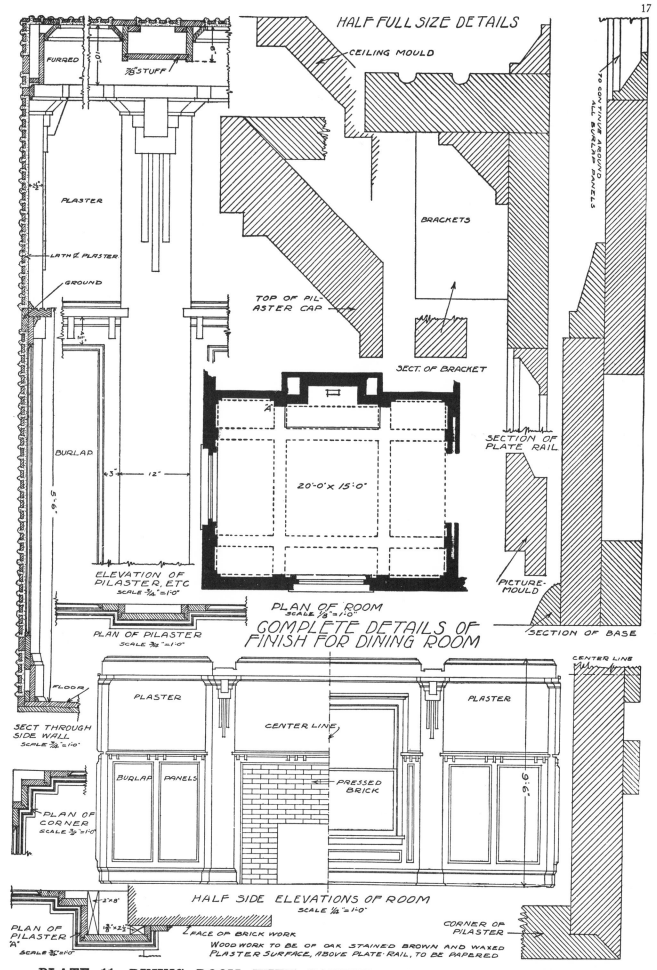

HALF FULL SIZE DETAILS

CEILING MOULD

FURRED

⅞" STUFF

PLASTER

LATH & PLASTER

GROUND

BURLAP

ELEVATION OF
PILASTER, ETC
SCALE ¾"=1'0"

PLAN OF PILASTER
SCALE ¾"=1'0"

SECT THROUGH
SIDE WALL
SCALE ¾"=1'0"

FLOOR

PLAN OF
CORNER
SCALE ¾"=1'0"

PLAN OF
PILASTER
'A'
SCALE ¾"=1'0"

2×8

TOP OF PIL-
ASTER CAP

BRACKETS

SECT. OF BRACKET

PLAN OF ROOM
SCALE ⅛"=1'0"

20'-0" X 15'-0"

COMPLETE DETAILS OF
FINISH FOR DINING ROOM

TO CONTINUE AROUND
ALL BURLAP PANELS

SECTION OF
PLATE RAIL

PICTURE-
MOULD

SECTION OF BASE

CENTER LINE

PLASTER

CENTER LINE

BURLAP PANELS

PRESSED
BRICK

9'-6"

PLASTER

HALF SIDE ELEVATIONS OF ROOM
SCALE ¼"=1'0"

FACE OF BRICK WORK

CORNER OF
PILASTER

WOOD WORK TO BE OF OAK STAINED BROWN AND WAXED
PLASTER SURFACE, ABOVE PLATE-RAIL, TO BE PAPERED

## PLATE 11—DINING ROOM WITH PANELED CEILING AND SIDEWALLS

Floor plan and complete details of a typical modern dining room elaborately finished with beam ceiling, plate rail and paneled wainscot. The ornamental pilasters supporting the ceiling beams make a novel and effective feature. The cornice mould is a modified ceiling beam.

18

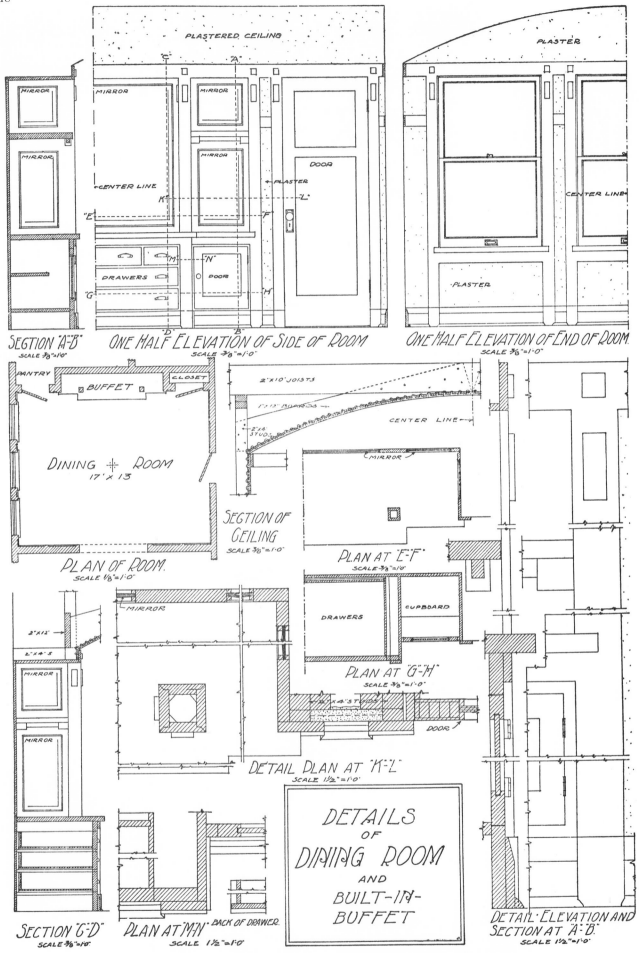

SECTION "A"-"B"
SCALE ⅜"=1'-0"

ONE HALF ELEVATION OF SIDE OF ROOM
SCALE ⅜"=1'-0"

ONE HALF ELEVATION OF END OF ROOM
SCALE ⅜"=1'-0"

PLASTERED CEILING

MIRROR

MIRROR

MIRROR

MIRROR

CENTER LINE

PLASTER

DOOR

DRAWERS

DOOR

PLASTER

CENTER LINE

PLASTER

PANTRY

BUFFET

CLOSET

DINING + ROOM
17' X 13

PLAN OF ROOM.
SCALE ⅛"=1'-0"

2"X10" JOISTS

2"X4" STUD

CENTER LINE

SECTION OF CEILING
SCALE ⅜"=1'-0"

MIRROR

PLAN AT "E"-"F"
SCALE ⅜"=1'-0"

DRAWERS

CUPBOARD

PLAN AT "G"-"H"
SCALE ⅜"=1'-0"

2"X12"

2"X4"S

MIRROR

MIRROR

MIRROR

2"X4" STUDS

DOOR

DETAIL PLAN AT "K"-"L"
SCALE 1½"=1'-0"

SECTION "G"-"D"
SCALE ⅜"=1'-0"

PLAN AT "M"-"N"
SCALE 1½"=1'-0"

BACK OF DRAWER.

DETAILS
OF
DINING ROOM
AND
BUILT-IN-
BUFFET

DETAIL ELEVATION AND
SECTION AT "A"-"B"
SCALE 1½"=1'-0"

**PLATE 12—DINING ROOM WITH ARCHED CEILING**

Floor plan, elevations and complete details of this beautiful dining room having built-in buffet and a continuous head casing, but without plate rail. The arched ceiling is easily and cheaply constructed by nailing 1 by 12 inch boards, sawed to the curve, to the regular joists before the lathing is done. Design and details of construction for beautiful built-in sideboard.

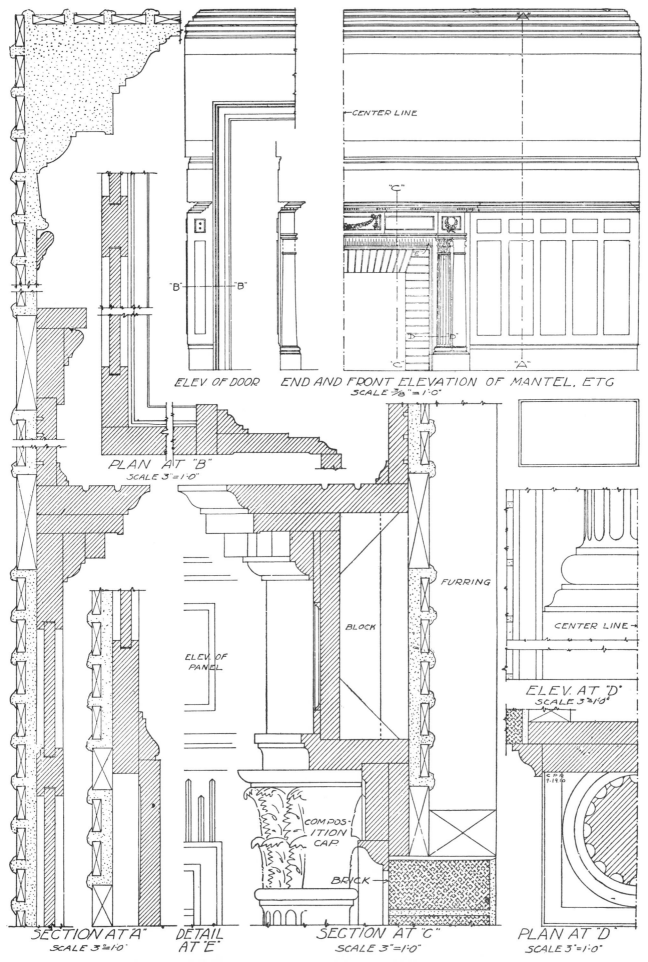

CENTER LINE

"C"

"B" — — "B"

ELEV. OF DOOR       END AND FRONT ELEVATION OF MANTEL, ETC
                              SCALE ⅜"=1'-0"

PLAN AT "B"
SCALE 3"=1'-0"

"E"

"A"

"C"        "C"

FURRING

BLOCK

ELEV. OF
PANEL

CENTER LINE

ELEV. AT "D"
SCALE 3"=1'-0"

COMPOS-
ITION
CAP.

BRICK

SECTION AT "A"        DETAIL        SECTION AT "C"        PLAN AT "D"
  SCALE 3"=1'-0"        AT "E"         SCALE 3"=1'-0"       SCALE 3"=1'-0"

## PLATE 13—DETAILS OF TRIM FOR COLONIAL DINING ROOM

This dining room has a high paneled wainscot, finished in white enamel, with the plate rail placed well below its top line so that the plates will be below the level of the wall decorations. A wood mantel of typical Colonial design adds to the beauty of this room. A beautiful landscape frieze (wall paper) is used effectively between the wainscot and the plaster cove.

20

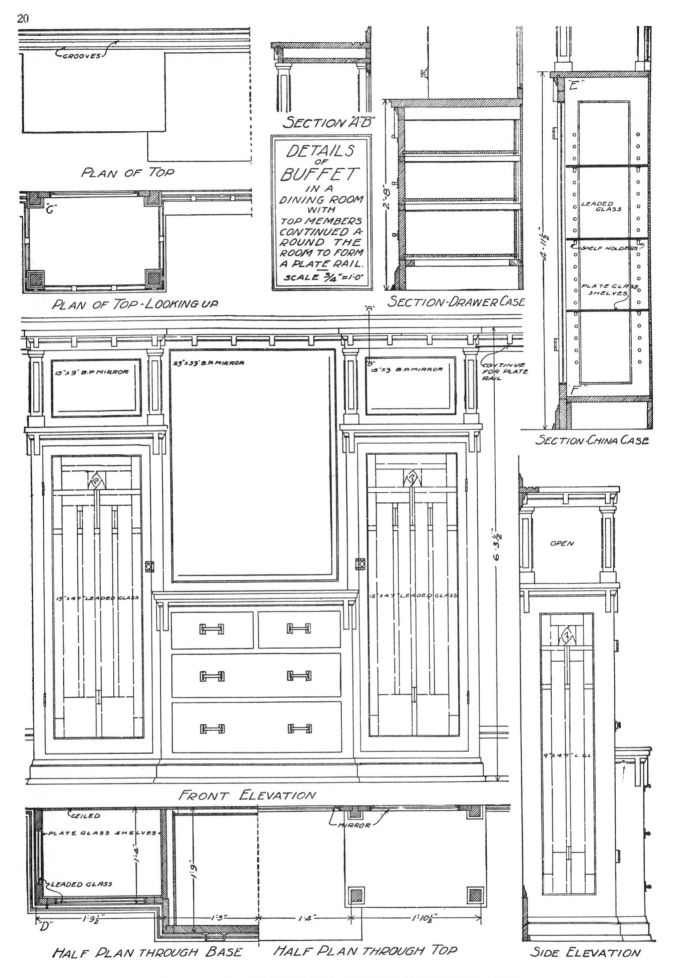

GROOVES

PLAN OF TOP

SECTION "A"-"B"

PLAN OF TOP-LOOKING UP.

DETAILS
OF
BUFFET
IN A
DINING ROOM
WITH
TOP MEMBERS
CONTINUED A-
ROUND THE
ROOM TO FORM
A PLATE RAIL.
SCALE ¾"=1'0"

SECTION-DRAWER CASE

"E"

LEADED GLASS

SHELF HOLDERS

PLATE GLASS SHELVES

SECTION-CHINA CASE

"F"

13"x9" B.P. MIRROR

29"x39" B.P. MIRROR

15"x9" B.P. MIRROR

CONTINUE FOR PLATE RAIL

"A"

"B"

15"x47" LEADED GLASS

15"x47" LEADED GLASS

6'-3½"

OPEN

9"x47" L GL

FRONT ELEVATION

CEILED

PLATE GLASS SHELVES

1'-4"

LEADED GLASS

"D"

1'-9½"

MIRROR

1'-9"

1'-5"

1'-4"

1'-10½"

HALF PLAN THROUGH BASE

HALF PLAN THROUGH TOP

SIDE ELEVATION

## PLATE 14—BEAUTIFUL DINING ROOM BUFFET

A modern design for a dining room buffet, or built-in sideboard, with top member continuing around the room to form the plate rail. The china cases have leaded glass doors and sides. Additional details for this buffet are given in the lower portion of Plate 15.

**PLATE 15B—TWO KITCHEN CABINET DESIGNS**

Arrangement of two convenient cabinets or cases for the kitchen in which all utensils and supplies can be stored away.

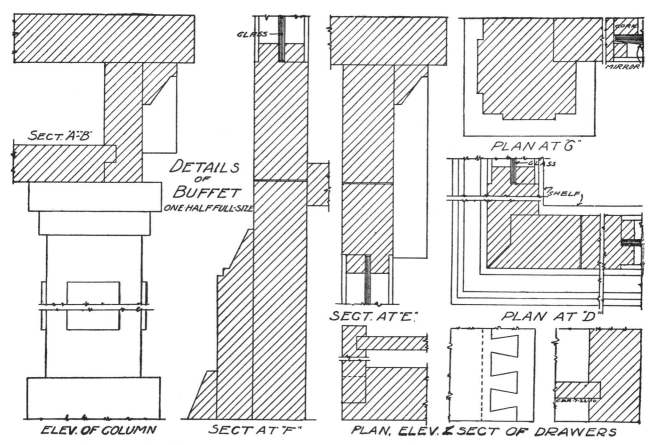

SECT. "A-B"

DETAILS OF BUFFET ONE-HALF FULL-SIZE

GLASS

PLAN AT "G"

GLASS

SHELF

SECT. AT "E"

PLAN AT "D"

ELEV. OF COLUMN

SECT AT "F"

PLAN, ELEV. & SECT OF DRAWERS

**PLATE 15A—DETAILS OF DINING ROOM BUFFET**

Working details, drawn one-half full size, of the beautiful dining room buffet shown in Plate 14.

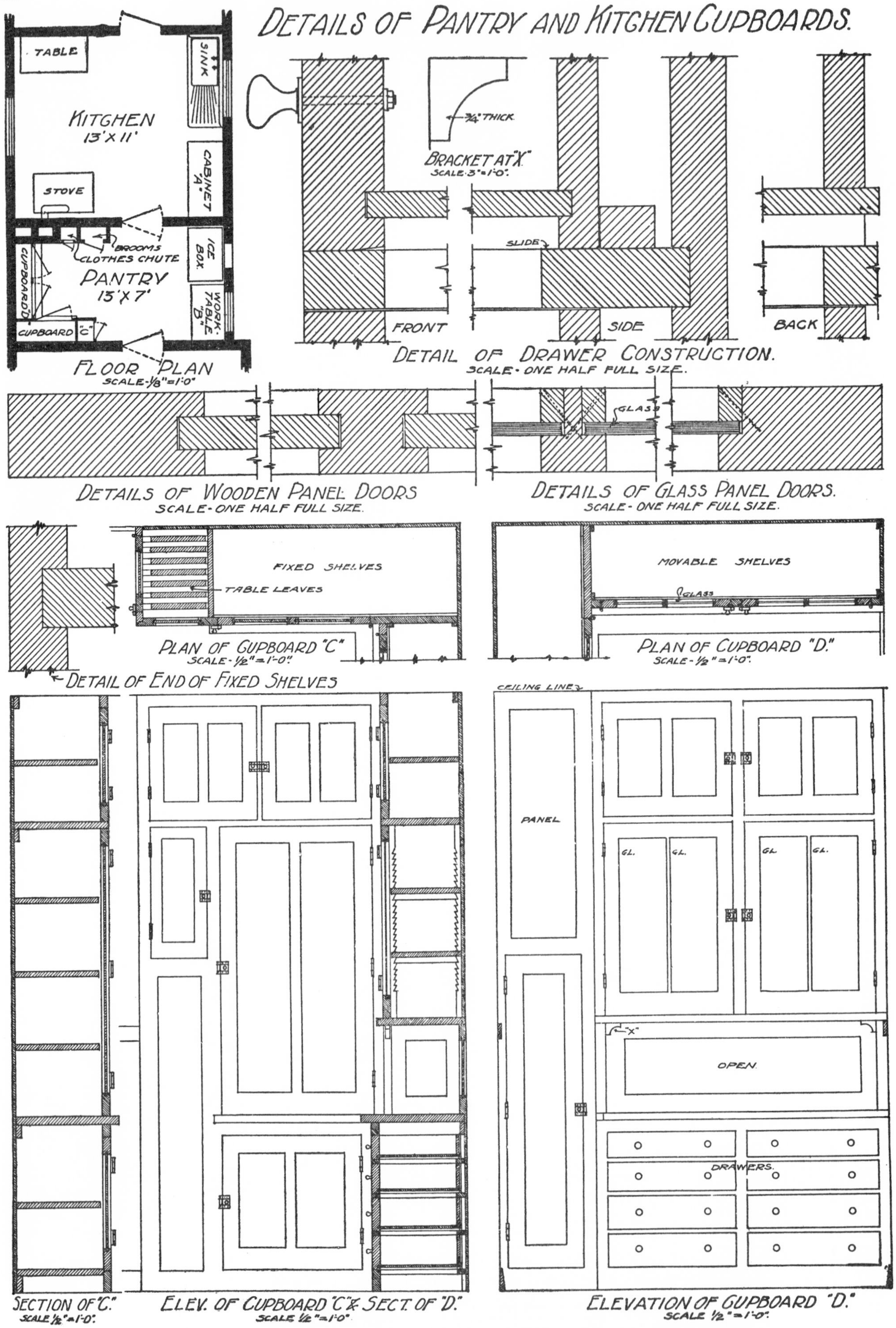

22

DETAILS OF PANTRY AND KITCHEN CUPBOARDS.

KITCHEN
13' X 11'

TABLE

SINK

STOVE

CABINET "A"

ICE BOX

BROOMS
CLOTHES CHUTE

PANTRY
15' X 7'

WORK TABLE "B"

CUPBOARD "C"

FLOOR PLAN
SCALE-1/8"=1'-0"

BRACKET AT "X"
SCALE-3"=1'-0"

3/4" THICK

FRONT

SLIDE

SIDE

BACK

DETAIL OF DRAWER CONSTRUCTION.
SCALE-ONE HALF FULL SIZE.

DETAILS OF WOODEN PANEL DOORS
SCALE-ONE HALF FULL SIZE.

GLASS

DETAILS OF GLASS PANEL DOORS.
SCALE-ONE HALF FULL SIZE.

FIXED SHELVES

TABLE LEAVES

PLAN OF CUPBOARD "C"
SCALE-1/2"=1'-0"

MOVABLE SHELVES

GLASS

PLAN OF CUPBOARD "D."
SCALE-1/2"=1'-0"

DETAIL OF END OF FIXED SHELVES

CEILING LINE

PANEL

GL. GL. GL. GL.

"X"

OPEN.

DRAWERS.

SECTION OF "C."
SCALE 1/2"=1'-0"

ELEV. OF CUPBOARD "C" & SECT. OF "D."
SCALE 1/2"=1'-0"

ELEVATION OF CUPBOARD "D."
SCALE 1/2"=1'-0"

**PLATE 16—KITCHEN AND PANTRY WITH BUILT-IN CASES**

Floor plan showing ideal arrangement, together with details of convenient kitchen and pantry cupboards. Additional details are shown in Plate 17.

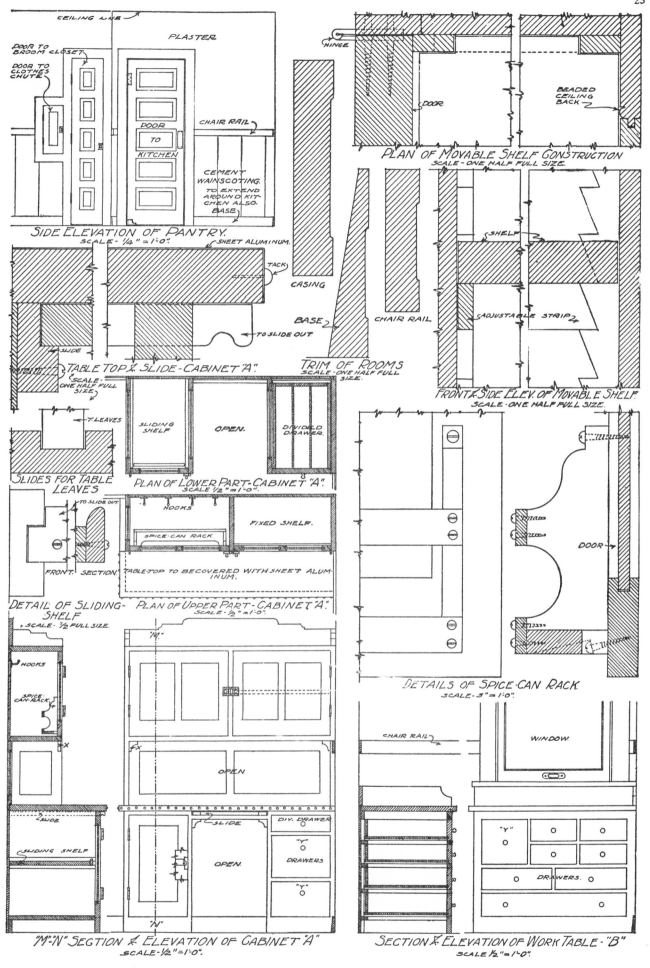

# PLATE 17—KITCHEN AND PANTRY WITH BUILT-IN CASES

Additional details for the kitchen and pantry cupboards indicated in the floor plan, Plate 16. Complete working details to scale are presented in these two plates, covering completely the interior finish of this conveniently arranged housekeeping workshop.

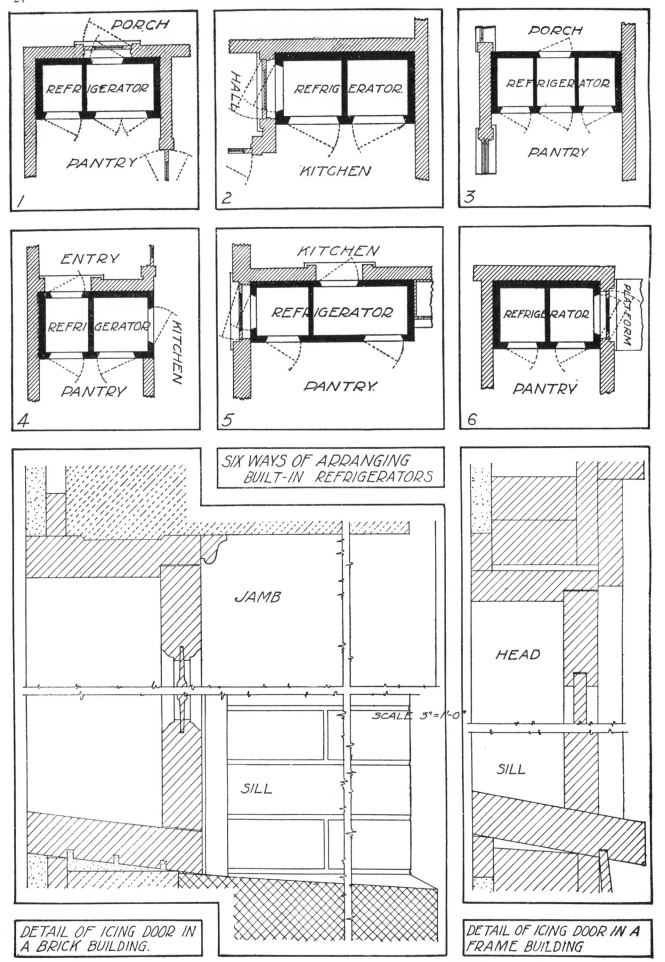

SIX WAYS OF ARRANGING BUILT-IN REFRIGERATORS

DETAIL OF ICING DOOR IN A BRICK BUILDING.

DETAIL OF ICING DOOR IN A FRAME BUILDING

**PLATE 17 A—BUILT-IN REFRIGERATOR FOR KITCHEN OR PANTRY**

Floor plan diagrams showing six different arrangements for built-in refrigerators to be iced from the outside. Working details for the icing door in both brick and frame buildings. This door in the wall of a house should be larger than the icing door in a refrigerator by two inches at the top, two inches at the bottom, three inches at the fastener side and five inches at the hinge side. In case of very thick walls, the opening should be still larger to allow the ice being handled easily.

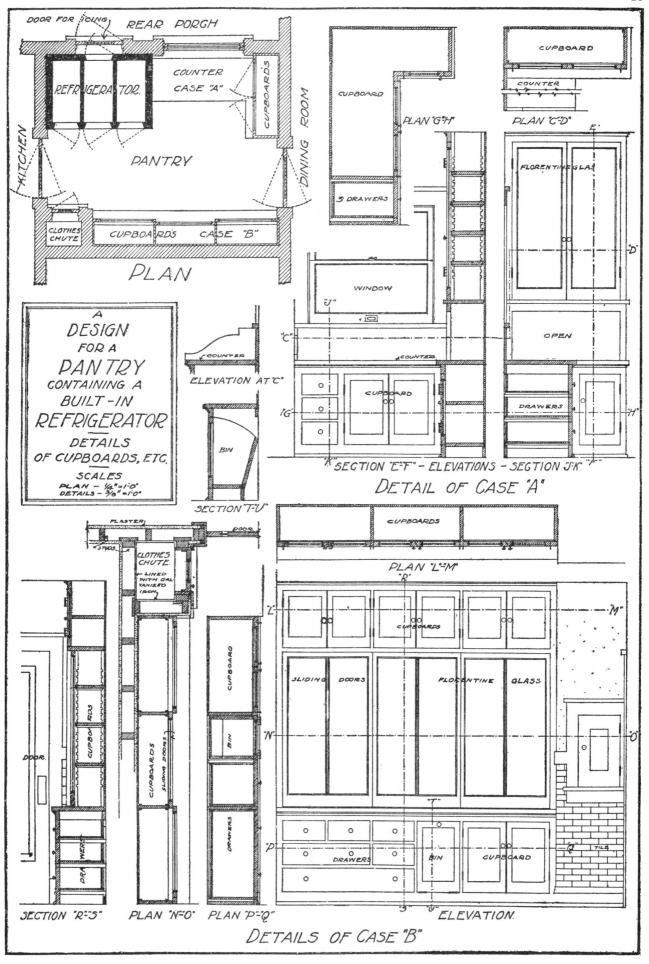

**PLATE 17 B—BUILT-IN REFRIGERATORS FOR KITCHEN OR PANTRY**

Floor plan of pantry showing arrangement of built-in refrigerator to be iced from the outside, also other convenient built-in cases and cupboards for a room of this kind. Refrigerators specially made for purposes of this kind can be had from the manufacturers, it being no economy for the carpenter to attempt to build the refrigerator himself. Refrigerators are shipped "in the white" and should be finished to match the balance of the wood trim.

26

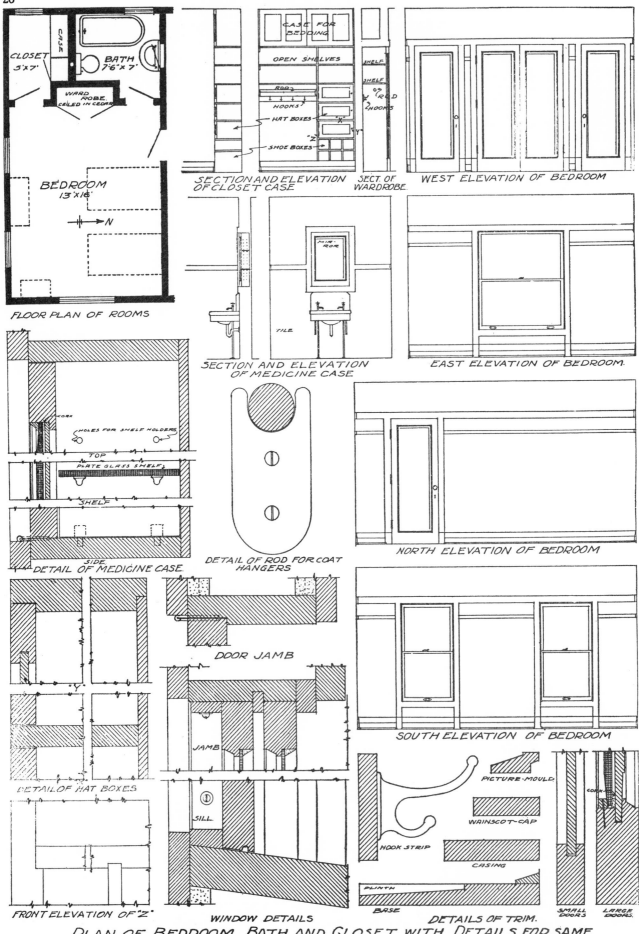

CLOSET 5'X7'

CASE

BATH 7'6"X7'

WARD ROBE CEILED IN CEDAR

BEDROOM 13'X16'

N

FLOOR PLAN OF ROOMS

CASE FOR BEDDING

OPEN SHELVES

ROD

HOOKS

HAT BOXES

SHOE BOXES

SHELF

SHELF

ROD

2 HOOKS

SECTION AND ELEVATION OF CLOSET CASE

SECT. OF WARDROBE.

WEST ELEVATION OF BEDROOM

MIR-ROR

TILE

SECTION AND ELEVATION OF MEDICINE CASE

EAST ELEVATION OF BEDROOM.

CORK

HOLES FOR SHELF HOLDERS

TOP

PLATE GLASS SHELF

SHELF

SIDE

DETAIL OF MEDICINE CASE.

DETAIL OF ROD FOR COAT HANGERS

NORTH ELEVATION OF BEDROOM

"Y"

DETAIL OF HAT BOXES

DOOR JAMB

JAMB

SILL.

FRONT ELEVATION OF "Z"

WINDOW DETAILS

SOUTH ELEVATION OF BEDROOM

PICTURE MOULD

WAINSCOT CAP

HOOK STRIP

CASING

PLINTH

BASE

DETAILS OF TRIM.

CORK

SMALL DOORS

LARGE DOORS.

PLAN OF BEDROOM, BATH AND CLOSET WITH DETAILS FOR SAME

SCALE OF PLANS AND ELEVATIONS = 1/8"=1'-0"

3"=1'-6"=SCALE OF DETAILS.

## PLATE 18—BEDROOM WITH WARDROBE AND CLOTHES CLOSET

Floor plan and complete details of a bedroom with a communicating bathroom and clothes closet elaborately furnished with shelves, built-in boxes and cases. The wardrobe is lined with cedar.

Attention is called to the omission of the ordinary stool and apron from the window sills and the use instead of simply a piece of the side casing. One of the doors should be a full-length mirror.

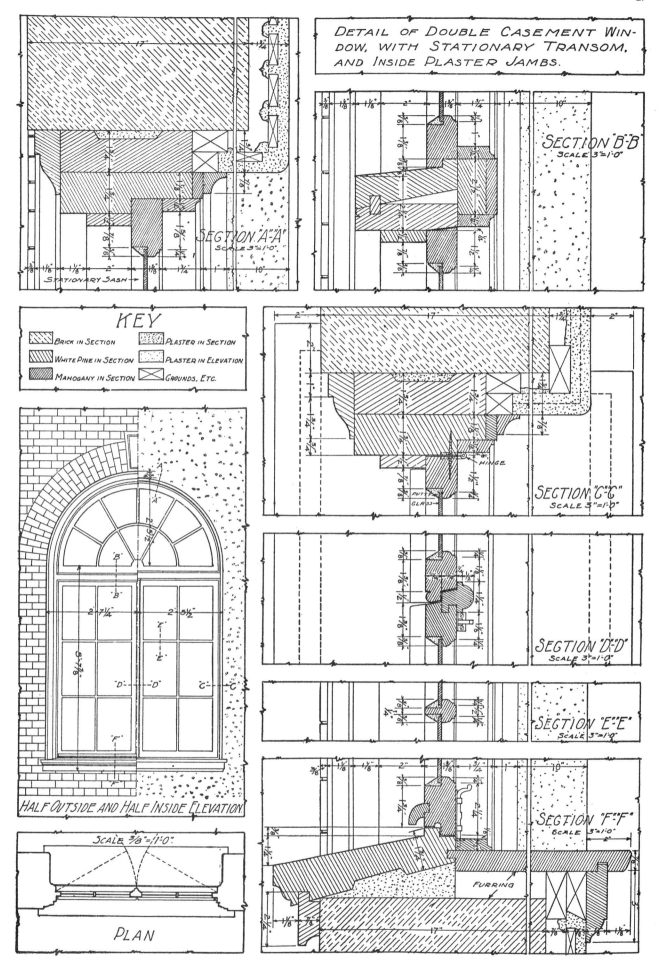

DETAIL OF DOUBLE CASEMENT WINDOW, WITH STATIONARY TRANSOM, AND INSIDE PLASTER JAMBS.

SECTION "A"-"A"
SCALE 3"=1'-0"

STATIONARY SASH

SECTION "B"-"B"
SCALE 3"=1'-0"

KEY

| | | | |
|---|---|---|---|
| ▨ | BRICK IN SECTION | ▦ | PLASTER IN SECTION |
| ▨ | WHITE PINE IN SECTION | ▦ | PLASTER IN ELEVATION |
| ▨ | MAHOGANY IN SECTION | ⊠ | GROUNDS, ETC. |

HALF OUTSIDE AND HALF INSIDE ELEVATION.

PLAN
SCALE 3/8"=1'-0"

SECTION "C"-"C"
SCALE 3"=1'-0"

HINGE
PUTTY
GLASS

SECTION "D"-"D"
SCALE 3"=1'-0"

SECTION "E"-"E"
SCALE 3"=1'-0"

SECTION "F"-"F"
SCALE 3"=1'-0"

FURRING

## PLATE 19—DOUBLE CASEMENT WINDOWS WITH STATIONARY TRANSOM

Inward opening casement windows with inside jambs plastered. A method desirable in public or semi-public buildings, as it eliminates nearly all the inside finish. Windows of this kind may be used equally as well with a square top transom, or with no transom at all.

28

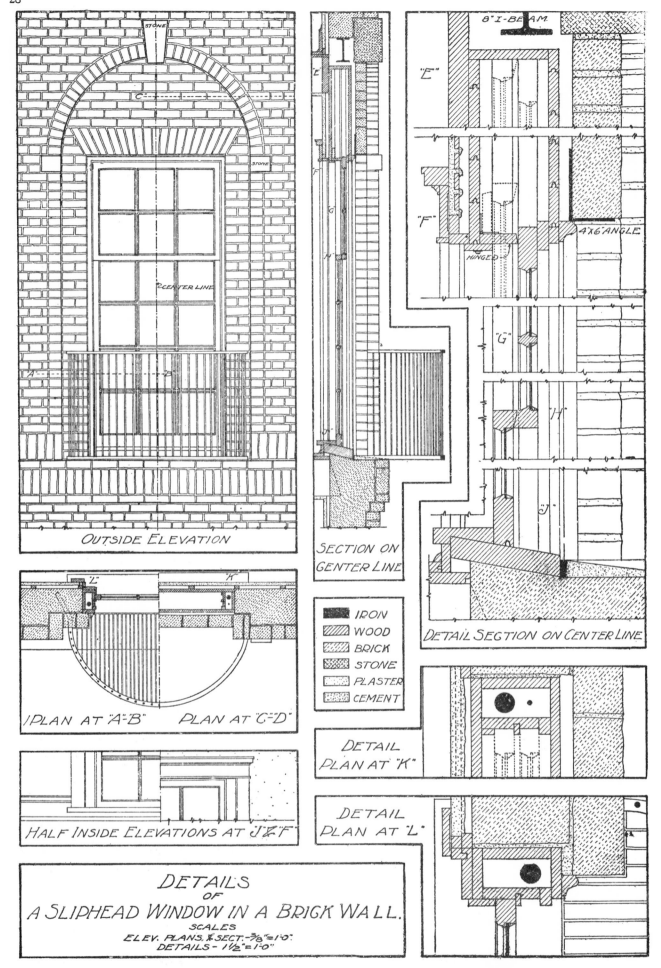

OUTSIDE ELEVATION

SECTION ON CENTER LINE

8" I-BEAM

"E"

"F"

4"X6" ANGLE

HINGED

"G"

"H"

"J"

DETAIL SECTION ON CENTER LINE

PLAN AT "A-B"    PLAN AT "C-D"

IRON
WOOD
BRICK
STONE
PLASTER
CEMENT

DETAIL PLAN AT "K"

HALF INSIDE ELEVATIONS AT "J" & "F"

DETAIL PLAN AT "L"

DETAILS
OF
A SLIPHEAD WINDOW IN A BRICK WALL.
SCALES
ELEV. PLANS, & SECT.-3/8"=1'-0".
DETAILS - 1½"=1'-0"

**PLATE 20—SLIP-HEAD WINDOW IN A BRICK WALL**

This window is popular, especially in the South, for Colonial residences both brick and frame. Attention is called to the hinged head which is lifted by the sash when raised and which falls again into position by its own weight as soon as the sash is lowered.

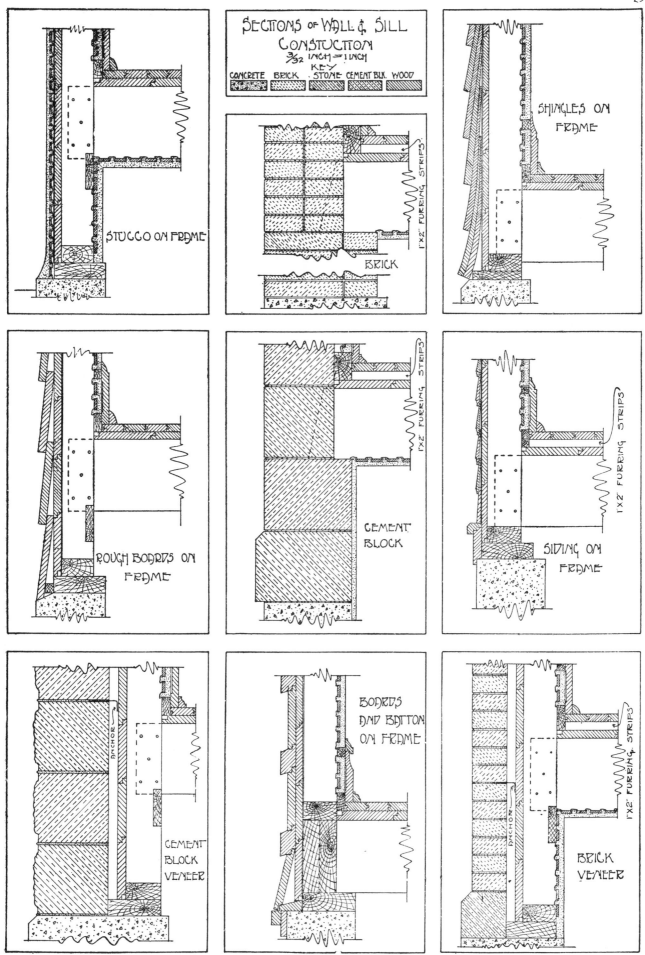

SECTIONS OF WALL & SILL
CONSTUCTION
3/32 INCH = 1 INCH
KEY
CONCRETE  BRICK  STONE  CEMENT BLK.  WOOD

STUCCO ON FRAME

BRICK

SHINGLES ON FRAME

ROUGH BOARDS ON FRAME

CEMENT BLOCK

SIDING ON FRAME

CEMENT BLOCK VENEER

BOARDS AND BATTON ON FRAME

BRICK VENEER

## PLATE 21—WALL SECTIONS AND SILL CONSTRUCTION

Approved construction for the twelve leading types of building, using the various common materials: stucco on frame, rough boards on frame, cement block veneer, brick, cement blocks, boards and batton on frame, shingles on frame, siding on frame, and brick veneer.

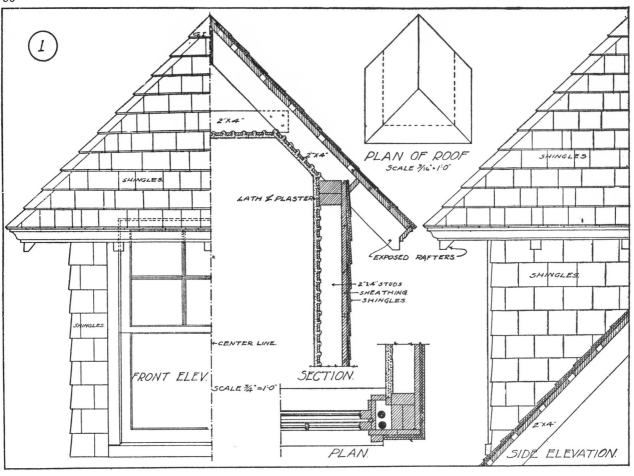

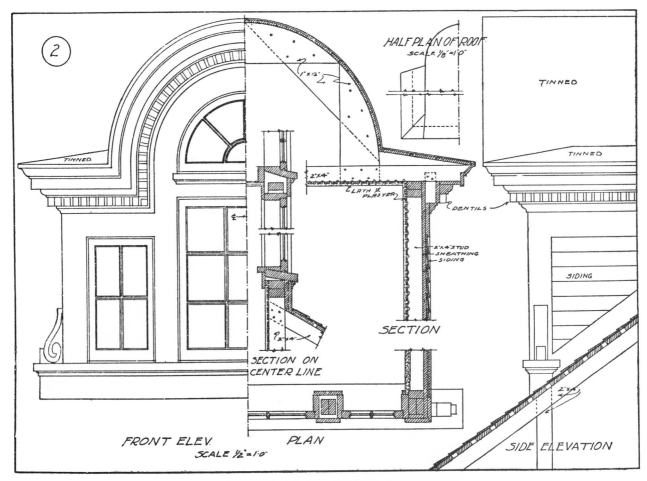

## PLATE 22—ROOF DORMER WINDOWS

1—A shingled hip-roof dormer of the popular inexpensive type used with many variations on shingled houses.

2—Colonial dormer with semi-circular end gable. The sides of this dormer are preferably covered with lap siding and the roof is tinned.

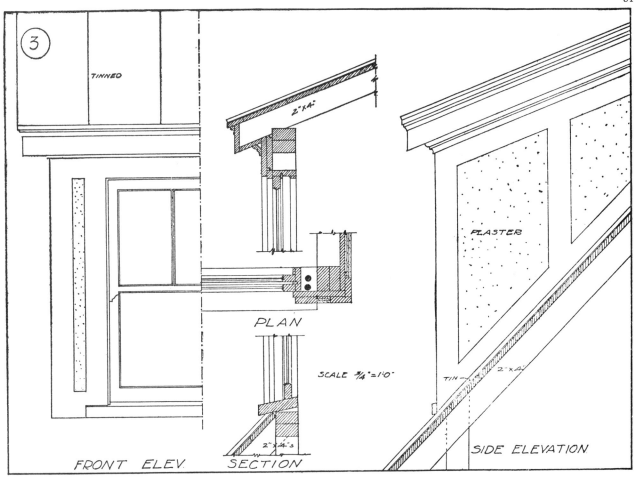

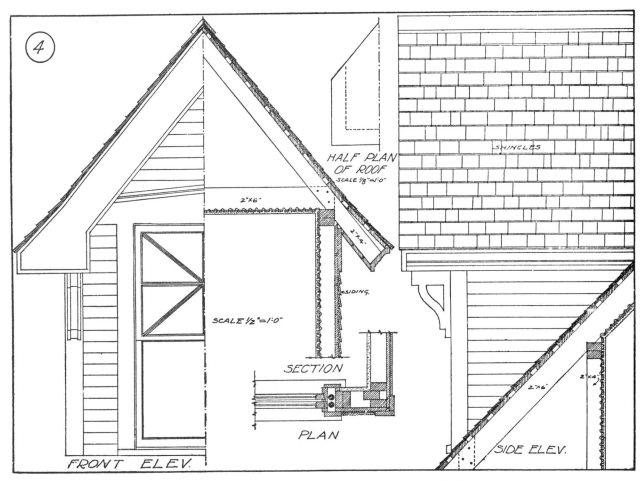

**PLATE 23—ROOF DORMER WINDOWS**

3—Sloping roof dormer. The simplest kind of a dormer and very satisfactory if the main roof rises high enough to allow it.

4—Gable end dormer, appropriate on steep-roofed buildings. All of these dormers are well suited for both new and remodeling work.

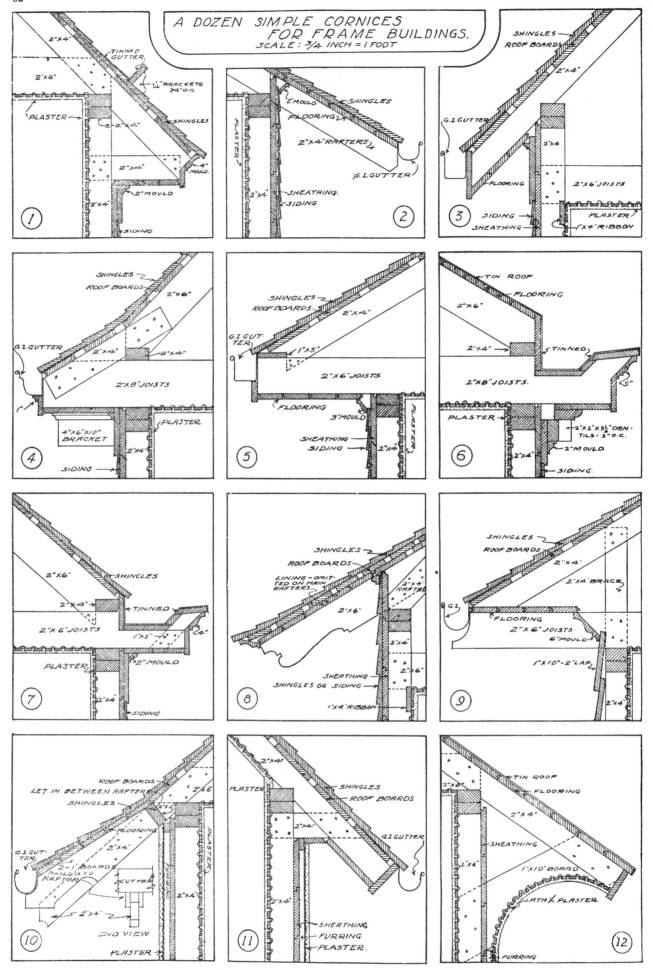

A DOZEN SIMPLE CORNICES
FOR FRAME BUILDINGS.
SCALE: 3/4 INCH = 1 FOOT

## PLATE 24—CORNICE CONSTRUCTION FOR FRAME BUILDINGS

1—Narrow box cornice; 2—Simple open rafter cornice; 3—Soffit nailed direct to rafter ends; 4—Box cornice bracketed; 5—Wide box cornice; 6—Dentil cornice with concealed gutter; 7—Simple cornice with concealed gutter; 8—Curved bungalow cornice with ornamental rafter ends; 9—Square box cornice with show rafters; 10—Curved cornice with ornamental rafter ends; 11—Simple closed cornice for cement plaster house; 12—Circular stucco cornice.

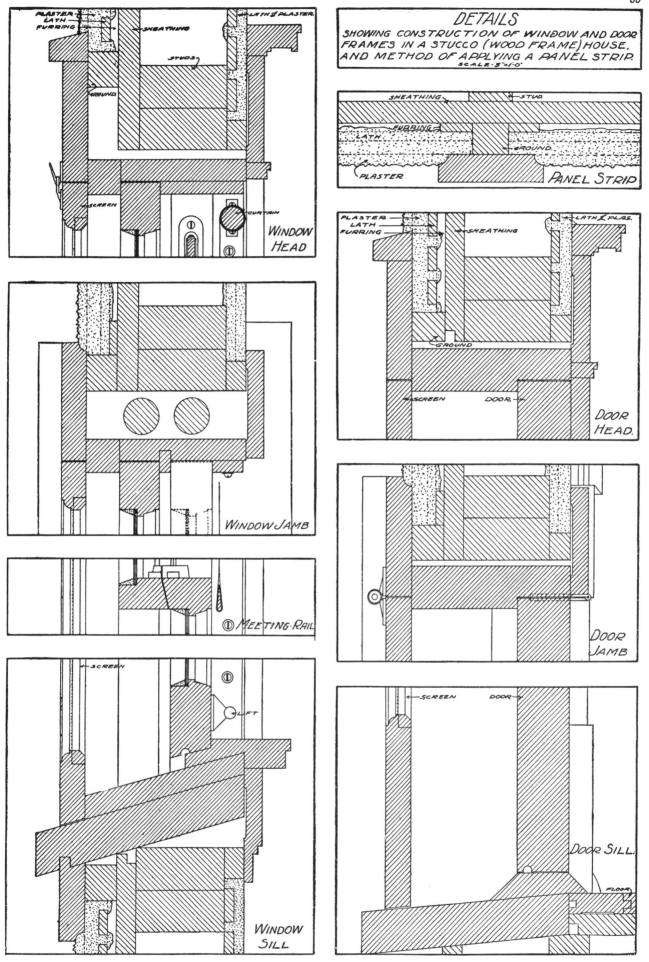

DETAILS
SHOWING CONSTRUCTION OF WINDOW AND DOOR FRAMES IN A STUCCO (WOOD FRAME) HOUSE, AND METHOD OF APPLYING A PANEL STRIP.
SCALE 3"=1'-0"

PANEL STRIP

WINDOW HEAD

WINDOW JAMB

① MEETING RAIL

WINDOW SILL

DOOR HEAD.

DOOR JAMB

DOOR SILL.

## PLATE 25—FRAMING FOR CEMENT PLASTER HOUSES

Full details showing the construction of window and door frames in stucco, wood frame houses. Attention is called to the fact that all casings, bands, panel strips, etc., are applied directly on the grounds after the first coat of plaster is in place and that the second coat is put on after all woodwork has been placed in position. Wood lath used for plaster work.

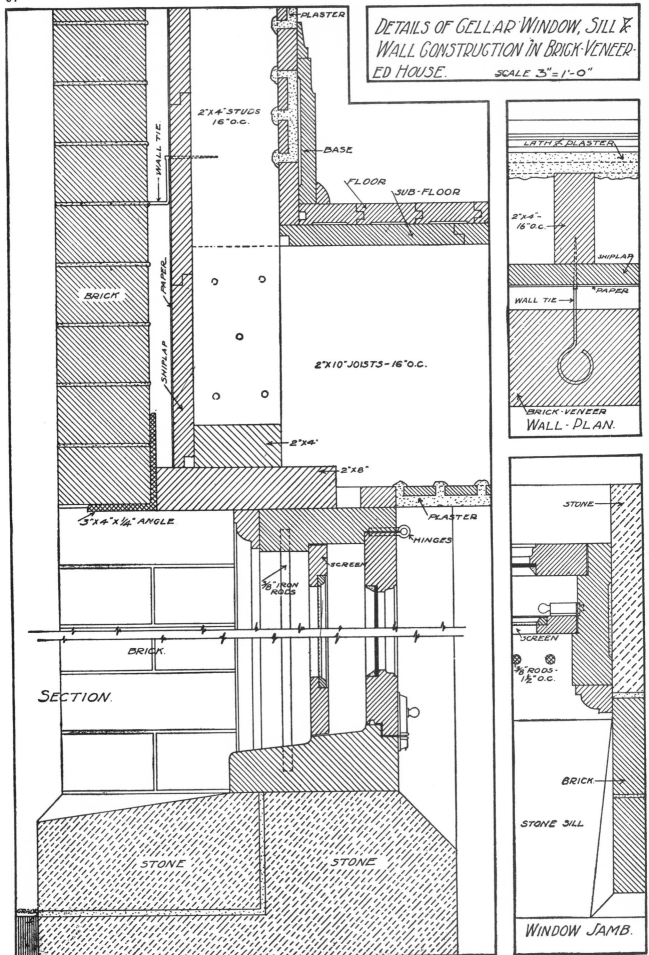

PLASTER

DETAILS OF CELLAR WINDOW, SILL &
WALL CONSTRUCTION IN BRICK-VENEER-
ED HOUSE.    SCALE 3"=1'-0"

2"X4" STUDS
16" O.C.

BASE

FLOOR    SUB-FLOOR

LATH & PLASTER

2"X4"-
16" O.C.

SHIPLAP

WALL TIE    PAPER

BRICK-VENEER

WALL-PLAN.

WALL TIE

PAPER

SHIPLAP

BRICK

2"X10" JOISTS-16" O.C.

2"X4"

2"X8"

3"X4"X1/4" ANGLE.

PLASTER

HINGES

STONE

SCREEN

7/8" IRON
RODS

SCREEN

7/8" RODS-
1 1/2" O.C.

BRICK.

BRICK

SECTION.

STONE SILL

STONE    STONE

GRADE

WINDOW JAMB.

PLATE 26—BRICK VENEER CONSTRUCTION

Details of cellar-window, sill and wall construction. Details drawn to large scale showing
approved construction for this popular building
method, using brick veneer over timber frame.

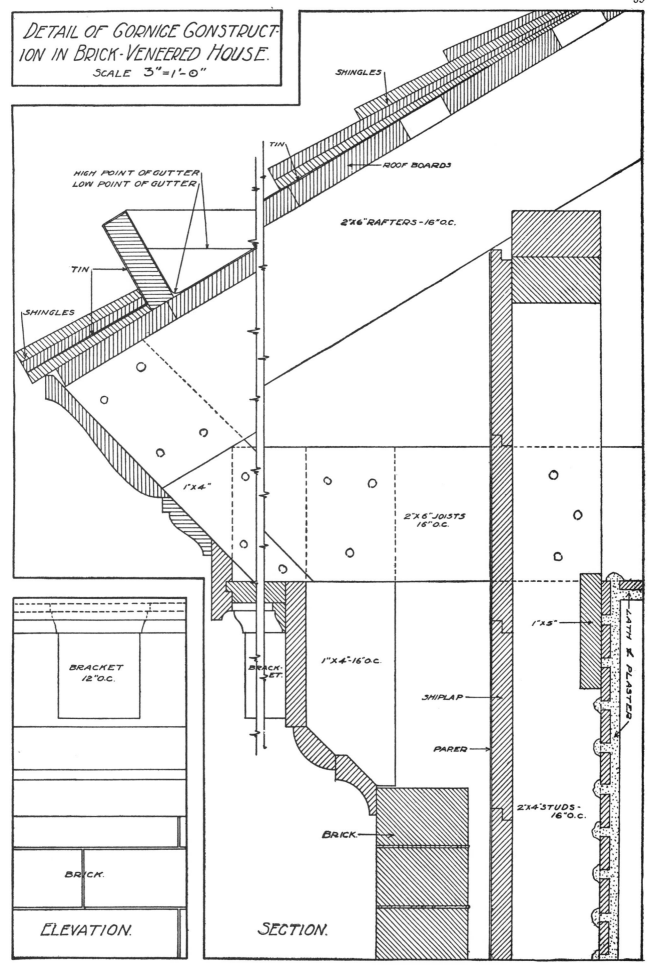

DETAIL OF CORNICE CONSTRUCTION IN BRICK-VENEERED HOUSE.
SCALE 3"=1'-0"

SHINGLES

TIN

ROOF BOARDS

HIGH POINT OF GUTTER
LOW POINT OF GUTTER

2"X6" RAFTERS - 16" O.C.

TIN

SHINGLES

1"X4"

2"X6" JOISTS
16" O.C.

1"X5"

BRACKET
12" O.C.

BRACK-
ET.

1"X4"-16" O.C.

SHIPLAP

PARER

LATH & PLASTER

2"X4" STUDS -
16" O.C.

BRICK.

BRICK.

ELEVATION.

SECTION.

**PLATE 27—BRICK VENEER CONSTRUCTION**

Cornice framing. Details drawn to large scale showing approved method of framing at the
cornice for brick veneer houses.

36

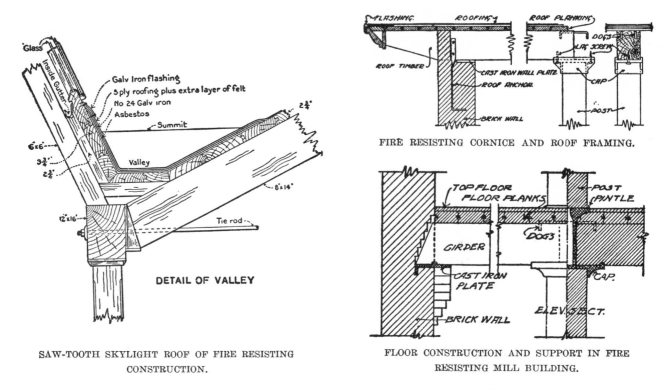

**DETAIL OF VALLEY**

SAW-TOOTH SKYLIGHT ROOF OF FIRE RESISTING
CONSTRUCTION.

FIRE RESISTING CORNICE AND ROOF FRAMING.

FLOOR CONSTRUCTION AND SUPPORT IN FIRE
RESISTING MILL BUILDING.

## PLATE 28B—FIRE RESISTING TIMBER FACTORY CONSTRUCTION

Details of approved or standard mill and warehouse framing.

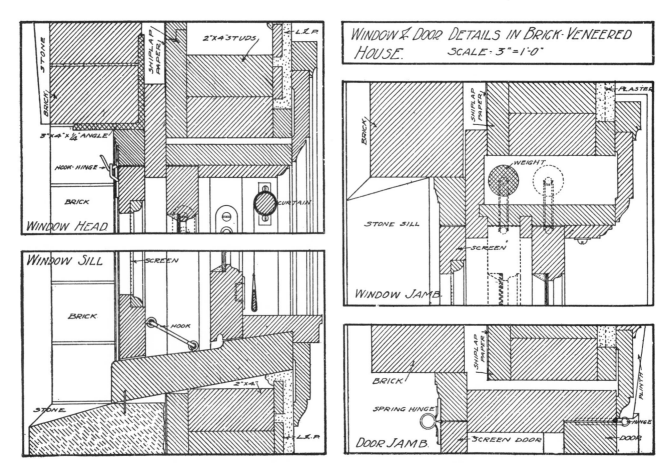

## PLATE 28A—BRICK VENEER CONSTRUCTION

Details of double hung windows with outside screens; also details of door jamb, all using brick veneer.

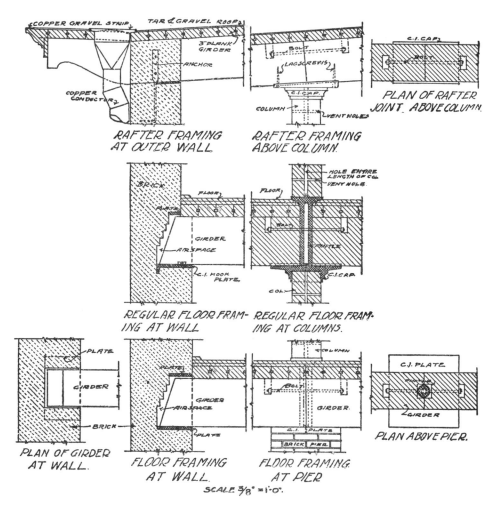

RAFTER FRAMING AT OUTER WALL.
RAFTER FRAMING ABOVE COLUMN.
PLAN OF RAFTER JOINT ABOVE COLUMN.
REGULAR FLOOR FRAMING AT WALL.
REGULAR FLOOR FRAMING AT COLUMNS.
PLAN OF GIRDER AT WALL.
FLOOR FRAMING AT WALL.
FLOOR FRAMING AT PIER.
PLAN ABOVE PIER.
SCALE ⅜" = 1'-0".

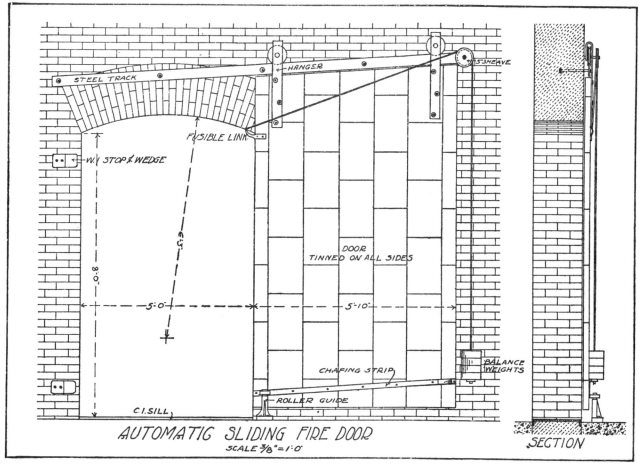

AUTOMATIC SLIDING FIRE DOOR
SCALE ⅜" = 1'-0"
SECTION

**PLATE 29—FIRE RESISTING TIMBER FACTORY CONSTRUCTION**

Arrangement for a fire resisting warehouse door, made to close automatically in case of fire. Wrought iron stop and wedge forces the door tight shut. Complete details are also presented above, showing construction and support for roof and floors.

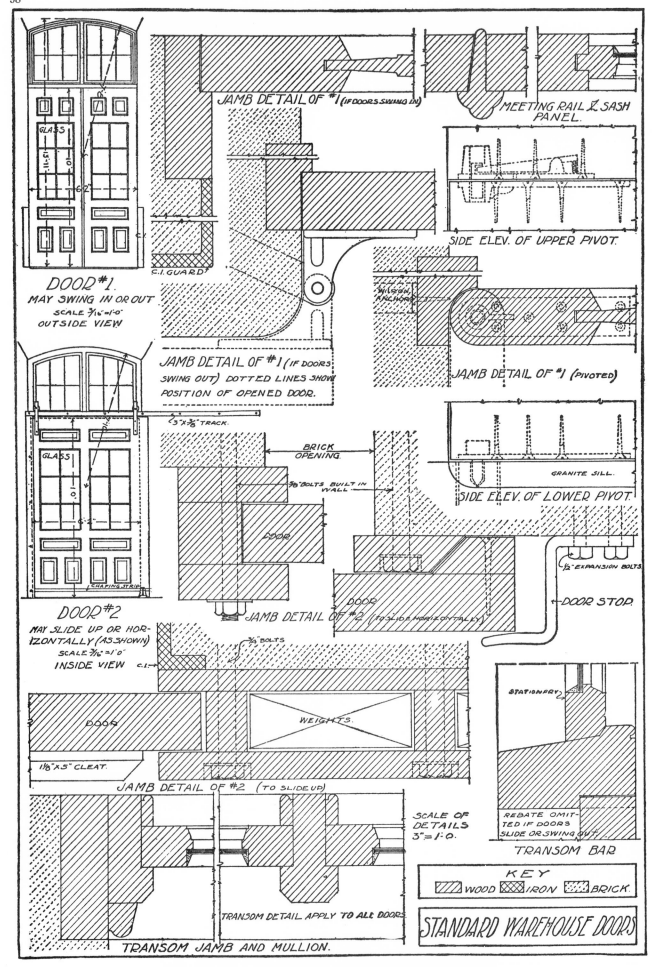

DOOR #1.
MAY SWING IN OR OUT
SCALE 7/16"=1'-0"
OUTSIDE VIEW

GLASS
13'-11"
6'-2"

JAMB DETAIL OF #1 (IF DOORS SWING IN)

MEETING RAIL & SASH PANEL.

SIDE ELEV. OF UPPER PIVOT.

C.I. GUARD

JAMB DETAIL OF #1 (IF DOORS SWING OUT) DOTTED LINES SHOW POSITION OF OPENED DOOR.

WROUGHT IRON ANCHORS

JAMB DETAIL OF #1 (PIVOTED)

3"x3/8" TRACK.

BRICK OPENING.

5/8" BOLTS BUILT IN WALL

DOOR

GRANITE SILL.

SIDE ELEV. OF LOWER PIVOT.

1/2" EXPANSION BOLTS

DOOR STOP.

DOOR

JAMB DETAIL OF #2 (TO SLIDE HORIZONTALLY)

DOOR #2
MAY SLIDE UP OR HOR-IZONTALLY (AS SHOWN)
SCALE 7/16"=1'-0"
INSIDE VIEW

GLASS
1'-0"

3/4" BOLTS

C.I.

STATIONARY

WEIGHTS.

DOOR

REBATE OMIT-TED IF DOORS SLIDE OR SWING OUT

1 1/8"x5" CLEAT.

JAMB DETAIL OF #2 (TO SLIDE UP)

SCALE OF DETAILS 3"=1'-0".

TRANSOM BAR

CHAFING STRIP

KEY
WOOD    IRON    BRICK.

STANDARD WAREHOUSE DOORS

TRANSOM DETAIL APPLY TO ALL DOORS

TRANSOM JAMB AND MULLION.

## PLATE 30—STANDARD WAREHOUSE DOORS

Complete details for heavy fire resisting doors, both sliding and swinging, for use in mills, factories and warehouses. The transoms over such doors are usually stationary. Note that door stop is put on with bolts passing clear through the brick wall.

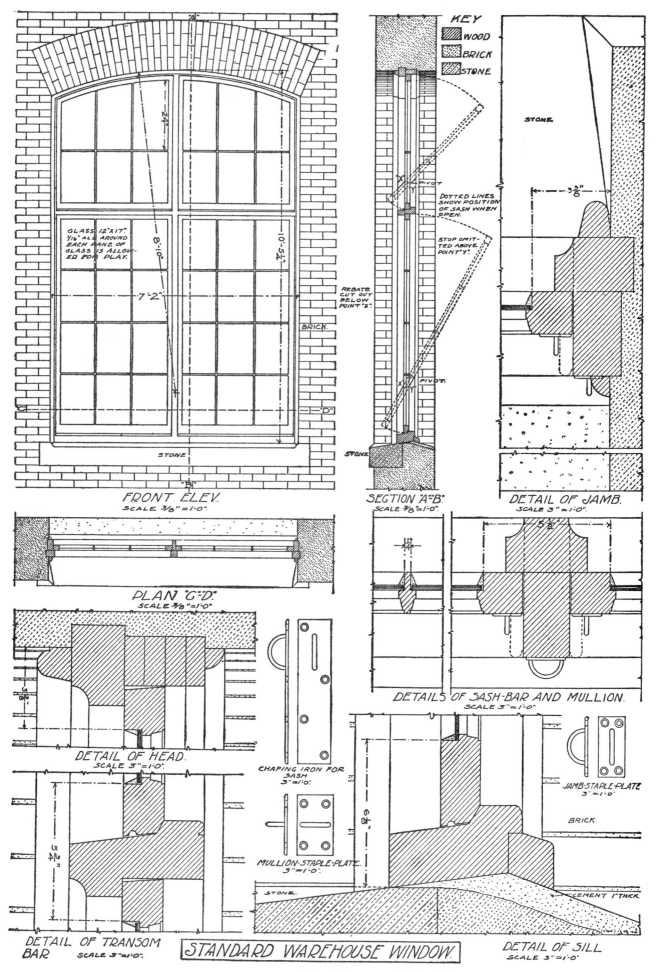

KEY
WOOD
BRICK
STONE

GLASS 12"X17" 1/16" ALL AROUND EACH PANE OF GLASS IS ALLOWED FOR PLAY.

STONE

BRICK

FRONT ELEV.
SCALE 3/8"=1'-0".

PIVOT

DOTTED LINES SHOW POSITION OF SASH WHEN OPEN.

STOP OMITTED ABOVE POINT "Y".

REBATE CUT OUT BELOW POINT "X".

PIVOT.

STONE.

SECTION "A"-"B".
SCALE 3/8"=1'-0".

STONE

DETAIL OF JAMB.
SCALE 3"=1'-0".

PLAN "C"-"D".
SCALE 3/8"=1'-0".

DETAILS OF SASH-BAR AND MULLION.
SCALE 3"=1'-0".

DETAIL OF HEAD.
SCALE 3"=1'-0".

CHAFING IRON FOR SASH
3"=1'-0".

MULLION-STAPLE-PLATE.
3"=1'-0".

JAMB-STAPLE-PLATE
3"=1'-0"

BRICK.

DETAIL OF TRANSOM BAR    SCALE 3"=1'-0".

STANDARD WAREHOUSE WINDOW.

STONE.

CEMENT 1" THICK.

DETAIL OF SILL
SCALE 3"=1'-0"

## PLATE 31—STANDARD WAREHOUSE WINDOWS

Complete details for double pivoted windows (wood frames) suitable for mills, factories and warehouses. The arched window heads should be made of small pieces of wood glued together and sawed to fit the curve. Interior jambs are of rounded corner bricks.

40

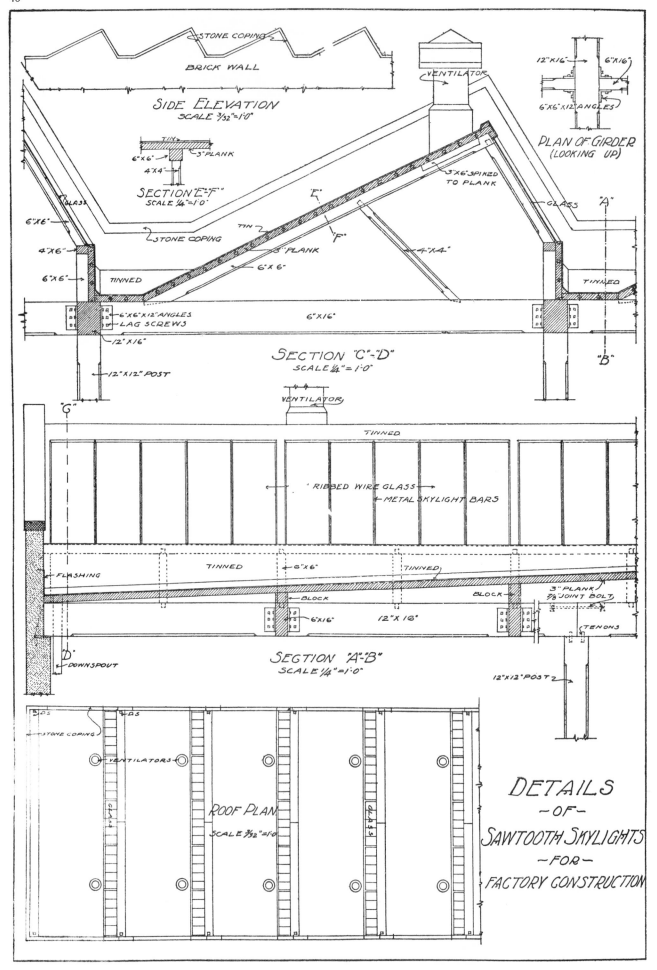

SIDE ELEVATION
SCALE 3/32"=1'0"

STONE COPING
BRICK WALL

VENTILATOR

PLAN OF GIRDER
(LOOKING UP)

12"X16"    6"X16"

6"X6"X12" ANGLES

SECTION "E"-"F"
SCALE 1/4"=1'0"

TIN
6"X6"
3"PLANK
4"X4"

GLASS
6"X6"
4"X6"
6"X6"

STONE COPING
TINNED

TIN
3"PLANK
6"X6"

3"X6"SPIKED
TO PLANK

4"X4"

E
F

GLASS    "A"
TINNED

6"X6"X12" ANGLES
LAG SCREWS
12"X16"

6"X16"

SECTION "C"-"D"
SCALE 1/4"=1'0"

"B"

12"X12" POST

"C"

VENTILATOR

TINNED

RIBBED WIRE GLASS
METAL SKYLIGHT BARS

FLASHING
TINNED    6"X6"    TINNED
BLOCK    BLOCK
3"PLANK
7/8" JOINT BOLT

6"X16"    12"X16"
TENONS

"D"
DOWNSPOUT

SECTION "A"-"B"
SCALE 1/4"=1'0"

12"X12" POST

STONE COPING
DS    DS

VENTILATORS

GLASS    GLASS

ROOF PLAN
SCALE 3/32"=1'0"

DETAILS
-OF-
SAWTOOTH SKYLIGHTS
-FOR-
FACTORY CONSTRUCTION

## PLATE 32—SAW-TOOTH SKYLIGHT ROOF

Arrangement and complete details of lighted roof—fire resisting—for shops and factories. The glass in the "saw teeth" should face north. Ribbed glass should be used for diffusing the light; with all interior work painted white there will be no shadows. Supporting rafters should not be less than 6 by 6 nor roofing less than 3 inch plank, if this construction is to be fire resisting. Supporting posts and girders are of yellow pine, fastened together by means of angles.

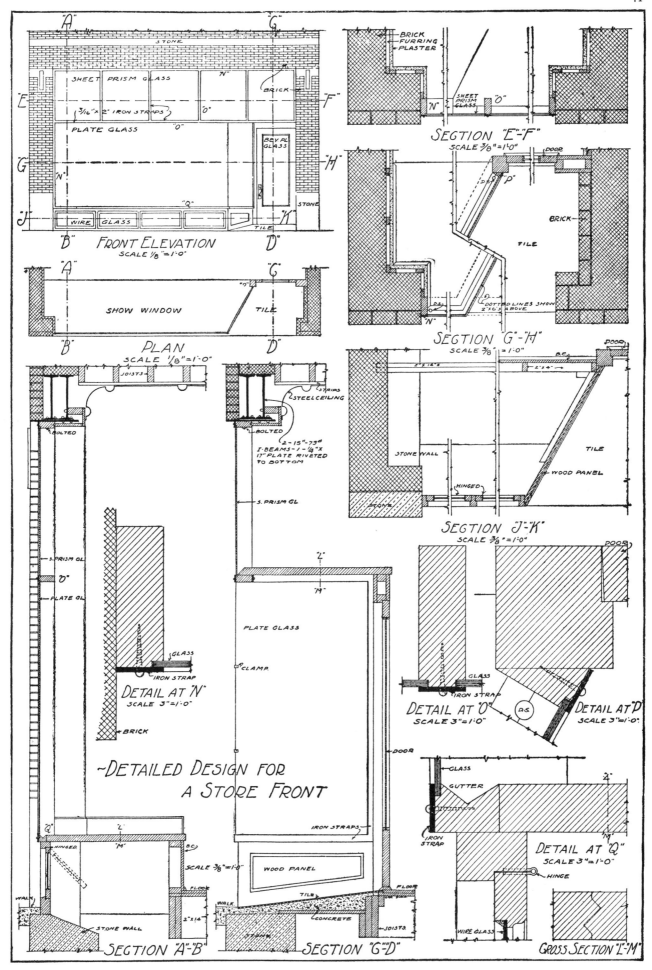

**PLATE 33—MODERN STORE FRONT**

Arrangement and complete details of store front giving maximum amount of light and good display space. Brick work is carried above the window on a double I beam girder. Sheet prism glass at the top of the window and over the door throws light to the interior of the store. Plate glass is held in place by neat iron straps. Hinged sash with wire glass light the store basement.

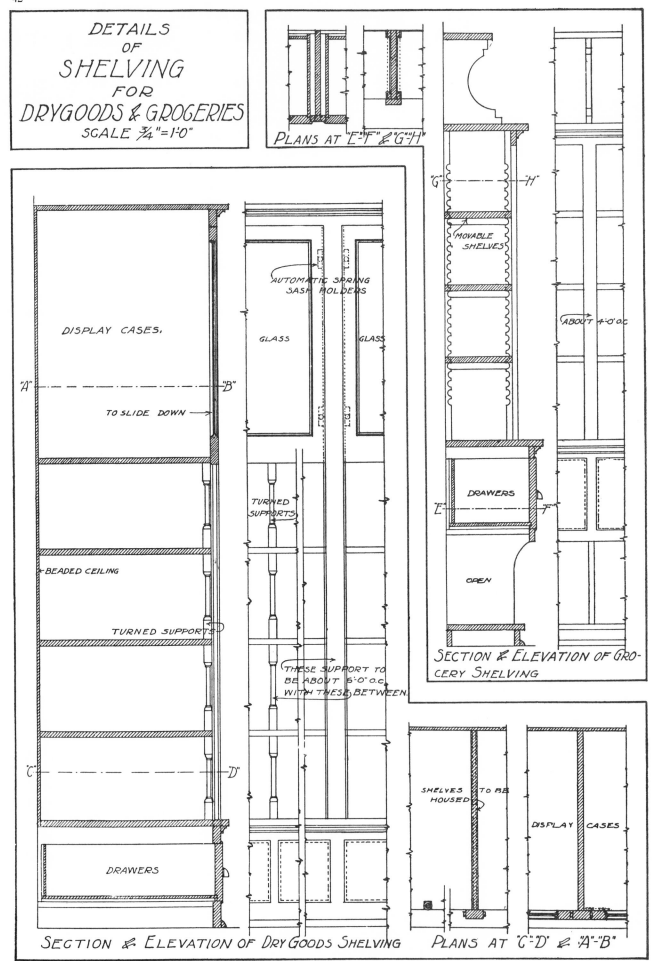

DETAILS
OF
SHELVING
FOR
DRYGOODS & GROCERIES
SCALE ¾"=1'0"

PLANS AT "E"-"F" & "G"-"H"

"G"————————"H"

MOVABLE
SHELVES

ABOUT 4'-0" O.C.

DISPLAY CASES.

"A"————————"B"

TO SLIDE DOWN →

GLASS          GLASS

AUTOMATIC SPRING
SASH HOLDERS

TURNED
SUPPORTS

BEADED CEILING

TURNED SUPPORTS

THESE SUPPORT TO
BE ABOUT 6'-0" O.C.
WITH THESE BETWEEN.

"C"————————"D"

DRAWERS

DRAWERS

"E"————————"F"

OPEN

SECTION & ELEVATION OF GRO-
CERY SHELVING

SHELVES TO BE
HOUSED

DISPLAY CASES

SECTION & ELEVATION OF DRY GOODS SHELVING

PLANS AT "C"-"D" & "A"-"B"

## PLATE 34—SHELVING AND STORE FIXTURES

Details of shelving and stock drawers for the neat display and orderly storage of drygoods and groceries. For drygoods the shelves are stationary and should be supported about every 6 feet with turned spindles; in place of the very high shelves, display cases with sliding glass doors are arranged as shown. For groceries the shelves are movable so as to be adjustable to the height of the packages to be placed on them; there is a broad fixed shelf at counter height.

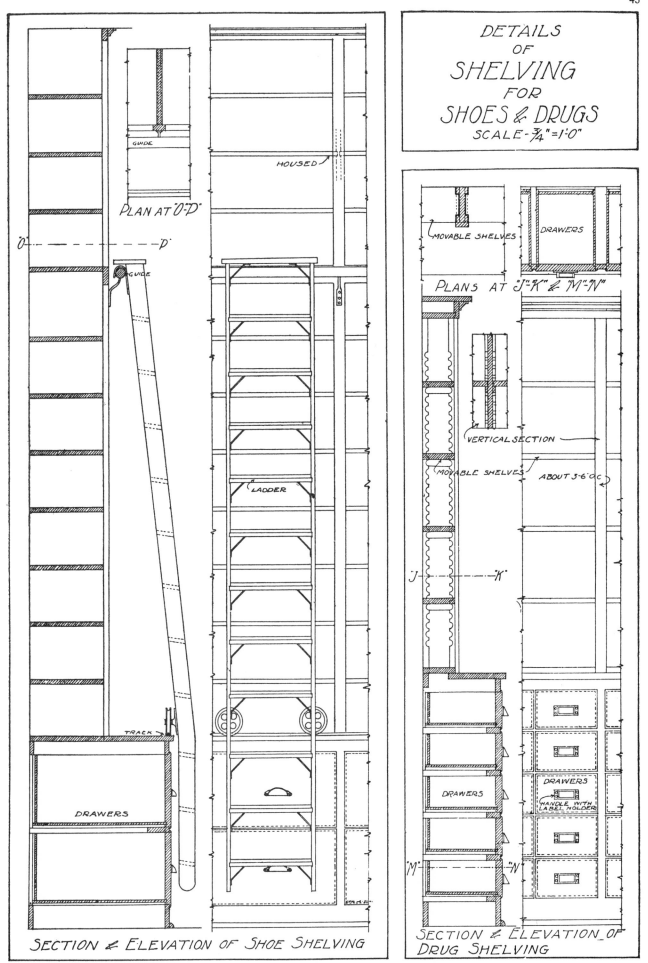

PLAN AT "O-D"

O — — — — — — — D

GUIDE

HOUSED

GUIDE

LADDER

TRACK

DRAWERS

SECTION & ELEVATION OF SHOE SHELVING

MOVABLE SHELVES

DRAWERS

PLANS AT "J"-"K" & "M"-"N"

VERTICAL SECTION

MOVABLE SHELVES

ABOUT 3'-6" O.C.

J — — — — — — K

DRAWERS

DRAWERS
HANDLE WITH LABEL HOLDER

M — — — — — N

SECTION & ELEVATION OF DRUG SHELVING

## PLATE 35—SHELVING AND STORE FIXTURES

Details of shelving, stock drawers, etc., for shoe stores and drug stores. For shoes there are two deep drawers under the broad counter shelf, and above, the shelving is just as deep as the shoe boxes are long, the shelves being just far enough apart to give room for two boxes. The shelving extends clear to the ceiling; rolling stock ladders are arranged as indicated. For drug stores combinations of narrow movable shelves and numerous small drawers are used.

44

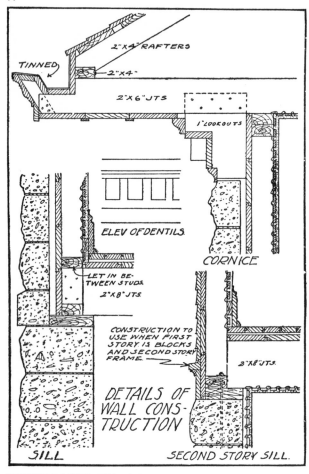

CEMENT BLOCKS USED IN COMBINATION, WALL SECTIONS
SHOWING CONSTRUCTION AND ARRANGEMENT.

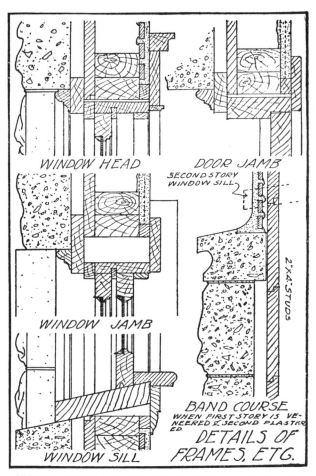

CEMENT BLOCK VENEER CONSTRUCTION, DETAILS OF
WINDOW AND DOOR FRAMES—BAND COURSE JOINT.

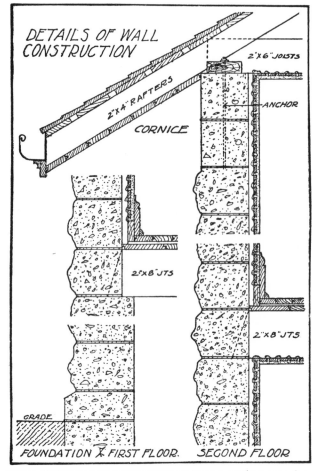

WALL SECTION SHOWING JOIST SEATING AT 1ST AND 2ND
FLOORS AND PLATE.

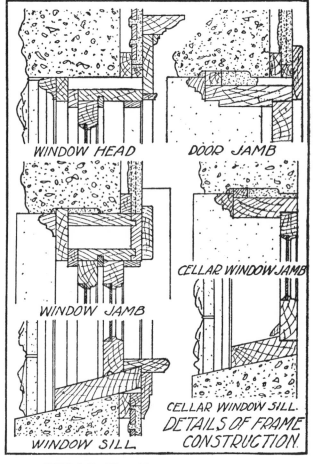

WINDOWS AND DOOR FRAMING DETAILS.

## PLATE 36—CONCRETE BLOCK CONSTRUCTION

Complete details of all wood framing occurring in connection with block work, both ordinary
block construction and block veneer.

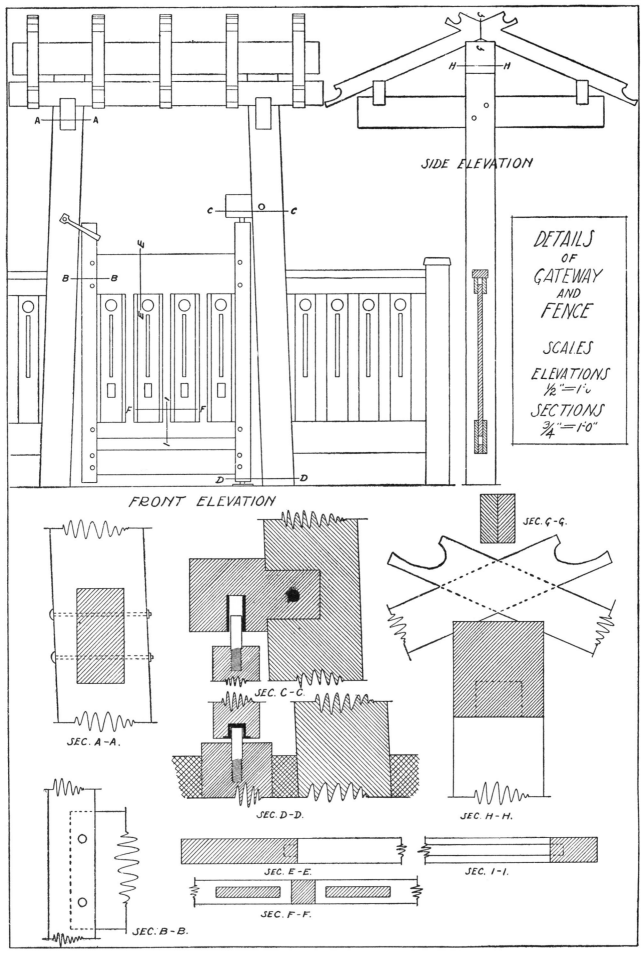

SIDE ELEVATION

DETAILS
OF
GATEWAY
AND
FENCE

SCALES

ELEVATIONS
½"=1'0"

SECTIONS
¾"=1'0"

FRONT ELEVATION

SEC. A-A.

SEC. C-C.

SEC. G-G.

SEC. D-D.

SEC. H-H.

SEC. B-B.

SEC. E-E.

SEC. I-I.

SEC. F-F.

## PLATE 37—ORNAMENTAL GATEWAY AND FENCE

Complete details for a very artistic timber gateway with pergola in the Japanese style. Note the method of hanging the gate. No hinges are used, the gate being hung on pins which work in sockets. A fence and gateway of this kind is preferably made of undressed lumber and stained.

# PART II. DETAILS OF FRAME AND MASONRY CONSTRUCTION

---

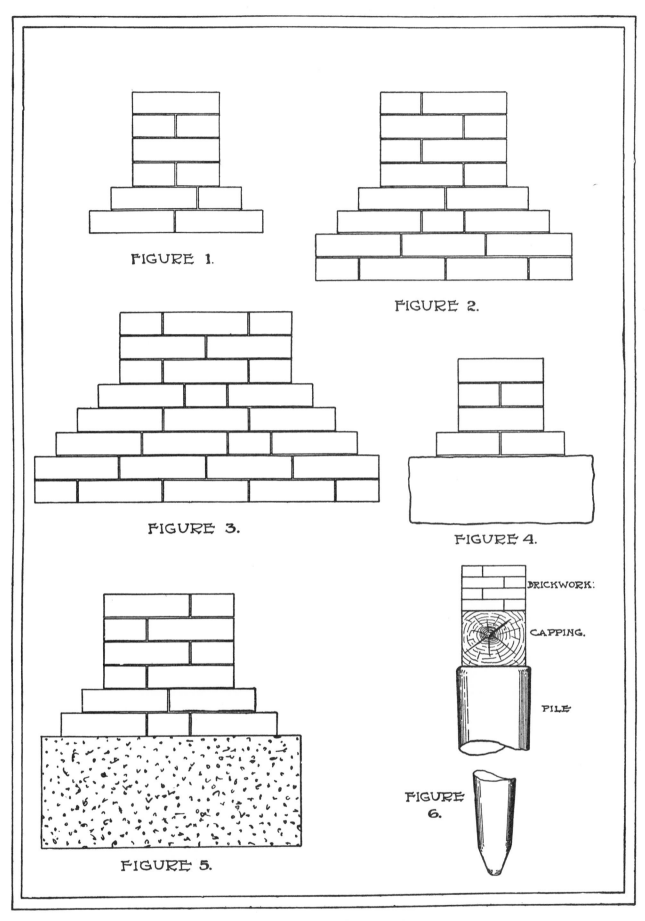

FIGURE 1.

FIGURE 2.

FIGURE 3.

FIGURE 4.

FIGURE 5.

BRICKWORK.

CAPPING.

PILE.

FIGURE 6.

## PLATE 38—FOUNDATIONS

Figs. 1, 2, 3, 4 and 5 show foundations where the soil is firm enough to bear the weight of the building; all foundations to be put down below frost. In Figs. 1, 2 and 3, the footings are made by spreading the brick wall itself by means of offsets. In Figs. 4 and 5, stone and concrete footings, respectively are used. In marshy soils a firm foundation is made by driving wooden piles as shown in Fig. 6. A concrete beam, poured in place, is often substituted for capping timber.

48

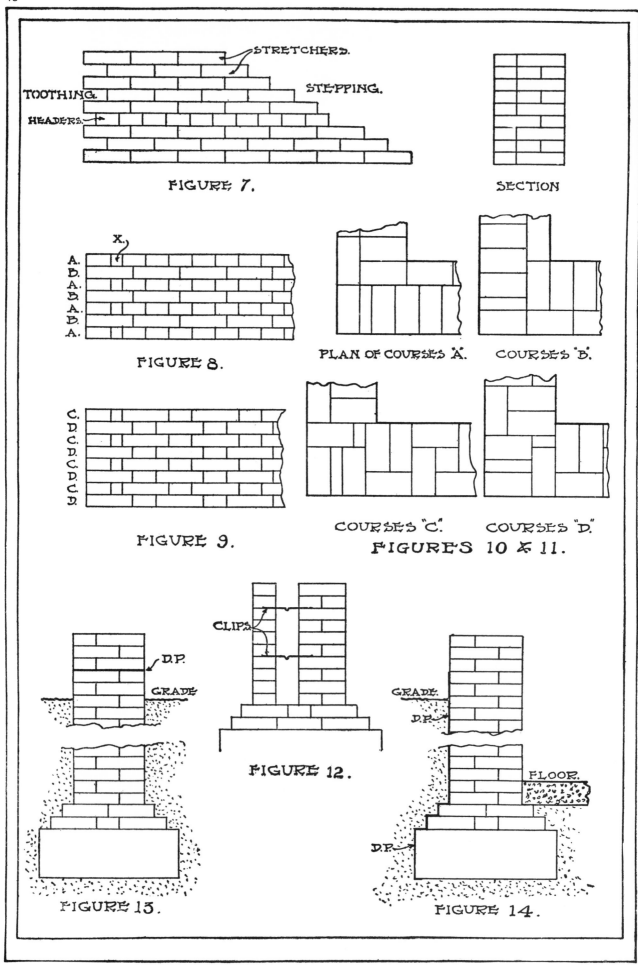

FIGURE 7.

SECTION

FIGURE 8.

PLAN OF COURSES "A".

COURSES "B".

FIGURE 9.

COURSES "C".    COURSES "D".

FIGURES 10 & 11.

FIGURE 12.

FIGURE 13.

FIGURE 14.

## PLATE 39—BRICK WORK AND BONDING

Fig. 7 shows the bond used in ordinary brick work, with headers every sixth course. Fig. 8, English bond. Fig. 9, Flemish bond. Figs. 10 and 11, plan views of English and Flemish bonds. Fig. 12, construction of hollow brick wall. Fig. 13, damp-proof course in brick wall where there is no basement. Fig. 14, damp-proof course protecting brick wall and foundation to make a dry basement. In extra wet locations the damp-proof course is carried under footings and floor.

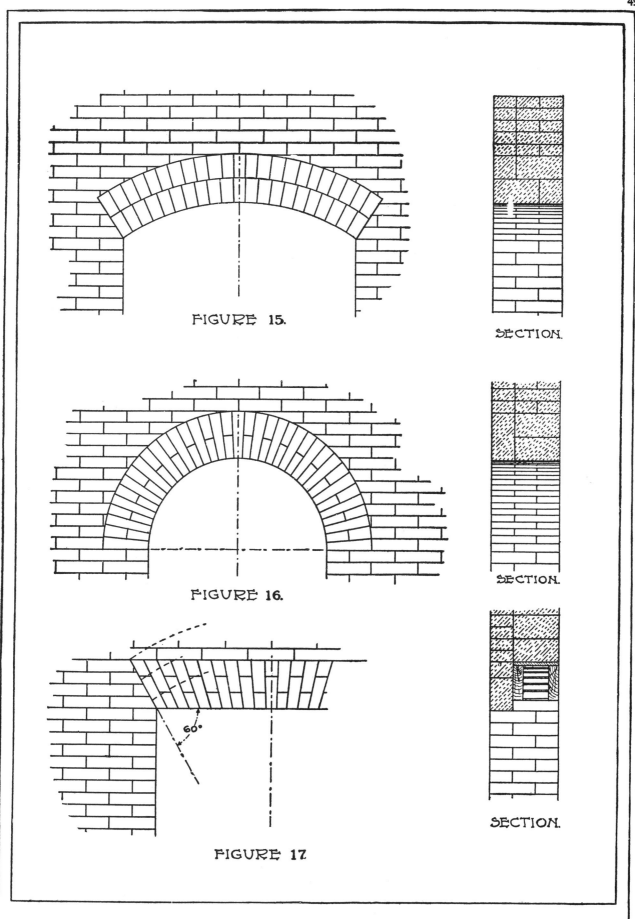

FIGURE 15.

SECTION.

FIGURE 16.

SECTION.

FIGURE 17

SECTION.

## PLATE 40—CONSTRUCTION OF BRICK ARCHES

Fig. 15, segmental arch with two-row-lock arch used in common work. The bricks are laid on edge in two concentric rings extending through the wall. Fig. 16, segmental arch formed of ordinary bricks rubbed or cut to the required shape and forming a perfect bond. Fig. 17, flat arch composed of bricks rubbed or cut to the required shape. Arches of this form should have a rise, or camber, equal to about one-eighth of an inch for every foot of span in order to prevent sagging. A concealed wooden lintel or arched frame work bears most of the weight above.

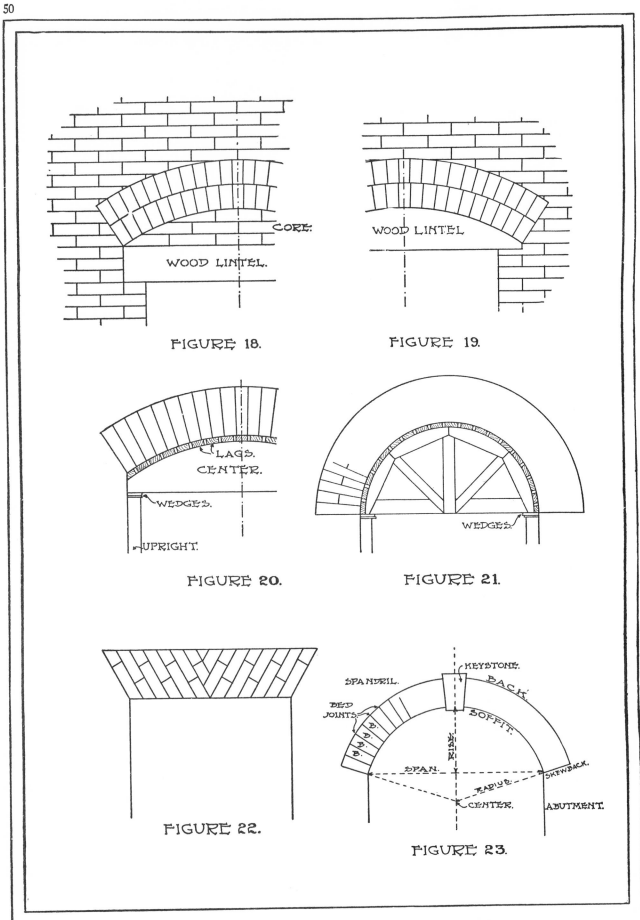

FIGURE 18.

FIGURE 19.

FIGURE 20.

FIGURE 21.

FIGURE 22.

FIGURE 23.

## PLATE 41—CONSTRUCTION OF BRICK ARCHES

Figs. 18 and 19, interior views of flat arches as shown in Fig. 17, Plate 40. The main weight of the wall is carried by the concealed wooden lintels and the rough brick relieving or discharging arch above. Figs. 20 and 21 show wooden false work used to support the bricks of an arch while the arch is being built. Fig. 22, Dutch arch; ornamental though weak in construction and suitable only for openings of narrow span. Bricks have to be specially cut to shape. Fig. 23 is a diagram giving the proper names for various parts of an arch.

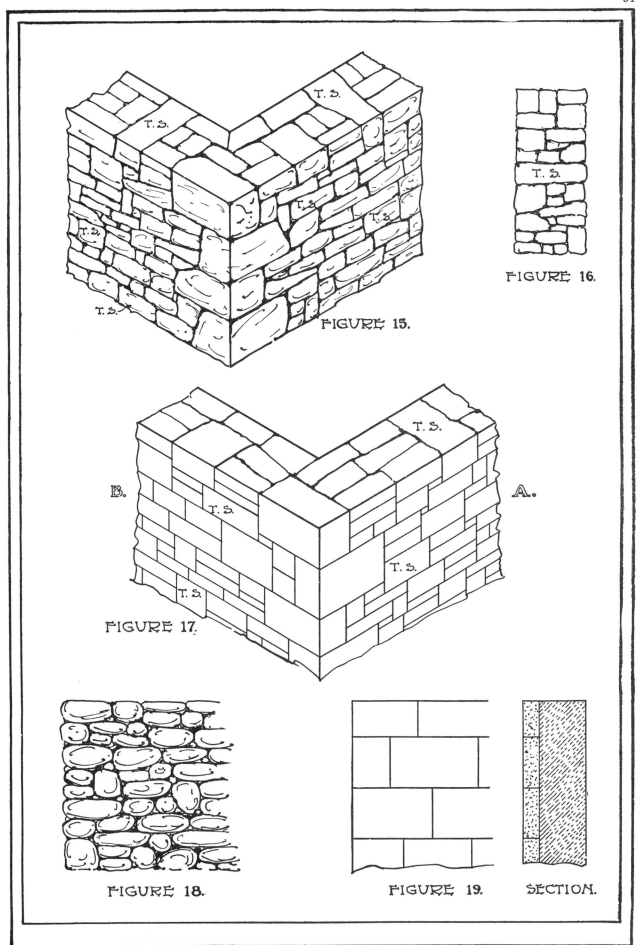

FIGURE 15.

FIGURE 16.

FIGURE 17.

FIGURE 18.

FIGURE 19.

SECTION.

## PLATE 42—STONE MASONRY WALLS

Figs. 15 and 16 show a wall with stones laid up random rubble. Proper bonding requires the insertion of "through stones," marked (T. S.), at intervals of four or five feet in the length, and about every eighteen inches in the height of the wall. Fig. 17, wall of squared rubble. At A the wall is uncoursed, at B laid up in courses. Fig. 18, wall of field or cobble stones. Fig. 19, elevation and section of coursed ashlar wall, showing veneer of stone backed up with stone or brick.

52

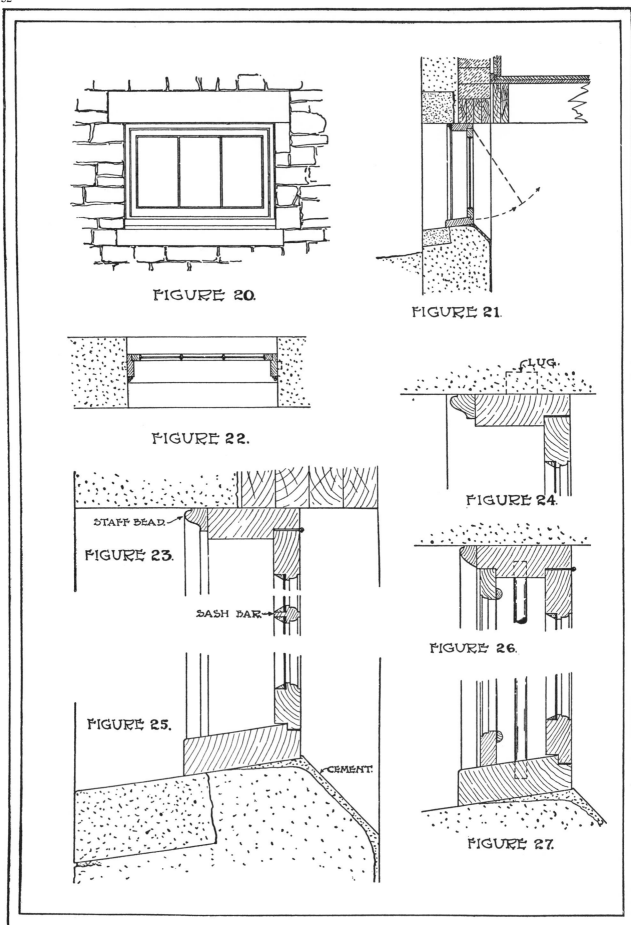

FIGURE 20.

FIGURE 21.

FIGURE 22.

FIGURE 24.

STAFF BEAD.

FIGURE 23.

SASH BAR.

PLUG.

FIGURE 26.

FIGURE 25.

CEMENT.

FIGURE 27.

## PLATE 43—CELLAR WINDOWS IN A STONE WALL

Fig. 20, elevation. Fig. 21, vertical section. Fig. 22, plan and horizontal section. Fig. 23, section through the head of the frame. Fig. 24, section through the jamb. Fig. 25, section through the sill. Figs. 26 and 27, head and sill of a window with an iron guard and window screen outside the sash. All details of approved construction for cellar windows.

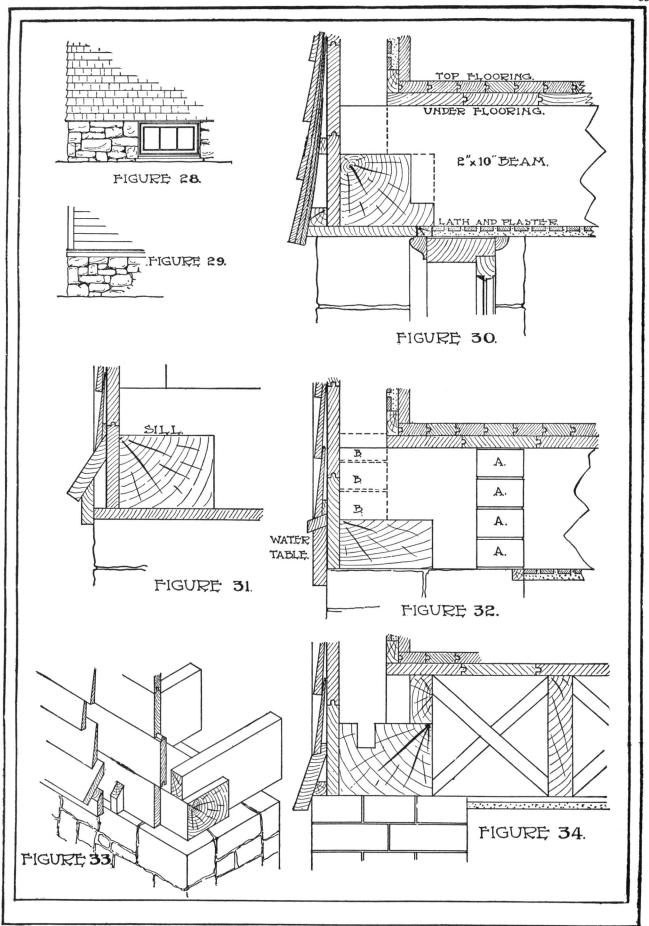

FIGURE 28.

FIGURE 29.

TOP FLOORING.

UNDER FLOORING.

2"x10" BEAM.

LATH AND PLASTER.

FIGURE 30.

SILL.

FIGURE 31.

B.
B.
B.

A.
A.
A.
A.

WATER TABLE.

FIGURE 32.

FIGURE 33

FIGURE 34.

## PLATE 44—SILL CONSTRUCTION FOR FRAME HOUSES

Figs. 28 and 29, exterior views showing stone foundation with shingles and clapboards respectively. Fig. 30, heavy timber sill with notched joist; base course of shingles. Fig. 31, base course as used with beveled siding. Fig. 32, at A is shown a fire stop of bricks, laid between the floor beams; also keeping out wind and vermin. This is frequently built on the sill as indicated by the dotted lines at B. Fig. 33, isometric view of the base of the frame work. Fig. 34, cross bridging between floor beams. Note studs mortised into the sill, a feature used only in the best work. Base course arranged to keep moisture away from sill timbers.

54

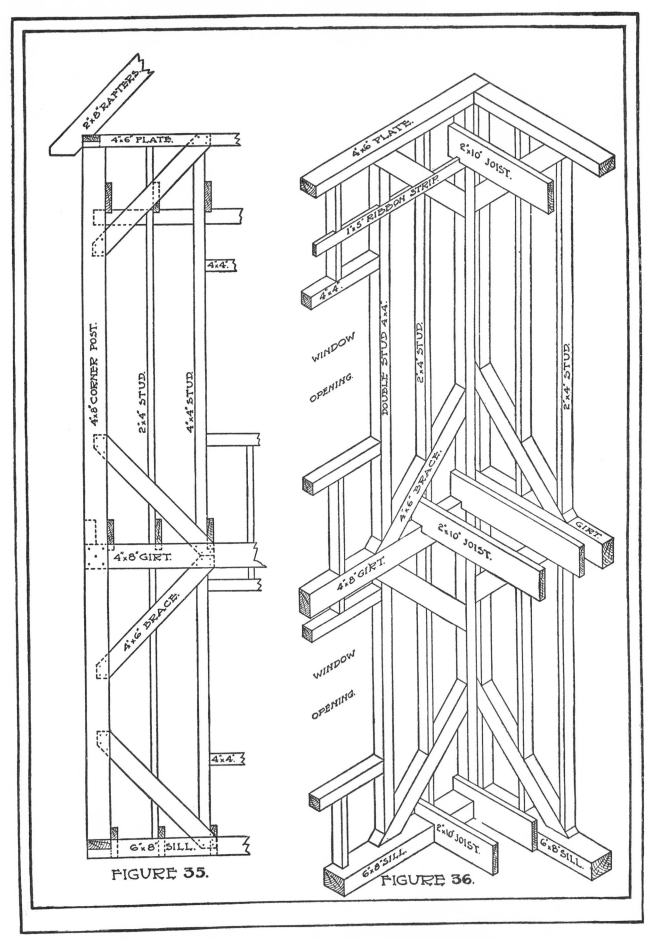

FIGURE 35.

FIGURE 36.

**PLATE 45—NEW ENGLAND BRACED FRAME CONSTRUCTION**

Fig. 35, elevation at the corner from sill to rafters. Fig. 36, perspective view of corner showing arrangement and placing of braces. This is a type of construction rarely seen in modern work.

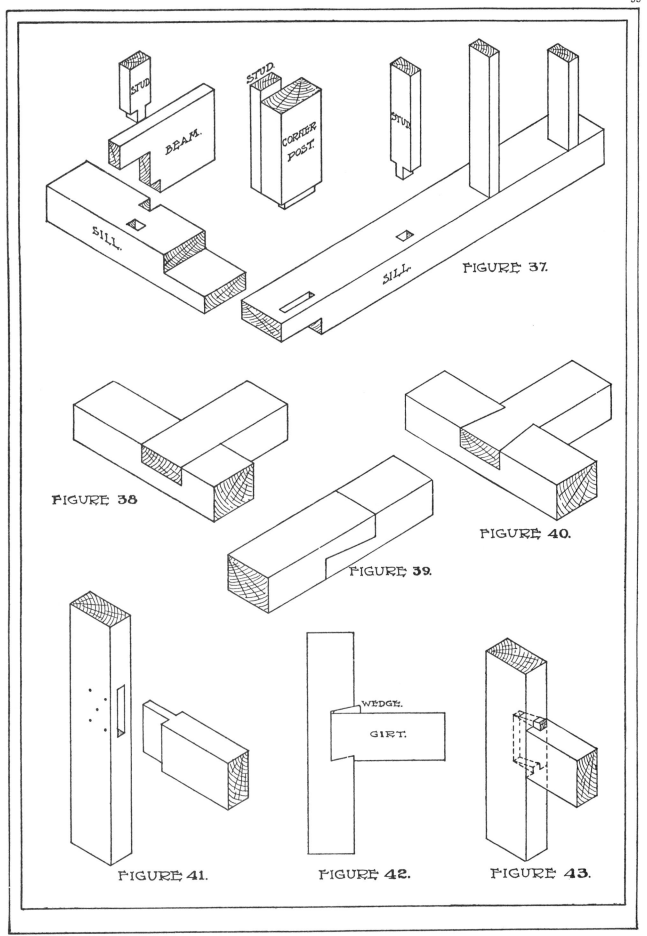

**PLATE 46—JOINTS USED IN HEAVY TIMBER FRAMING**

Fig. 37, main sill showing corner joint and the placing of joists, corner posts and studs. Fig. 38, tee halving. Fig. 39, beveled halving. Fig. 40, dove-tailed halving. Fig. 41, girth framed into corner post with mortise and tenon joint. Fig. 42, two views of girth framed into corner post with dove-tail tenon joint. All are approved practice for heavy timber framing.

56

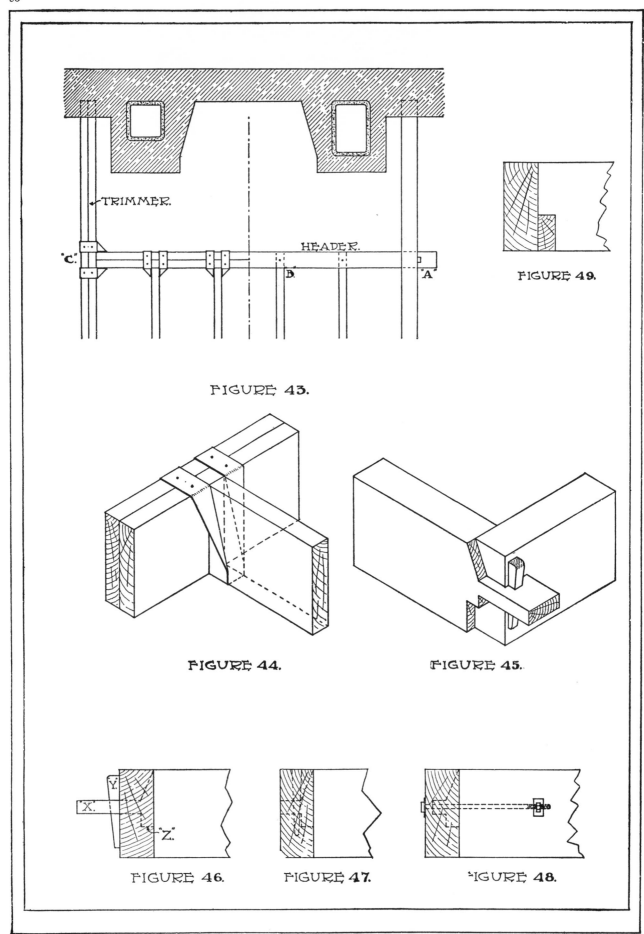

FIGURE 43.

FIGURE 49.

FIGURE 44.

FIGURE 45.

FIGURE 46.

FIGURE 47.

FIGURE 48.

## PLATE 47—JOIST FRAMING AND CONNECTIONS

Fig. 43, joist framing around a fireplace, the right half showing the headers, trimmers and tail beams framed together with the tusk and tenon joint; the other half fastened by means of wrought iron joist hangers. Fig. 44, detail of connection using joist hanger. Figs. 45, 46, 47 and 48, views of tusk and tenon joints. Fig. 49, the cheaper method of framing, the tail beams being supported by a 2 by 4 spiked to the header. A 2 by 4 is also to be spiked on to support brick arch.

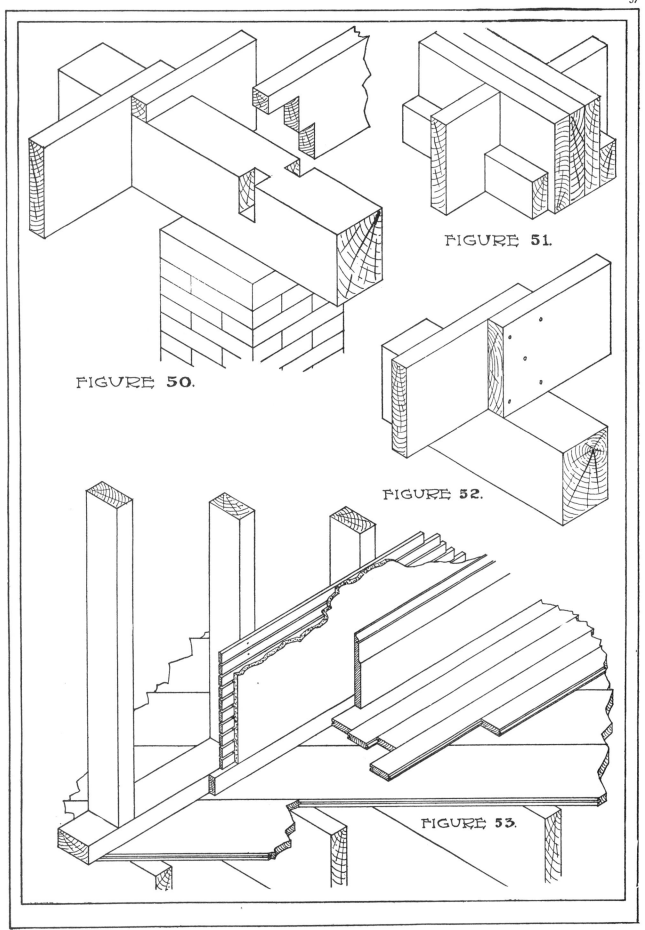

FIGURE 51.

FIGURE 50.

FIGURE 52.

FIGURE 53.

## PLATE 48—FLOOR CONSTRUCTION AND SUPPORT

Fig. 50, a 6 by 8 cellar girder resting on brick pier. Fig. 51, built-up flush girder consisting of three floor joists spiked together; 2 by 4 strips support the joist ends. Fig. 52, ordinary floor girder with joists resting on top and spiked together. Fig. 53, perspective view showing the interior partitions running at right angles to the direction of the floor beams. Note method of laying rough floor, finished floor and trim, which is somewhat unusual.

58

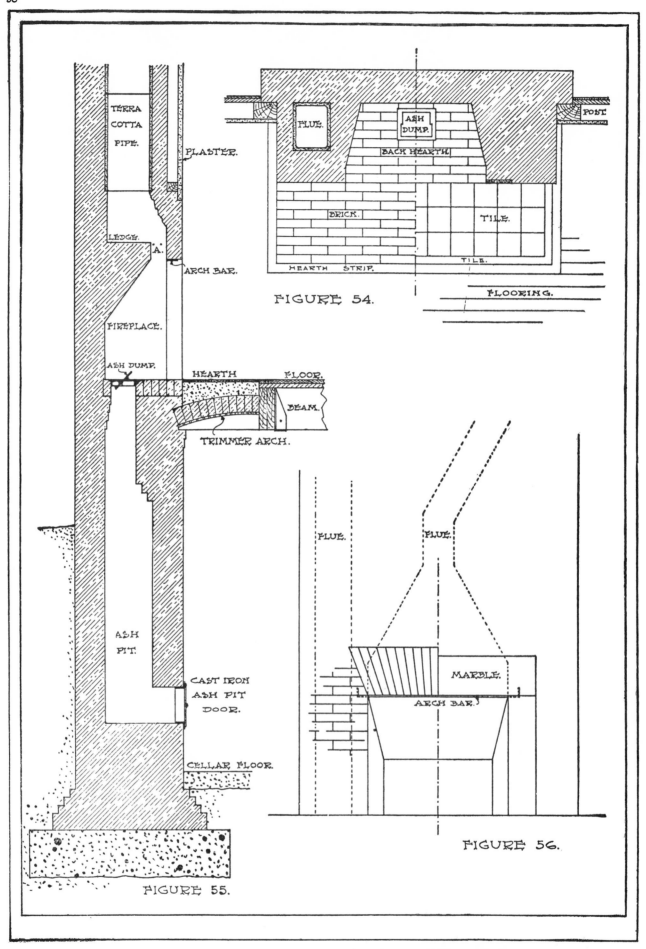

FIGURE 54.

FIGURE 55.

FIGURE 56.

**PLATE 49—FIRE PLACE CONSTRUCTION—NON SMOKING**

Fig. 54, plan view showing both tile and brick hearth. Fig. 55, vertical section through foundation, ash pit, fireplace and flue, showing construction and proper design to prevent smoking. Fig. 56, front elevation of fireplace, showing arrangement of parts.

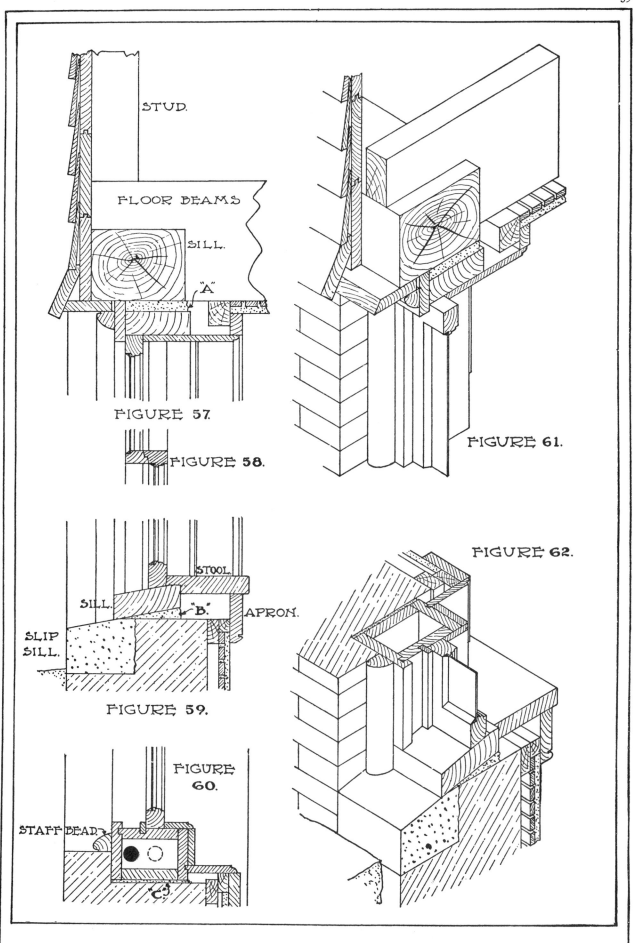

STUD.

FLOOR BEAMS

SILL.

"A"

FIGURE 57.

FIGURE 58.

FIGURE 61.

FIGURE 62.

STOOL.

SILL.

"B"

APRON.

SLIP
SILL.

FIGURE 59.

FIGURE
60.

STAFF BEAD.

"C"

## PLATE 50—DOUBLE HUNG CELLAR WINDOW

Construction for building where cellar is plastered and finished. Fig. 57, section through window head. Fig. 58, section through meeting rails. Fig. 59, section through window sill. Fig. 60, section through jamb. Fig. 61, isometric view showing relation of various members at the window head. Fig. 62, isometric view of window sill and jamb.

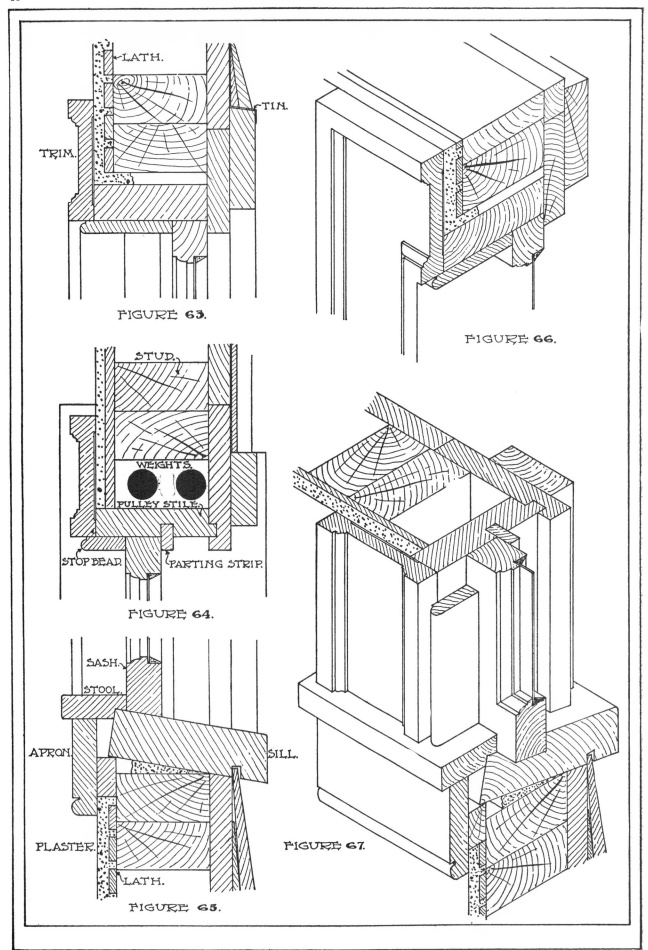

LATH.

TIN.

TRIM.

FIGURE 63.

FIGURE 66.

STUD.

WEIGHTS.

PULLEY STILE.

STOP BEAD.

PARTING STRIP.

FIGURE 64.

SASH.

STOOL.

APRON.

SILL.

PLASTER.

FIGURE 67.

LATH.

FIGURE 65.

## PLATE 51—CHEAP DOUBLE HUNG WINDOW

Arrangement and construction for ordinary inexpensive work, using skeleton frame without ground casings. Fig. 63, section through window head. Fig. 64, section through jamb. Fig. 65, section through sill. Fig. 66, isometric view of window head. Fig. 67, isometric view of jamb and sill. Note tin flashing above window and rabbeted sill to keep out water.

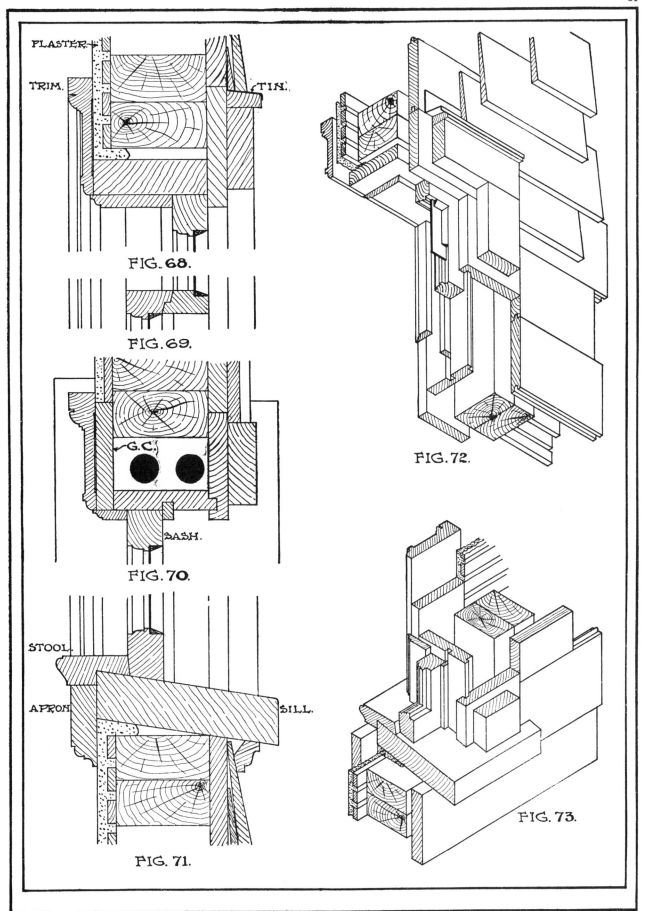

PLASTER.
TRIM.
TIN.
FIG. 68.

FIG. 69.

G.C.
SASH.
FIG. 70.

FIG. 72.

STOOL.
APRON.
SILL.
FIG. 71.

FIG. 73.

## PLATE 52—DOUBLE HUNG WINDOW WITH GROUND CASINGS

Skeleton frame construction in ordinary work. Fig. 68, section through window head. Note tin flashing to keep out the water. Fig. 69, section through meeting rails. Fig. 70, section through jamb showing ground casing (G. C.). Fig. 71, section through sill. Fig. 72, isometric view of head and jamb. Fig. 73, isometric view of sill and jamb.

62

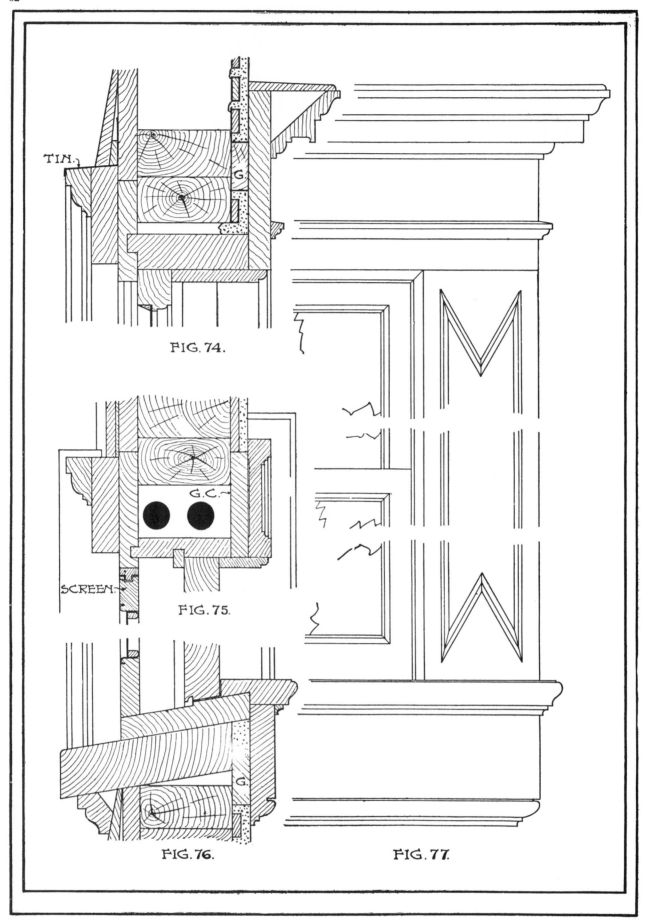

TIN.

G

FIG. 74.

G.C.

SCREEN

FIG. 75.

G

FIG. 76.

FIG. 77.

## PLATE 53—DOUBLE HUNG WINDOW WITH SCREEN

Construction in frame wall. Fig. 74, section through window head showing use of grounds (G). Note also tin flashing over window. Fig. 75, section through jamb showing sliding mosquito screen with running strip nailed to outside casing. Fig. 76, section through sill. Note that both sill and sub-sill are used in place of the single sill, common in cheaper work. Fig. 77, inside elevation showing elaborate interior finish, little used at the present time.

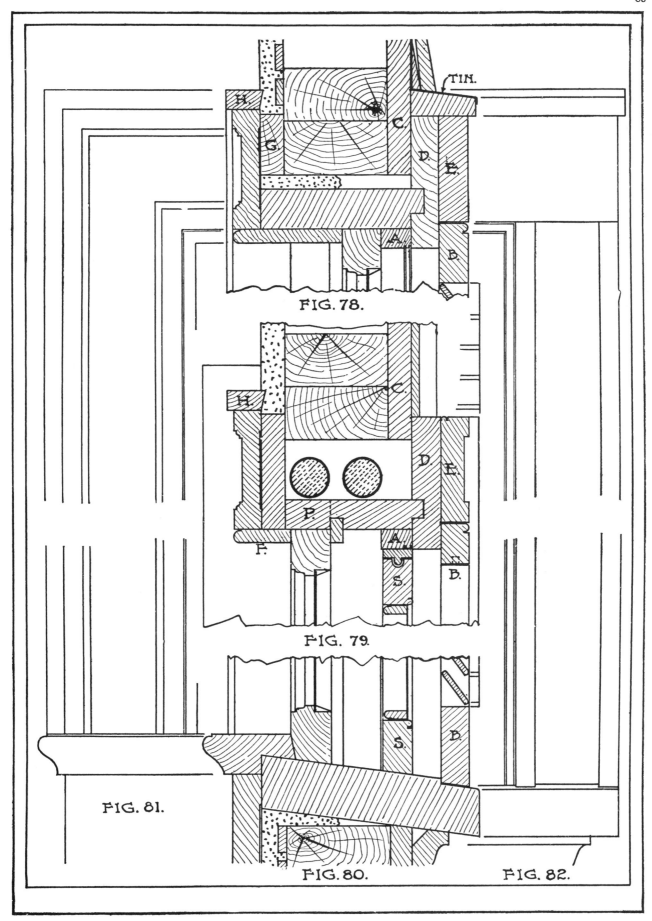

FIG. 78.

FIG. 79.

FIG. 81.

FIG. 80.

FIG. 82.

## PLATE 54—WINDOW WITH SCREEN AND OUTSIDE BLINDS

Double hung construction in frame wall. The extra space needed for mosquito screen and outside blinds is secured by putting the outside casing (D) over the sheathing boards (C), making a wider box for sash weights and allowing the piece (A) to be set for mosquito screen. The space between mosquito screen and blind (B) is required for the blind fasteners. Fig. 78, section through window head. Fig. 79, section through jamb. Fig. 80, section through window sill. Fig. 81, interior elevation showing inside trim. Fig. 82, exterior elevation of window.

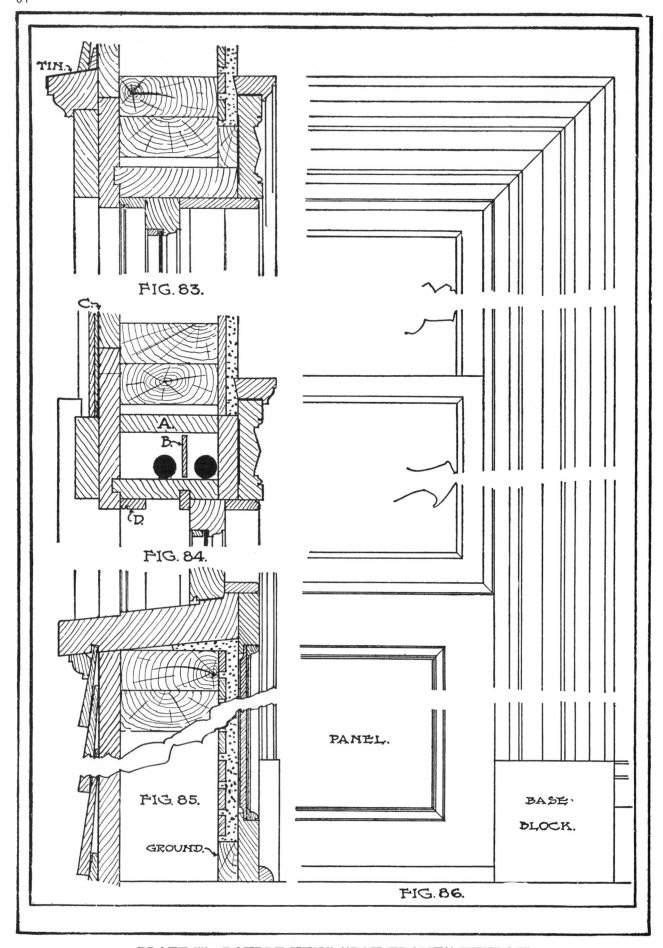

TIN.

FIG. 83.

C.

A.

B.

D.

FIG. 84.

FIG. 85.

GROUND.

PANEL.

BASE.

BLOCK.

FIG. 86.

## PLATE 55—DOUBLE HUNG "BOX FRAME" WINDOW

Construction in frame wall. The "box frame" is formed with back casing (A) completing the box and insuring a rigid pulley stile and consequently accurately fitting sashes. The extra space required for window screen and outside blinds is secured in this case by using 5 inch studs. Fig. 83, section through window head. Fig. 84, section through jamb; B is a strip of wood dividing the weight box, an improvement used only in the best grade of work. Fig. 85, section through sill, showing moulded panel under the window in place of the ordinary stool and apron finish. Fig. 86, interior elevation showing inside trim; base blocks very little used today.

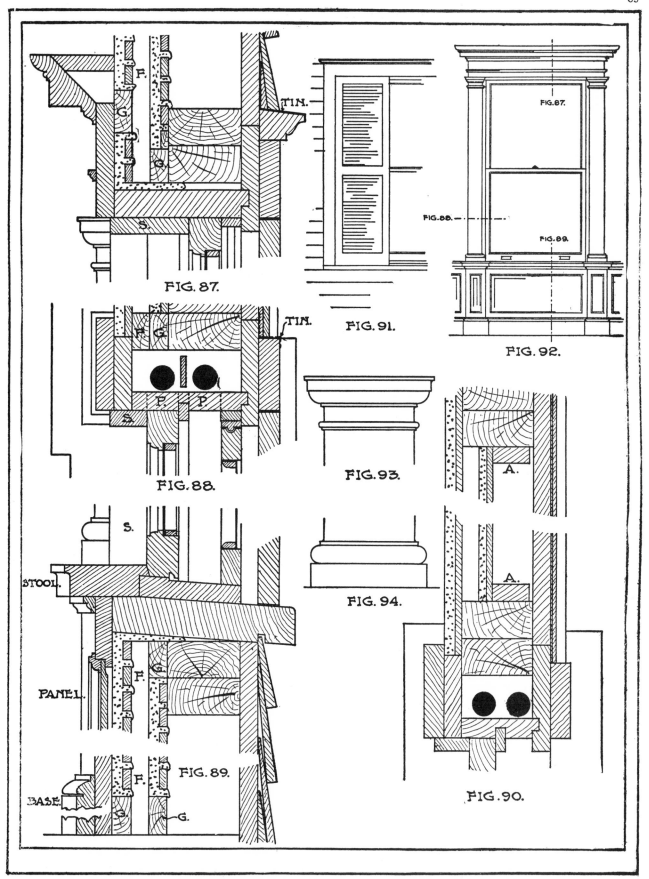

FIG. 87.

FIG. 91.

FIG. 92.

FIG. 88.

FIG. 93.

FIG. 94.

FIG. 89.

FIG. 90.

## PLATE 56—DOUBLE-PLASTERED WALLS—WINDOW FRAMING

In locations exposed to severe cold weather and penetrating winds the double plastered wall is desirable. The one-inch air space is formed, between the usual lath and plaster coat and the additional plaster surface, by means of 1 by 2 inch furring strips (F). Fig. 87, section through window head. Fig. 88, section through jamb. Fig.

89, section through window sill and base. Fig. 90, section through window jamb showing another method of constructing a double-plastered wall, in this case requiring no additional thickness. Fig. 91, exterior elevation of window. Fig. 92, interior elevation, showing inside trim. Figs. 93 and 94, details of pilaster cap and base.

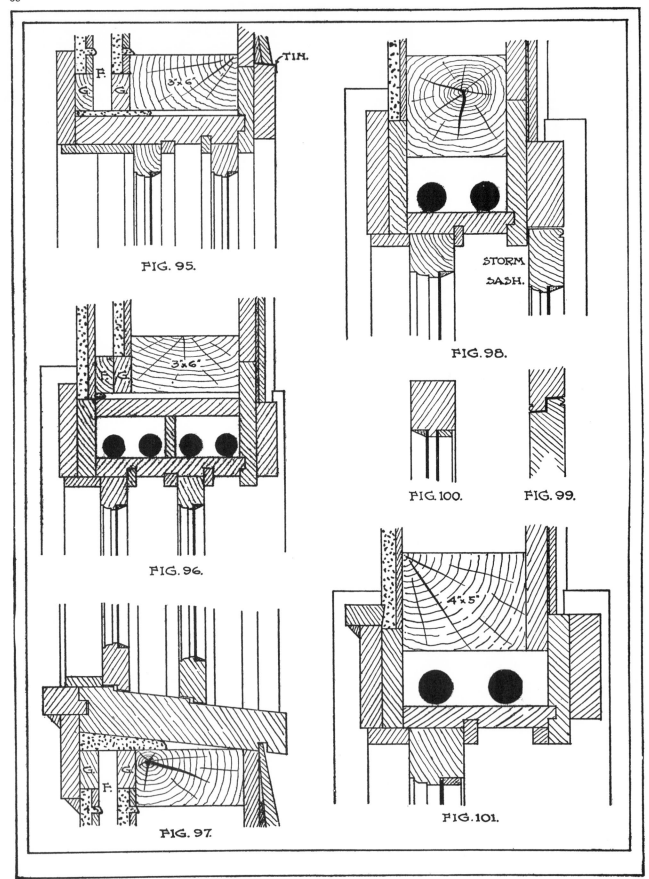

FIG. 95.

FIG. 98.

FIG. 96.

FIG. 100.     FIG. 99.

FIG. 97.

FIG. 101.

## PLATE 57—STORM SASH AND DOUBLE GLAZING

Fig. 95, section through window head of a very warm, storm resisting window for use in locations exposed to very severe weather throughout the greater part of the year. Note use of 3 by 6 studs and 1 by 2 furring strips (F) which form the double-plaster space. Fig. 96, section through jamb. Fig. 97, section through window sill. Fig. 98, another form of wall construction; section through window jamb showing storm sash substituted for blinds when cold weather sets in. Fig. 99, joint at meeting stiles of storm sash. Fig. 100, sectional view of double glazed sash for exposed locations. Fig. 101, frame for use with heavy sash; section through window jamb.

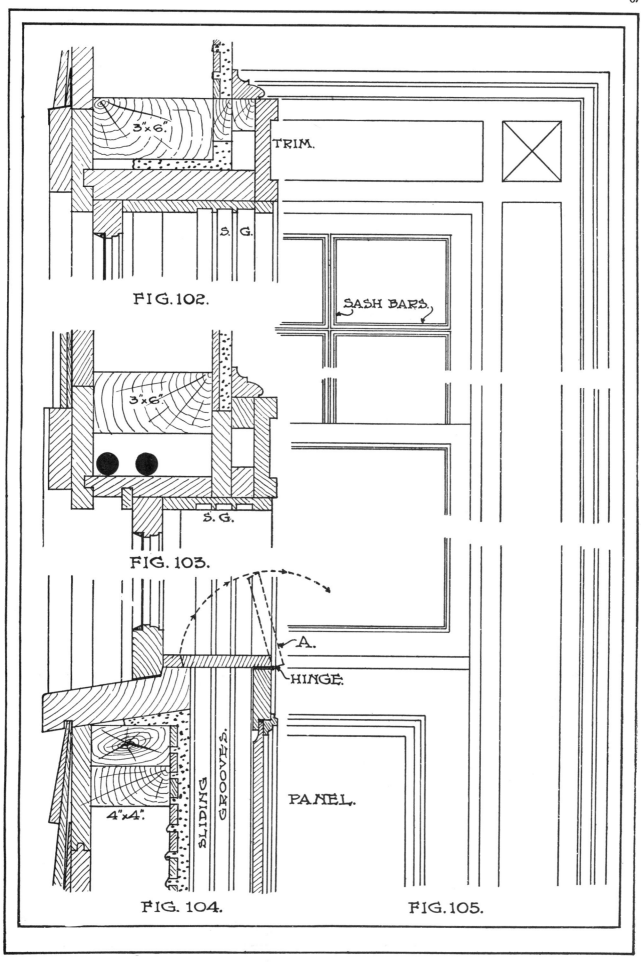

FIG. 102.

TRIM.

S. G.

3"x6".

FIG. 103.

3"x6".

S. G.

SASH BARS.

A.

HINGE.

SLIDING GROOVES.

PANEL.

4"x4".

FIG. 104.

FIG. 105.

## PLATE 58—INSIDE SLIDING WINDOW BLINDS

Double hung windows, construction in frame wall. This arrangement is for inside blinds sliding in grooves on the window jamb and when not in use sliding down into a pocket (Fig. 104) behind a moulded panel back. To provide the necessary space 3 by 6 studs are used. Fig. 102, section through window head. Note sliding grooves (S. G.). Fig. 103, section through jamb. Fig. 104, section through window sill showing pocket. Note plastering inside of pocket which should never be omitted. Fig. 105, inside elevation showing interior trim.

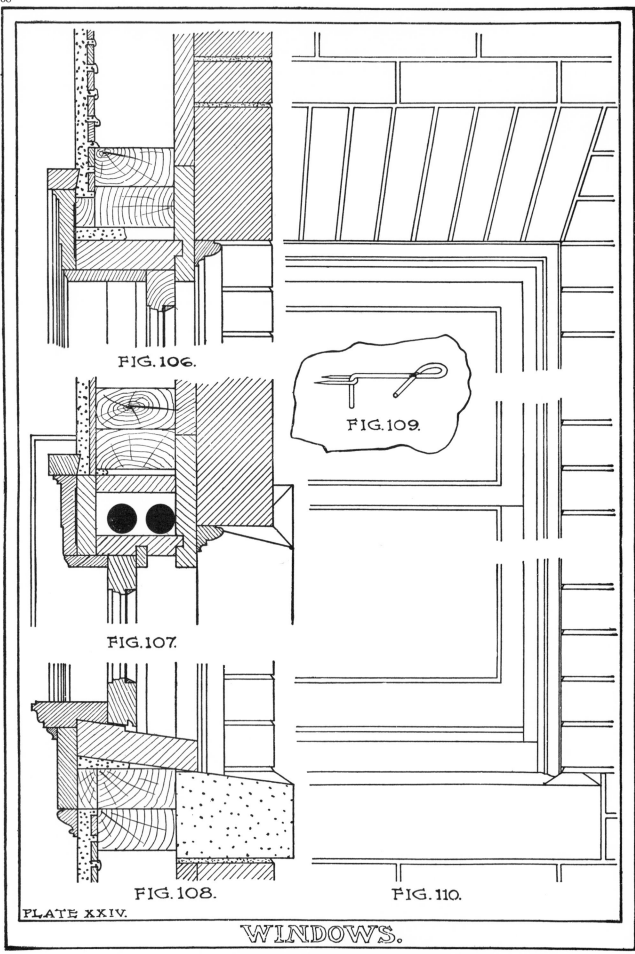

FIG. 106.

FIG. 109.

FIG. 107.

FIG. 108.

FIG. 110.

PLATE XXIV.

WINDOWS.

## PLATE 59—DOUBLE HUNG WINDOW IN BRICK-VENEER WALL

The wall is constructed of 2 by 4 studs, doubled at openings, plastered on the inside, sheathed diagonally on the outside with matched boards; then covered with waterproof sheathing paper and then with four inches of brick work. The brick wall is tied to the frame work every five courses and opposite every stud. Fig. 106, section through window head. Fig. 107, section through jamb. Fig. 108, section through sill. Fig. 109, detail wall tie. Fig. 110, exterior view.

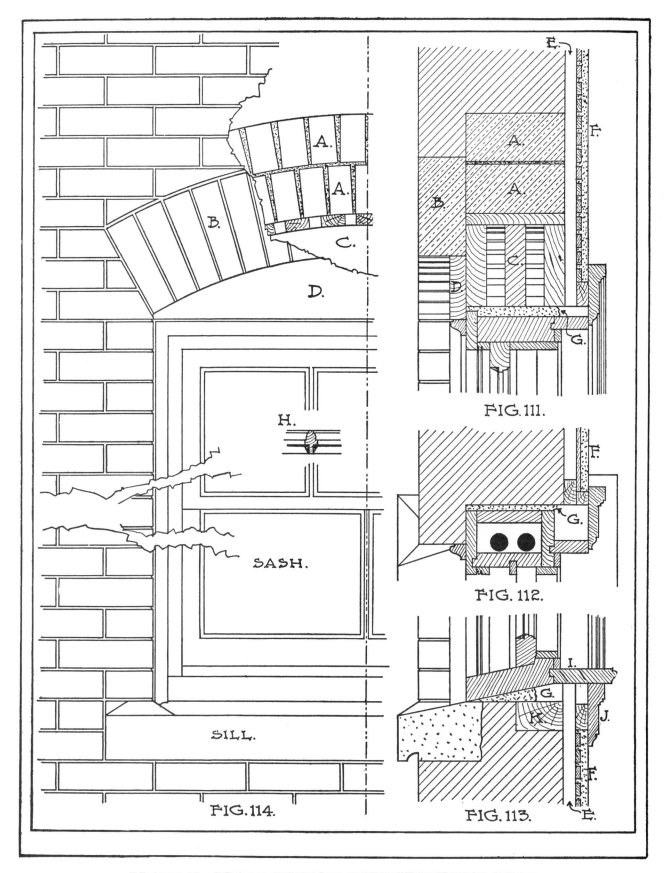

FIG. 111.

FIG. 112.

FIG. 114.

FIG. 113.

## PLATE 60—BROAD WINDOW WITH SEGMENTAL HEAD

Double hung windows construction in **13 inch** brick wall, the window finished with an arch **on** the outside and a square head on the inside. Fig. 111, section through window head, at center **line.** The opening is spanned on the outside by **the** segmental arch (B) of face brick. The **inner 8** inches are supported by a permanent **wood center** (C) and the two-row-lock relieving arch (AA).

E indicates the furring which should be used to prevent dampness. Fig. 112, section through jamb showing space (G) filled with mortar or hand-calked with oakum. Fig. 113, section through window sill. K is a 2 by 4 nailing strip. Fig. **114,** exterior elevation of the window. Note the piece D put in as a finish to cover the rough wood center C.

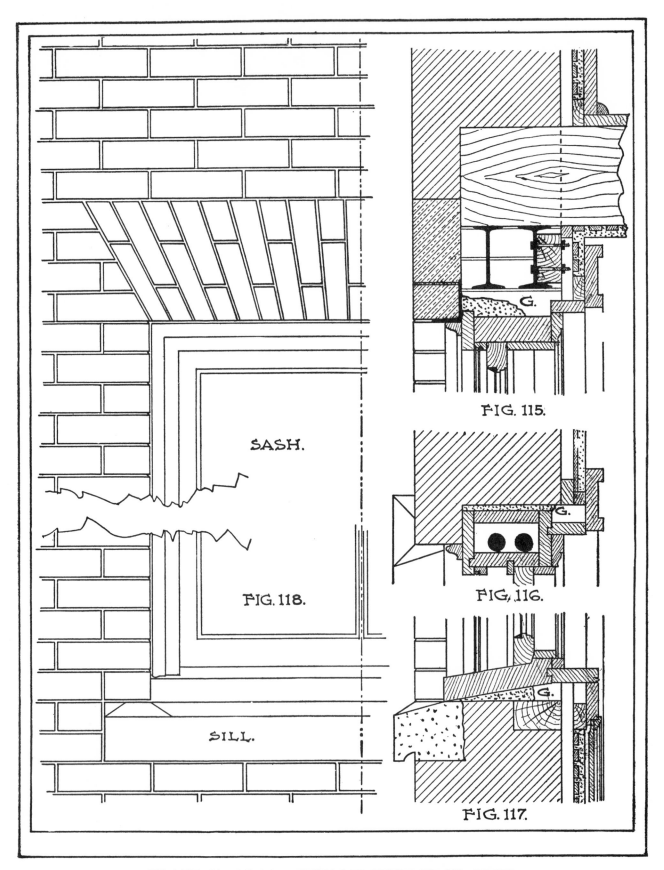

FIG. 115.

SASH.

FIG. 116.

FIG. 118.

SILL.

FIG. 117.

## PLATE 61—BROAD WINDOW WITH FLAT ARCH

Double hung windows, construction in 13 inch brick wall, the weight above the window opening, including floor joists, being supported by two steel I-beams. Such I-beams are necessary when there is not sufficient space between the window head and the underside of the floor joists to turn a brick relieving arch on top of a timber lintel. Fig. 115, section through window head, showing angle iron supporting flat brick arch and I-beams supporting floor joists. Fig. 116, section through jamb. Fig. 117, section through sill. Fig. 118, exterior view of window.

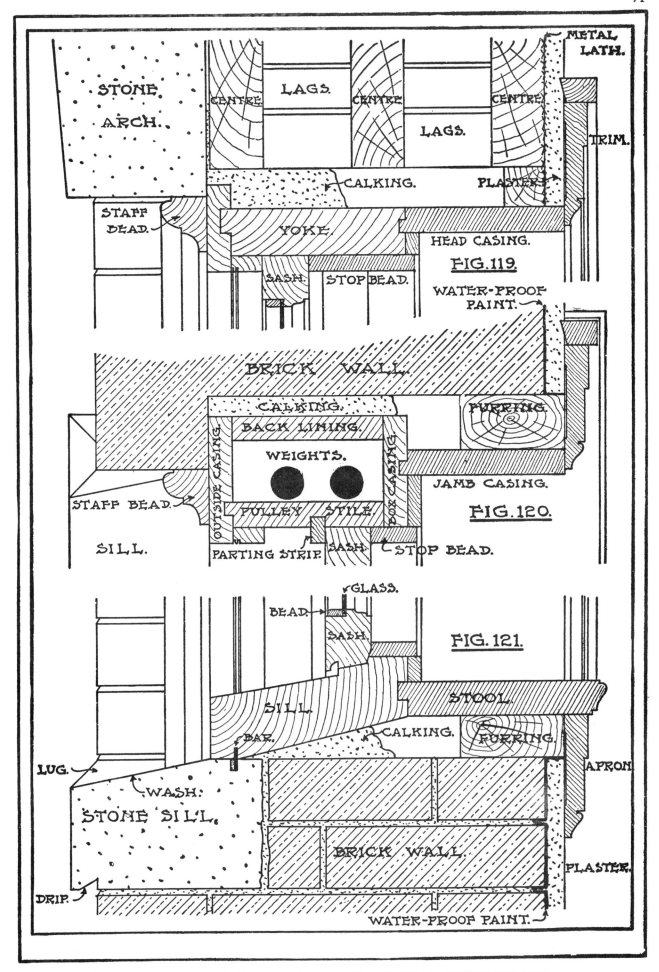

**PLATE 62—DOUBLE HUNG WINDOW IN 18″ BRICK WALL**

Fig. 119, section through window head. Fig. 120, section through window jamb. Fig. 121, section through window sill. Note that furring and lathing of inside walls are omitted and the plaster applied direct to the brick work. When this is done the wall should be thoroughly coated with a waterproofing coat so as to make it impervious to moisture which would discolor the finish plaster.

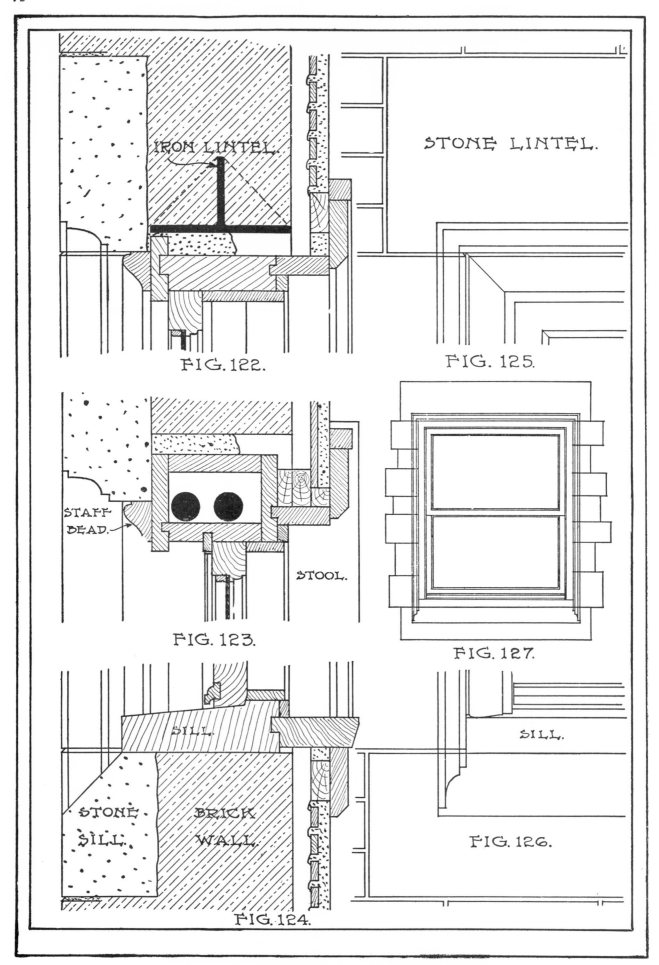

FIG. 122.

STONE LINTEL.

IRON LINTEL.

FIG. 125.

STAFF BEAD.

STOOL.

FIG. 123.

FIG. 127.

SILL.

STONE SILL.

BRICK WALL.

FIG. 126.

FIG. 124.

## PLATE 63—IRON LINTEL OVER WINDOWS

An iron lintel is preferred over wide window openings in masonry walls and where it is not convenient to turn a row-lock relieving arch over a timber lintel. Double hung window framing. Fig. 122, section through window head. Fig. 123, section through jamb. Fig. 124, section through sill. Figs. 125, 126 and 127, exterior elevations of window.

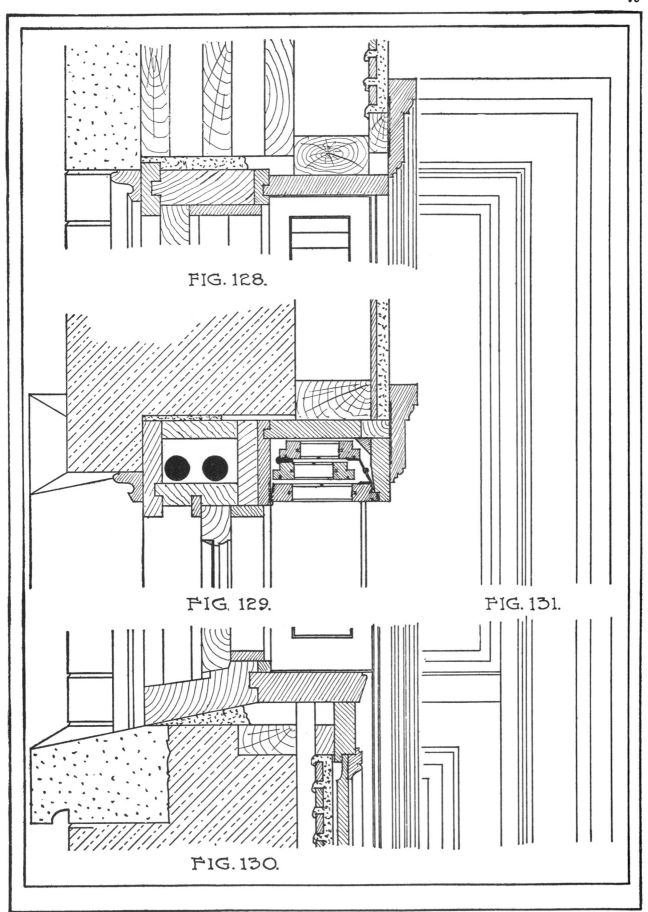

**PLATE 64—INSIDE BLINDS IN CONCEALED POCKETS**

With double hung windows, construction in 13 inch brick wall. Fig. 128, section through window head. Fig. 129, section through jamb showing construction of the blind box and the method of folding the blinds. All the woodwork of the box which would be exposed to view when the blinds are closed, should be made to conform with the finish of the balance of the room. Fig. 130, section through the window sill which is finished on the inside with a moulded stool and panel back. Plastering should always be provided back of panel back. Fig. 131, interior elevation.

74

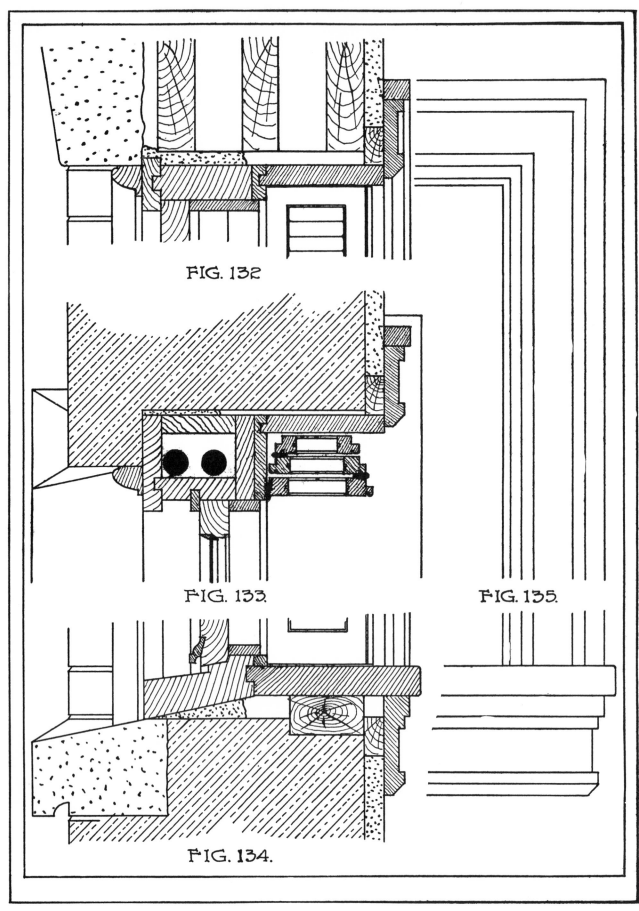

FIG. 132

FIG. 133.

FIG. 135.

FIG. 134.

## PLATE 65—INSIDE BLINDS—NOT CONCEALED

With double hung windows, construction in 16 inch brick wall. Fig. 132, section through window head. Fig. 133, section through jamb, showing arrangement of inside blinds. Fig. 134, section through sill. Fig. 135, interior elevation of window showing inside trim.

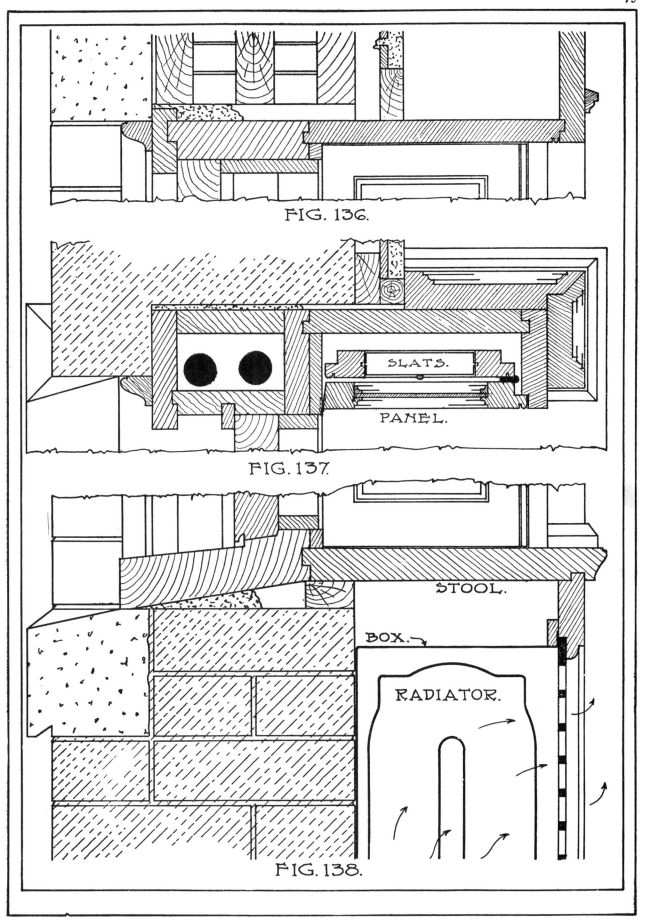

FIG. 136.

FIG. 137.

SLATS.

PANEL.

STOOL.

BOX.

RADIATOR.

FIG. 138.

## PLATE 66—INSIDE BLINDS SET IN PROJECTING BOXES

With double hung windows, construction in 13 inch brick wall. Fig. 136, section through window head. Fig. 137, section through window jamb and projecting blind box, showing arrangement of inside blinds. The blind box is treated architecturally, being nicely paneled; and the first leaf of the blinds is also paneled to match, so that when the blinds are folded back in the pocket the appearance is presented of a wide paneled jamb. Fig. 138, section through window sill. The space underneath the broad stool is utilized for a radiator box, making a good method of heating.

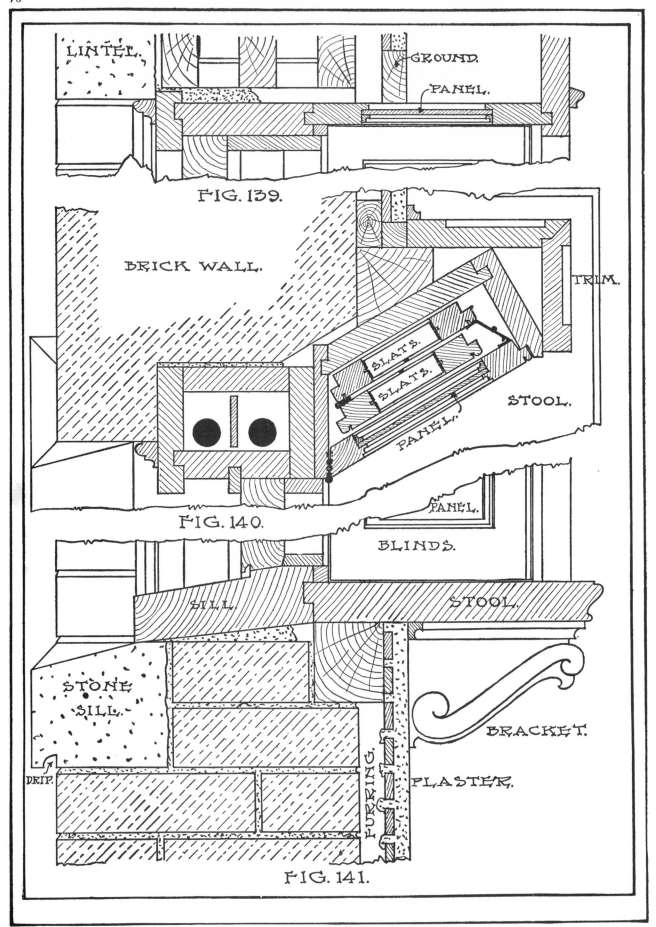

LINTEL.

GROUND.

PANEL.

FIG. 139.

BRICK WALL.

TRIM.

SLATS.

SLATS.

STOOL.

PANEL.

FIG. 140.

PANEL.

BLINDS.

SILL

STOOL.

STONE SILL.

DRIP.

FURRING.

BRACKET.

PLASTER.

FIG. 141.

## PLATE 67—INSIDE BLINDS SET IN SLANTING BOXES

With double hung windows, construction in 13 inch brick wall. Fig. 139, section through window head showing broad panel above projecting blind box with space above closed in tight up to the ceiling. Fig. 140, section through window jamb and slanting blind box, showing arrangement of blinds. Fig. 141, section through sill, showing bracketed stool.

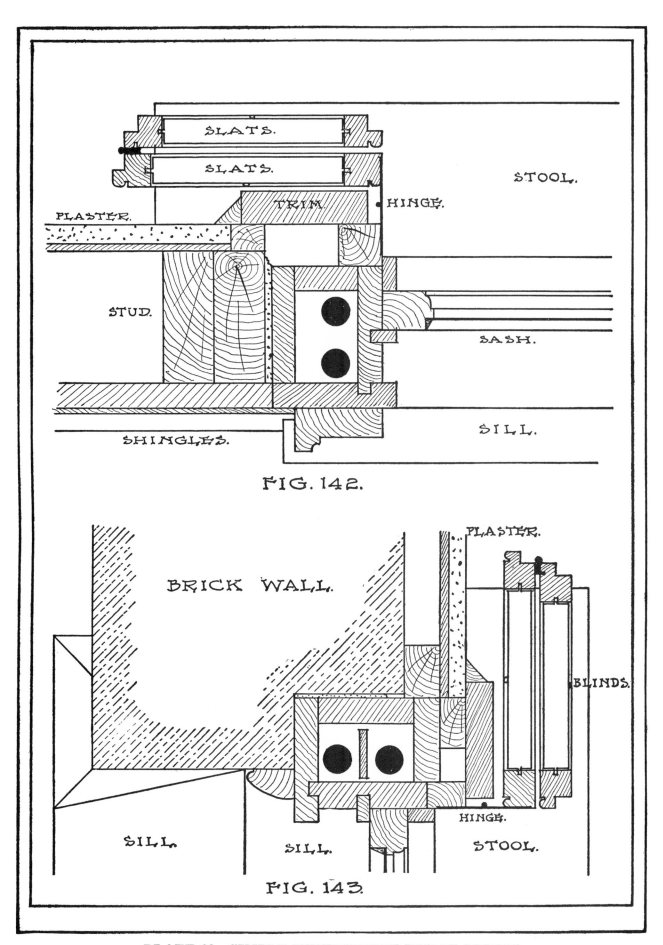

FIG. 142.

FIG. 143.

**PLATE 68—SIMPLE INEXPENSIVE INSIDE BLINDS**

With double hung windows. Fig. 142, section through window jamb, showing construction and **arrangement** for use in frame walls. Fig. 143, section through window jamb, showing construction and arrangement in 13-inch brick wall. Inside blinds are not used as much as they should be.

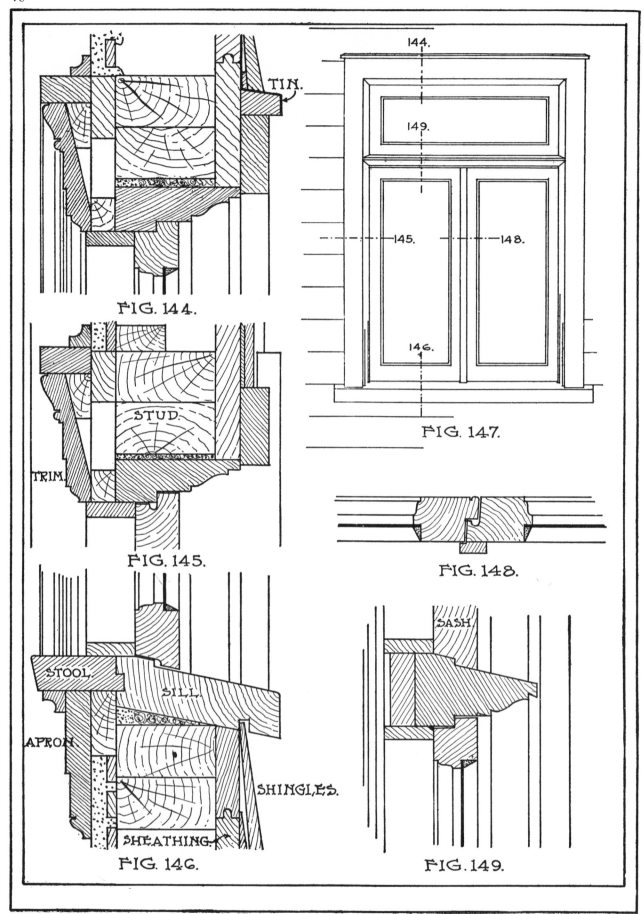

FIG. 144.

FIG. 145.

TRIM.

STUD.

FIG. 147.

144.

149.

145. 148.

146.

FIG. 148.

FIG. 146.

STOOL.

SILL

APRON

SHINGLES.

SHEATHING.

TIN.

SASH

FIG. 149.

## PLATE 69—DOUBLE CASEMENT WINDOWS WITH STATIONARY TRANSOM

Outward opening casement windows, construction in frame walls. Fig. 144, section through window head. Fig. 145, section through jamb. Fig. 146, section through window sill. Fig. 147, exterior elevation of window with dotted lines indicating the position of the sectional views. Fig. 148, horizontal section through meeting stiles of the sash. Fig. 149, section through transom bar. When the transom sash is to be hinged or pivoted a water box should be provided on lower rail.

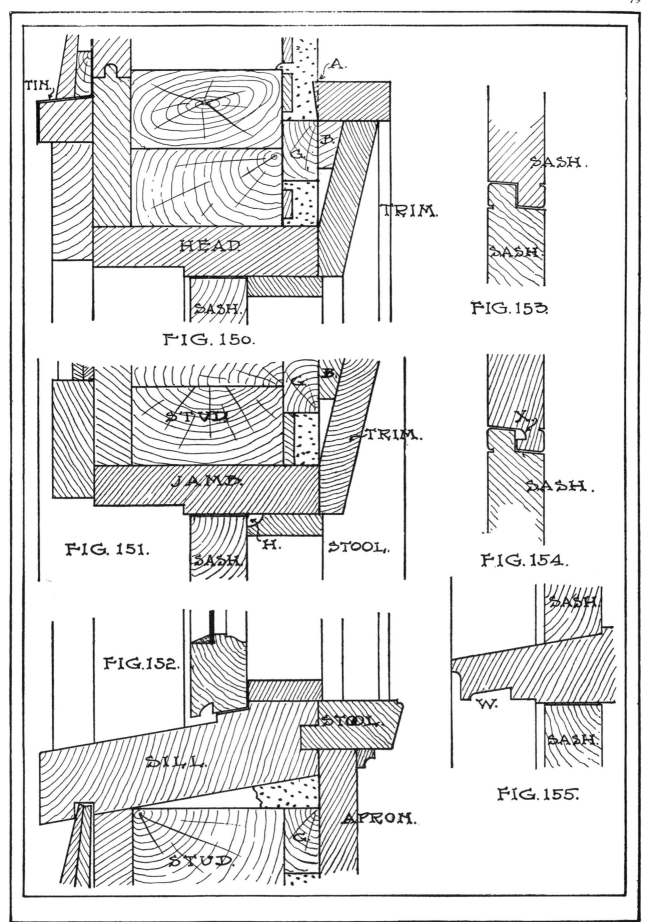

TIN.

A.

B.

TRIM.

HEAD.

SASH.

FIG. 150.

SASH.

SASH.

FIG. 153.

G.

B.

STUD.

TRIM.

JAMB.

H.

STOOL.

SASH.

FIG. 151.

SASH.

FIG. 154.

FIG. 152.

STOOL.

SILL.

APRON.

STUD.

SASH.

W.

SASH.

FIG. 155.

## PLATE 70—OUTWARD OPENING CASEMENT—ORDINARY CONSTRUCTION

Arrangement ordinarily used in frame dwellings. Fig. 150, section through window head. Note flashing of tin, or in better work, copper. Fig. 151, section through window jamb. Note that inside stop bead is hollowed at H to form a channel down which any water, which may beat in between sash and jamb, may pass. Fig. 152, section through window sill. Note how sash is grooved on the underside for a drip. Fig. 153, section showing construction of the meeting stiles of casements opening in two leaves. Fig. 154, same as Fig. 153, but of improved construction. Fig. 155, section through transom bar where stationary transom is used.

80

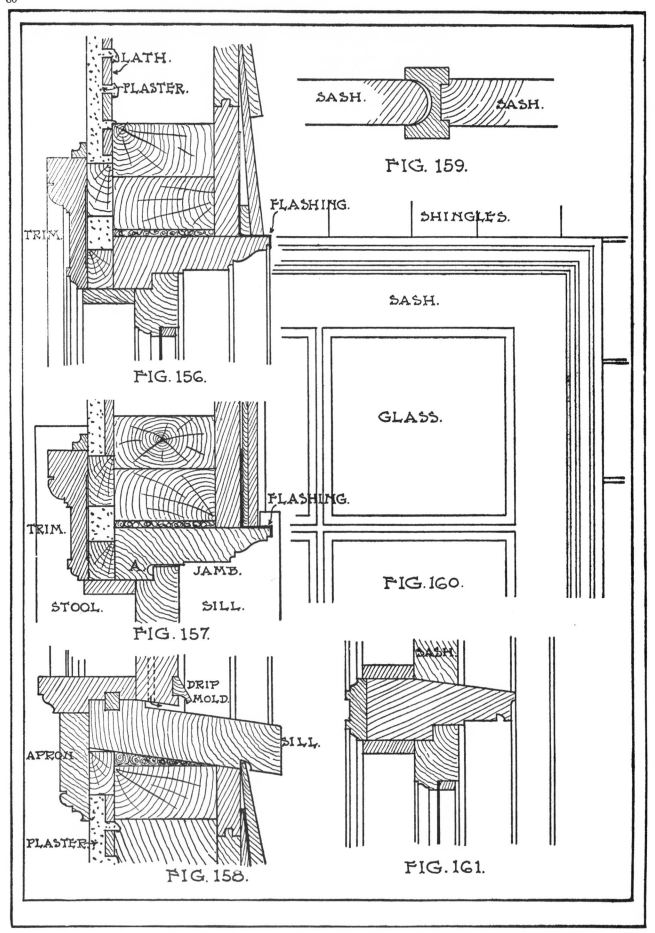

FIG. 159.

FIG. 156.

FIG. 157.

FIG. 160.

FIG. 158.

FIG. 161.

## PLATE 71—CASEMENT WINDOW WITHOUT OUTSIDE ARCHITRAVE

For outward opening casements of ordinary construction as in shingled dwellings where, for artistic reasons, no outside architrave is desired. Fig. 156, section through window head. Note method of flashing. Fig. 157, section through jamb. Fig. 158, section through window sill; casement provided with drip mould to insure water-tightness.

Fig. 159, horizontal section through the meeting stiles of casements in two leaves. This makes a tight joint but requires that both leaves be opened and closed together. Fig. 160, exterior elevation of the upper portion of window. Fig. 161, section through transom bar, transom sash being stationary.

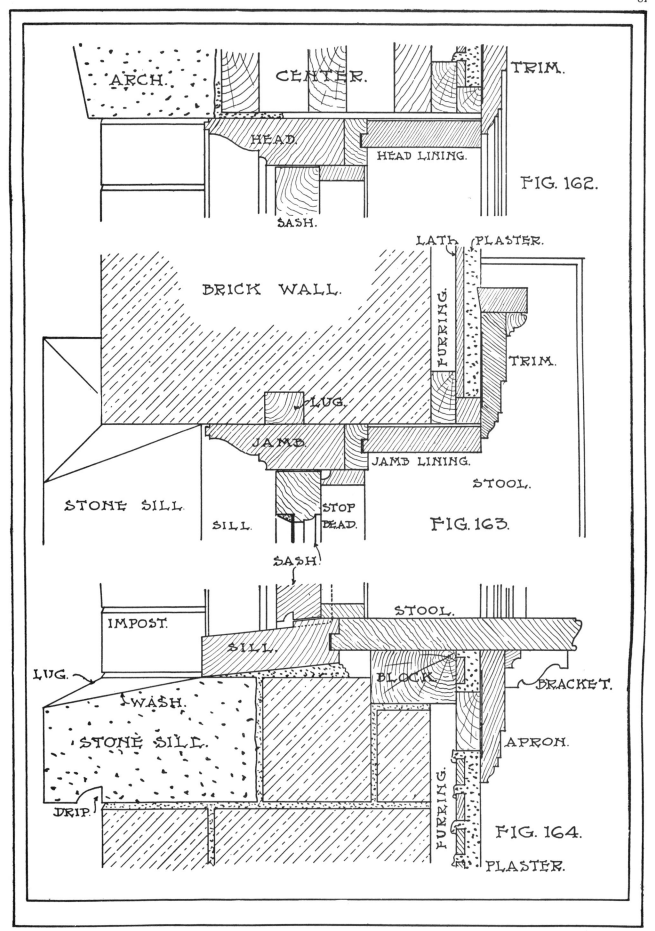

ARCH.    CENTER.    TRIM.

HEAD.    HEAD LINING.

SASH.

FIG. 162.

LATH    PLASTER.

BRICK WALL.

FURRING.

TRIM.

LUG.

JAMB.    JAMB LINING.

STOOL.

STONE SILL.    SILL.    STOP BEAD.    FIG. 163.

SASH.

IMPOST.    STOOL.

SILL.    BLOCK.    BRACKET.

LUG.

WASH.    APRON.

STONE SILL.

FURRING.    FIG. 164.

DRIP.    PLASTER.

## PLATE 72—INEXPENSIVE CASEMENT IN BRICK WALL

Outward opening casements of cheap construction; arrangement for 13 inch brick wall. Fig. 62, section through window head. Fig. 163, section through window jamb. Note arrangement of moulded stop bead and jamb lining. Fig. 164, section through window sill.

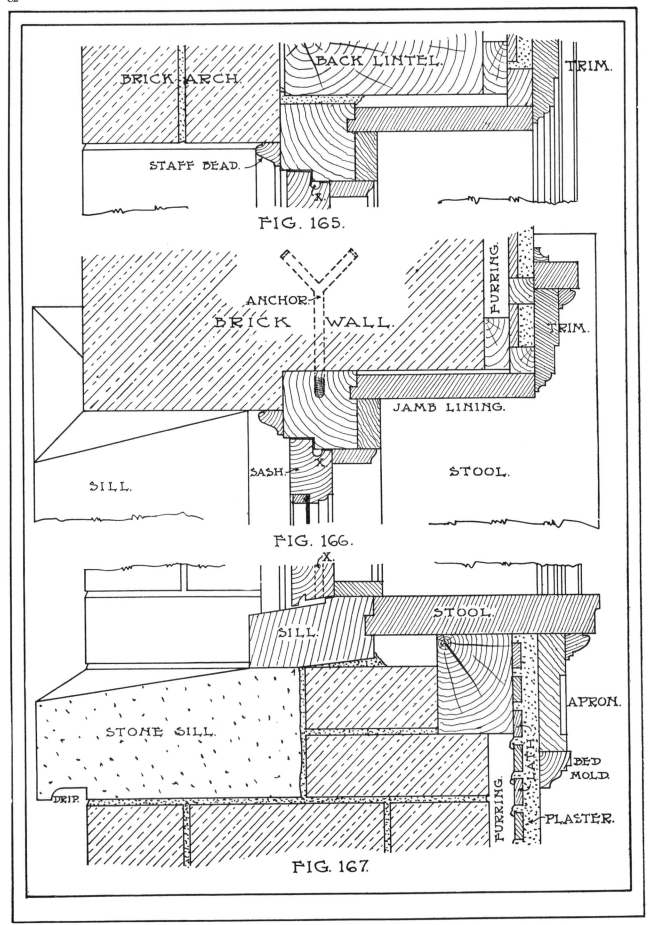

FIG. 165.

BRICK ARCH.　BACK LINTEL.　TRIM.

STAFF BEAD.

X

FIG. 166.

ANCHOR.

BRICK WALL.

FURRING.

TRIM.

JAMB LINING.

SILL.　SASH.　X　STOOL.

FIG. 167.

X.

STOOL.

SILL.

STONE SILL.

APRON.

BED MOLD.

FURRING.　LATH.

PLASTER.

DRIP.

## PLATE 73—OUTWARD OPENING CASEMENT—IMPROVED CONSTRUCTION

Arrangement for 16 inch brick wall. Fig. 165, section through window head. Fig. 166, section through jamb. Note how window frames are anchored tightly to the masonry, sitting in a recessed space and with joint covered with staff bead. Fig. 167, section through sill. X indicates channel to carry away any water which may beat in between jamb and sash.

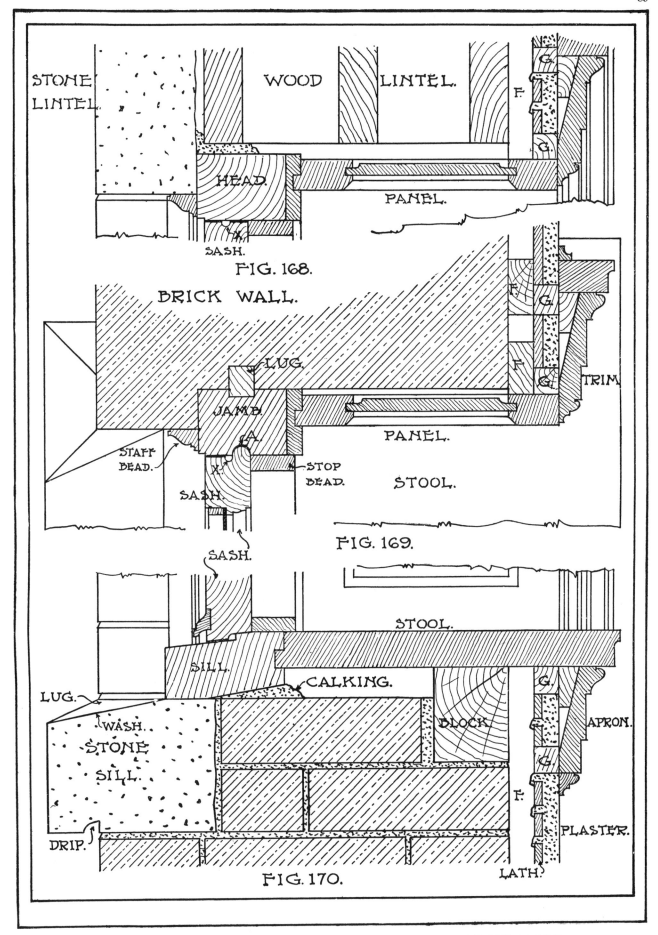

STONE LINTEL

WOOD LINTEL

F

G

HEAD.

PANEL.

SASH.

**FIG. 168.**

BRICK WALL.

F

G

F

G

TRIM

LUG.

JAMB.

PANEL.

STAFF BEAD.

A

STOP BEAD.

STOOL.

SASH.

X

SASH.

**FIG. 169.**

SASH.

STOOL.

SILL.

CALKING.

G

LUG.

WASH..

STONE SILL.

BLOCK

APRON.

F

DRIP.

PLASTER.

LATH.

**FIG. 170.**

## PLATE 74—OUTWARD OPENING CASEMENT IN BRICK WALL

Improved construction, arrangement for 16 inch brick wall. Fig. 168, section through window head. Fig. 169, section through window jamb. Fig. 170, section through sill. F is the furring to provide air space to keep out dampness. The interior trim is nailed to the grounds (G) and the window frames are securely fastened to wooden lugs built into the brick work.

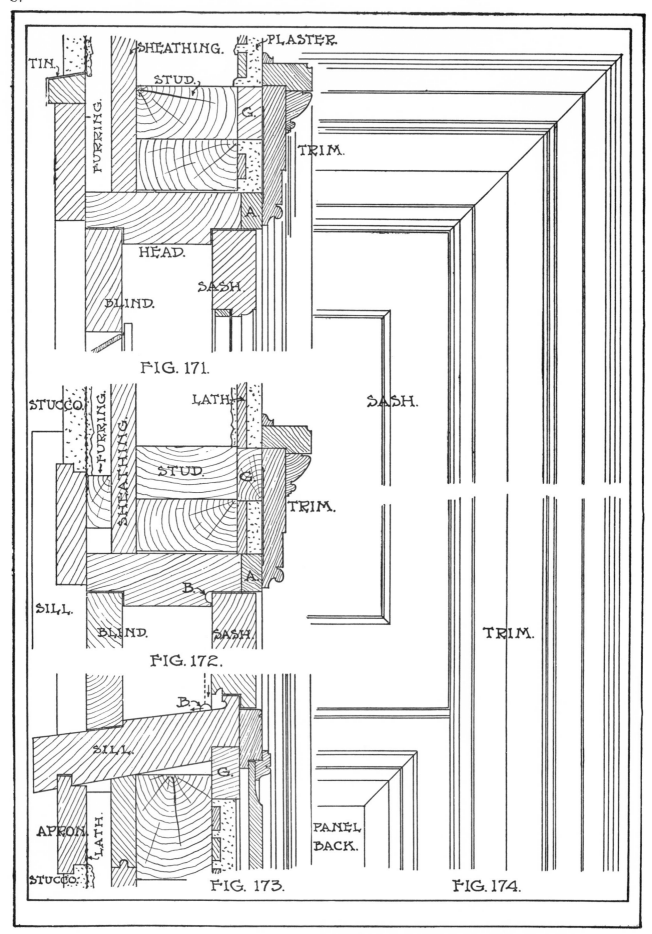

TIN.

SHEATHING. PLASTER.

STUD.

FURRING.

G.

TRIM.

A.

HEAD.

SASH.

BLIND.

FIG. 171.

STUCCO.

FURRING.

LATH.

SASH.

SHEATHING.

STUD.

G.

TRIM.

A.

B.

SILL.

BLIND.

SASH.

FIG. 172.

B.

SILL.

G.

APRON.

LATH.

PANEL BACK.

STUCCO.

FIG. 173.

FIG. 174.

TRIM.

## PLATE 75—INWARD OPENING CASEMENT IN CEMENT STUCCO WALL

The only serious objection to the use of casement windows in general is that it is difficult to make them proof against rain and wind, and with casements opening inward this difficulty is much greater than with those opening outward. The construction here illustrated will be found perfectly weather-tight except in exposed locations.

Fig. 171, section through window head. Fig. 172, section through jamb. Notice construction of wall and application of outside trim to cement plaster. Fig. 173, section through window sill. The double rabbeted channel and corner joint between sash and sill make this window perfectly water-tight, even against the most driving rains.

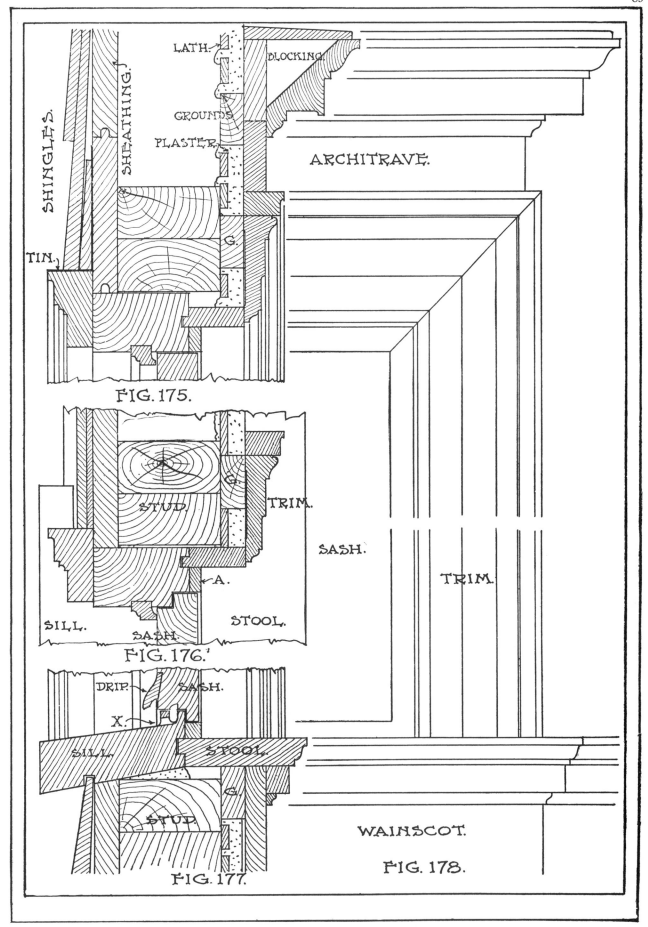

FIG. 175.

FIG. 176.

FIG. 177.

FIG. 178.

*Labels in figures:* SHINGLES. SHEATHING. LATH. GROUNDS. PLASTER. BLOCKING. ARCHITRAVE. G. TIN. STUD. G. TRIM. SASH. A. SILL. SASH. STOOL. DRIP. SASH. X. SILL. STOOL. G. STUD. WAINSCOT. TRIM.

## PLATE 76—WEATHER-PROOF INWARD OPENING CASEMENT

Arrangement in frame walls. The sash and frame are rabbeted at the sill and a small mould is tongued into the jambs outside of the sash in the manner shown. This mould is undercut so as to form a channel to catch any water which may beat in. This water discharges to the sill. Fig. 175, section through window head. Fig. 176, section through jamb. Fig. 177, section through window sill. Note extra drip mould attached to lower part of sash to protect the lower joint. Fig. 178, interior elevation showing inside trim. The projecting architrave above is now seldom used.

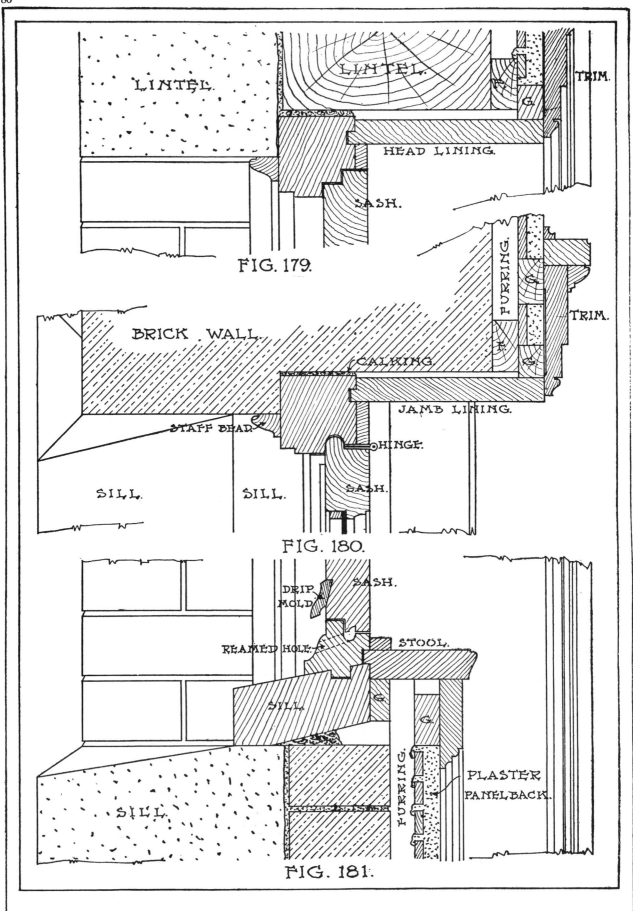

FIG. 179.

FIG. 180.

FIG. 181.

## PLATE 77—STORM-PROOF INWARD OPENING CASEMENT

Arrangement in brick wall. Details of a very successful method of constructing inward opening casement windows so as to be proof against wind and rain. The jamb of the frame is set in a rabbet in the masonry wall and has a semicircular groove cut in its outer edge for a corresponding semi-circular tongue on the stile of the sash. The sash tongue fits exactly into this groove and makes a perfectly water-tight joint. Fig. 179, section through window head. Fig. 180, section through jamb. Fig. 181, section through window sill.

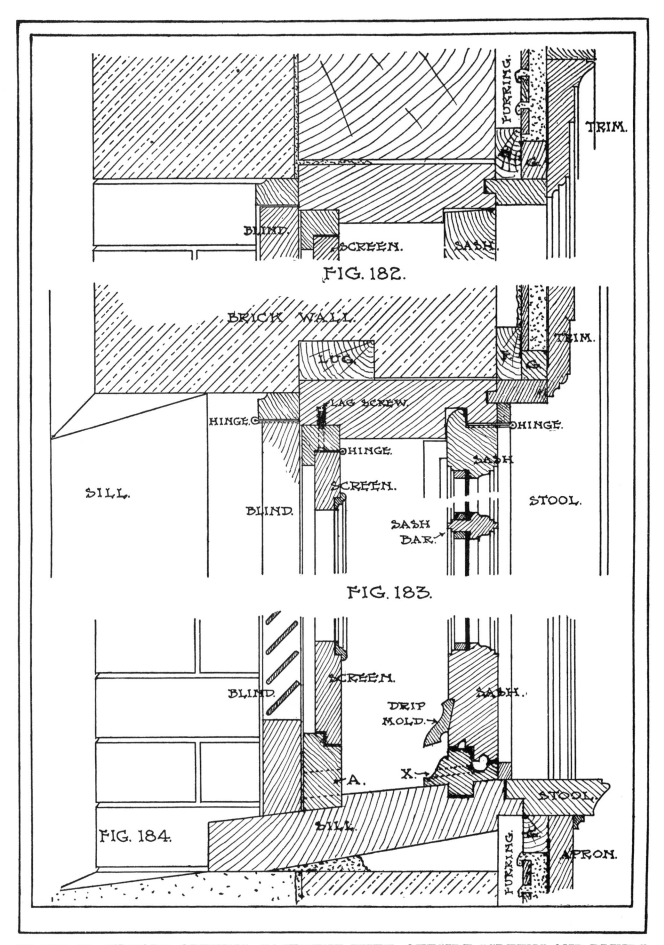

FIG. 182.

BRICK WALL.

FIG. 183.

FIG. 184.

**PLATE 78—INWARD OPENING CASEMENT WITH OUTSIDE SCREENS AND BLINDS**

Construction in brick wall. Fig. 182, section through window head. Fig. 183, section through jamb; note effective water-proof joint between casement and jamb. The screen is hinged to swing in same as casement. The blind swings out and is so arranged that storm sash can be hung in its place during cold weather. Fig. 184, section through sill showing arrangement to insure water tightness. Note drip mould and double rabbeted chambers to lead off moisture that might beat in.

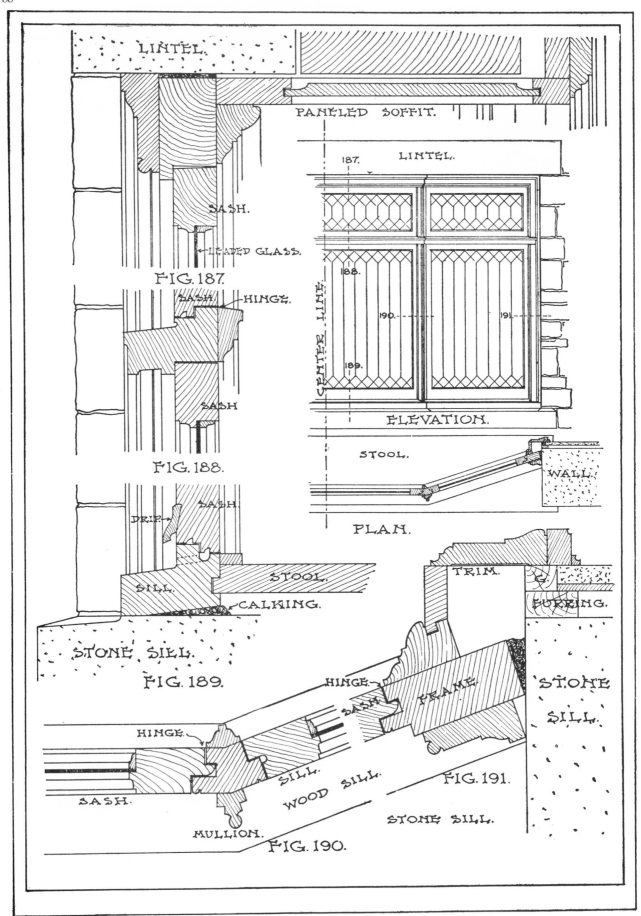

LINTEL.

PANELED SOFFIT.

SASH.

LEADED GLASS.

FIG. 187.

SASH. HINGE.

SASH.

FIG. 188.

187. LINTEL.

188.

CENTER LINE.

190. 191.

189.

ELEVATION.

STOOL.

WALL.

PLAN.

DRIP. SASH.

SILL. STOOL.

CALKING.

STONE SILL.

FIG. 189.

HINGE.

TRIM.

FURRING.

HINGE. SASH. FRAME.

STONE SILL.

HINGE.

SILL.

SASH. WOOD SILL.

FIG. 191.

MULLION.

STONE SILL.

FIG. 190.

## PLATE 79—INWARD OPENING CASEMENT BAY WINDOW

Construction in masonry wall. A popular and very satisfactory window arrangement. The exterior elevation shows the design; the dotted lines indicate the sections shown in the various details. Fig. 187, section through window head. Fig. 188, section through transom bar. Fig. 189, section through window sill. Fig. 190, enlarged plan view and horizontal section taken through the mullion of the bay window, and showing it to be of light construction and rabbeted for both sashes. Fig. 191, section through window jamb. Note arrangement in all parts for tightness.

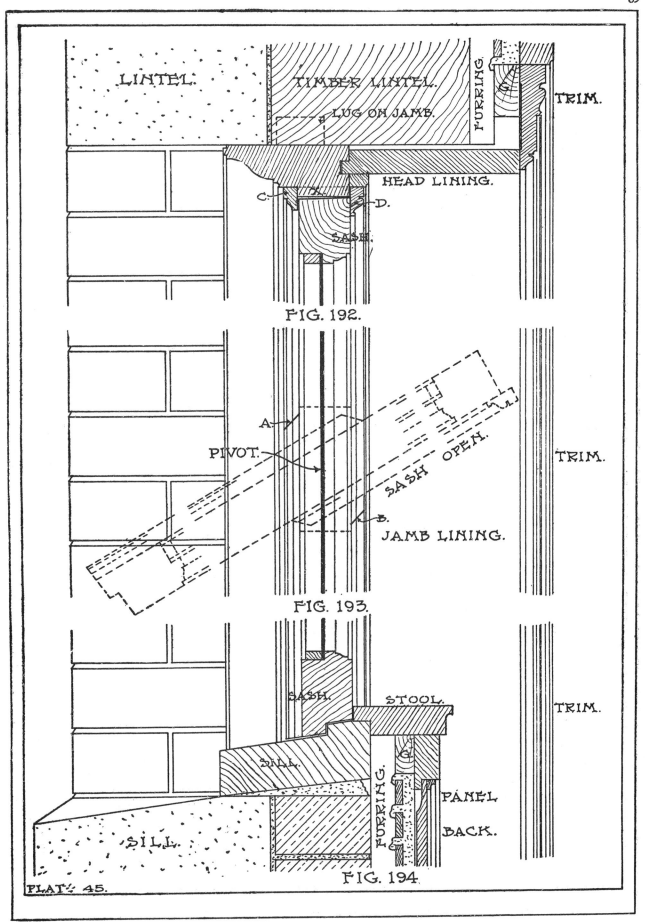

LINTEL.

TIMBER LINTEL.

FURRING.

TRIM.

LUG ON JAMB.

HEAD LINING.

C.  D.

SASH.

FIG. 192.

A

PIVOT.

SASH OPEN.

B.

JAMB LINING.

TRIM.

FIG. 193.

SASH.  STOOL.

TRIM.

SILL.

FURRING.

PANEL

BACK.

SILL.

FIG. 194.

PLATE 45.

## PLATE 80—HORIZONTALLY PIVOTED CASEMENT WINDOW

Construction in 16 inch brick wall. Pivoted casements should not be used in locations exposed to severe driving rain storms, as it is practically impossible to make them water-proof at the pivots. Fig. 192, section through window head. Fig. 193, vertical section taken through the window at the axis of the sash, showing the windows closed by means of the solid lines and open by means of the dotted lines. Fig. 194, vertical section through sill.

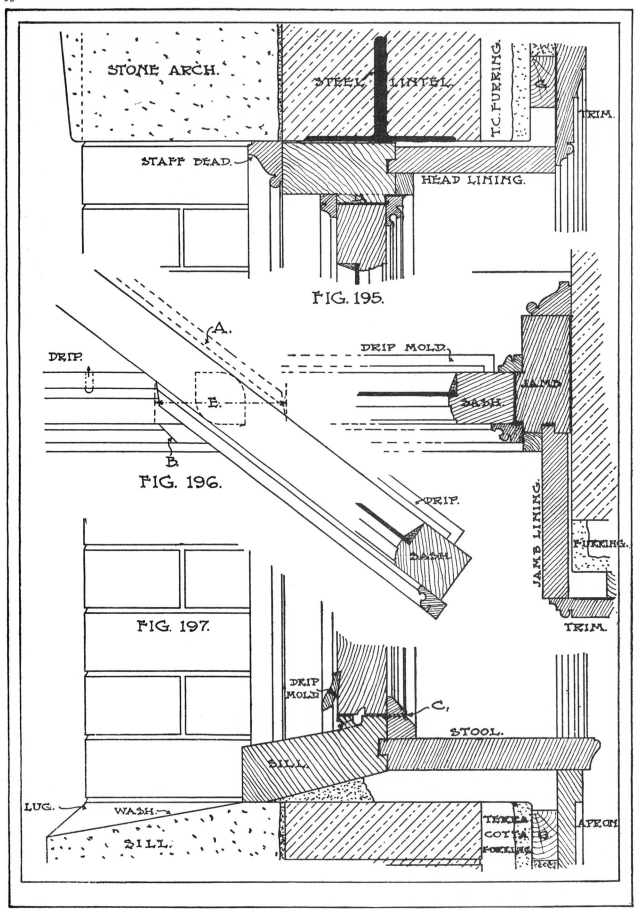

STONE ARCH.

STEEL LINTEL

T.C. FURRING.

TRIM.

STAFF BEAD.

HEAD LINING.

FIG. 195.

DRIP MOLD.

A.

DRIP

JAMB

SASH.

E.

B.

DRIP

FIG. 196.

SASH

JAMB LINING.

FURRING.

TRIM.

FIG. 197.

DRIP MOLD

C.

STOOL.

SILL

LUG.

WASH.

SILL.

TERRA COTTA FURRING

APRON

**PLATE 81—VERTICALLY PIVOTED CASEMENT WINDOW**

Construction in 16 inch brick wall. It is difficult to make this type of window weather-tight, especially for windows in exposed positions. Fig. 195, section through window head. Fig. 196, horizontal section through the window, showing the position of the sash, both when open and when closed. Fig. 197, vertical section showing the construction at the window sill.

# PART III. DETAILS OF MISCELLANEOUS BUILDING

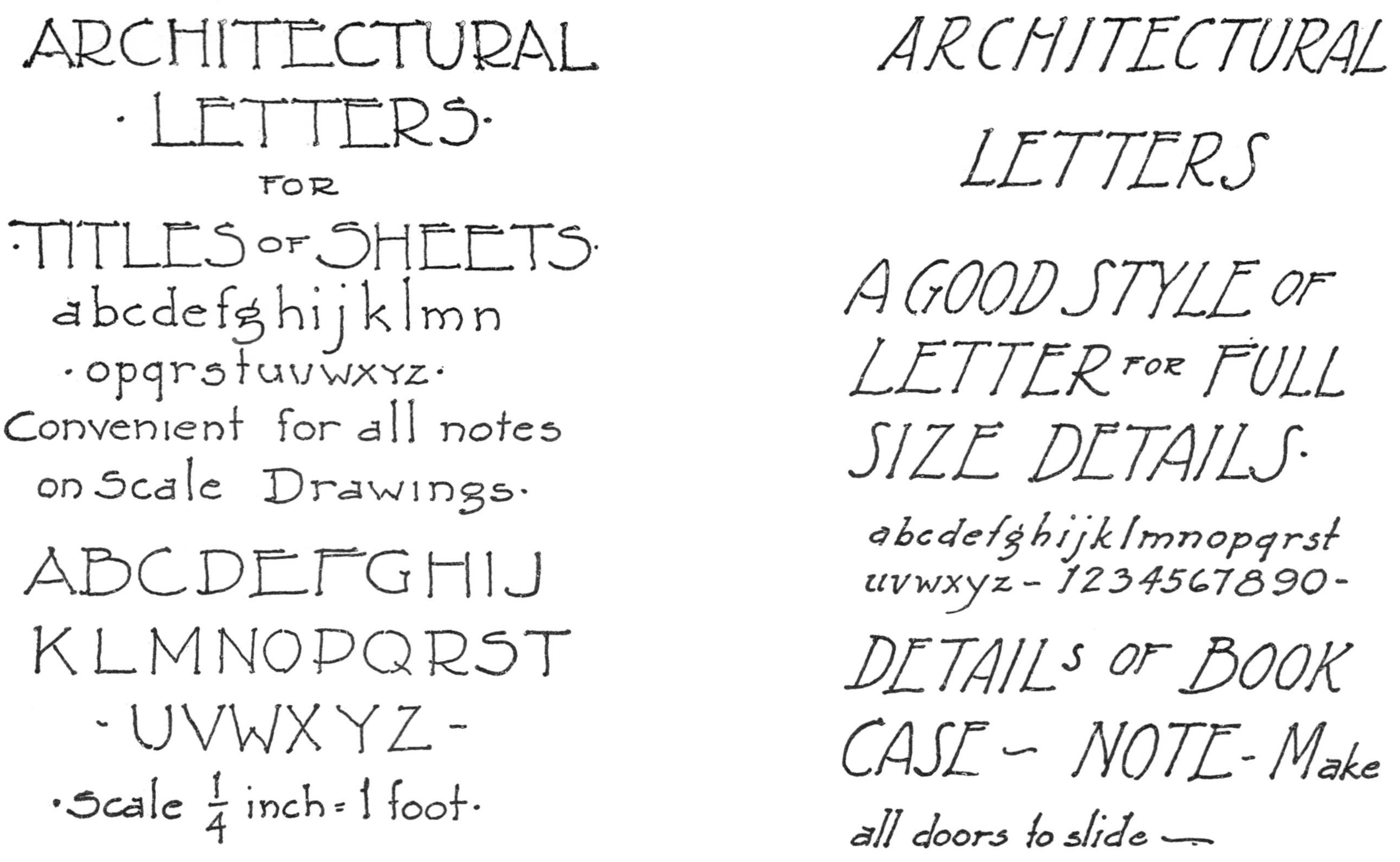

ARCHITECTURAL
LETTERS

A GOOD STYLE OF
LETTER FOR FULL
SIZE DETAILS.

abcdefghijklmnopqrst
uvwxyz - 1234567890-

DETAILS OF BOOK
CASE - NOTE - Make
all doors to slide —

ARCHITECTURAL
. LETTERS
FOR

TITLES OF SHEETS.
abcdefghijklmn
.opqrstuvwxyz.
Convenient for all notes
on Scale Drawings.

ABCDEFGHIJ
KLMNOPQRST
- UVWXYZ -
. Scale ¼ inch = 1 foot.

## PLATE 82—ARCHITECTURAL LETTERING

Two good styles of lettering for architect's plans. One shows easily made letters for general drawings; the other a good form of slanting letter for large work and full sized details. Good lettering is an absolute necessity for a good set of plans. A drawing poorly executed, but lettered attractively and well will look a great deal better than one well drawn, but poorly lettered. It is important to be a good draftsman, but more important still to be a good, neat letterer. All architectural lettering should be free hand work. Guide lines may be drawn but no instruments should be used.

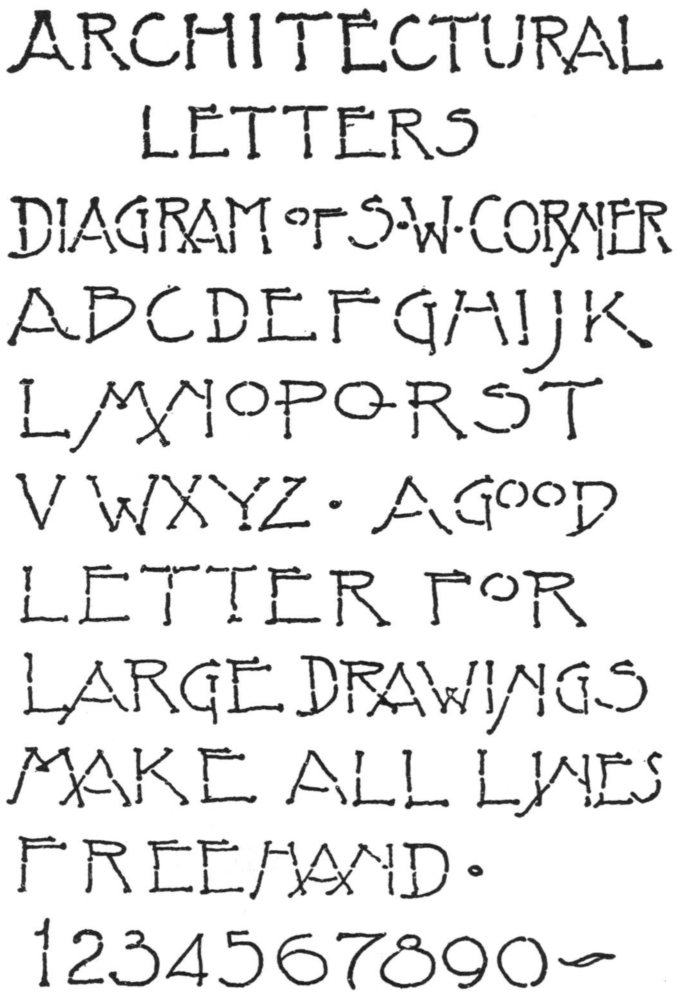

ARCHITECTURAL
LETTERS

ABCDEFGHIJKLMNO
PQRSTVVWXYZ-

ABCDEFGHIJKLMNO
PQRSTUVWXYZ·&

ABCDEFGHIJKL
MNOPQRSTUV
~WXYZ ~
-ELEVATION-
-SCALE $\frac{3}{4}$ INCH-

ARCHITECTURAL
LETTERS

DIAGRAM OF S.W. CORNER
ABCDEFGHIJK
LMNOPQRST
V WXYZ. A GOOD
LETTER FOR
LARGE DRAWINGS
MAKE ALL LINES
FREEHAND.
1234567890~

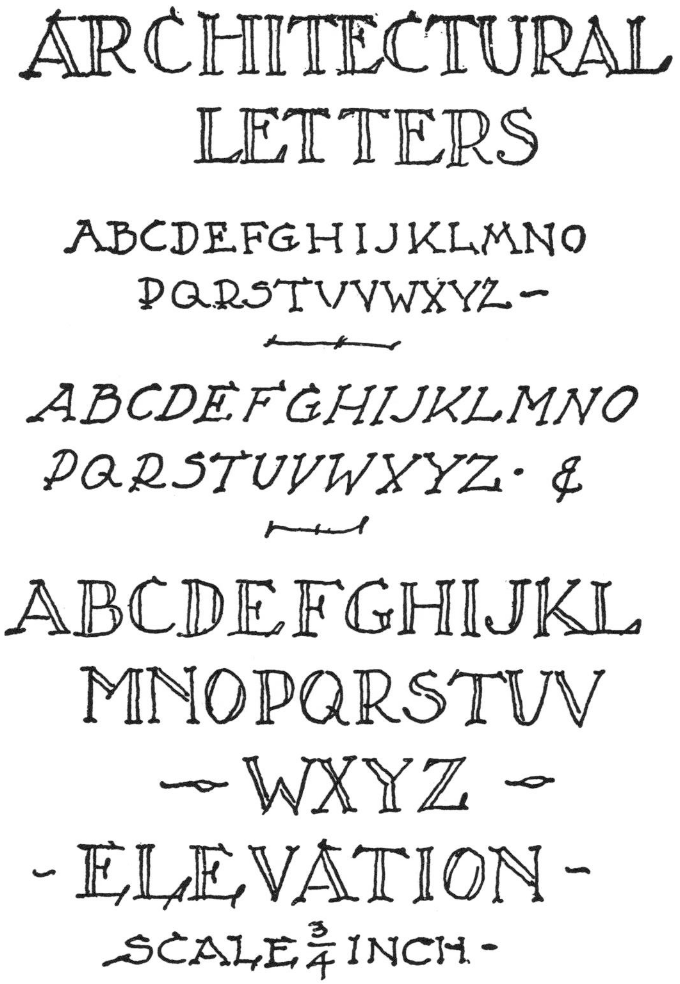

## PLATE 83—ARCHITECTURAL LETTERING

Two styles of ornamental lettering for architectural drawings. One uses a broken line, the other uses double line caps. Grace and ease are far more important for architectural lettering than mechanical precision. Uniform spacing of the letters is very important and it is well to see that the size of the letters used corresponds to the importance of the words being lettered. After careful and persistent practicing good lettering becomes as second nature to the experienced draftsman and can be done very rapidly. Use guide lines at first and practice.

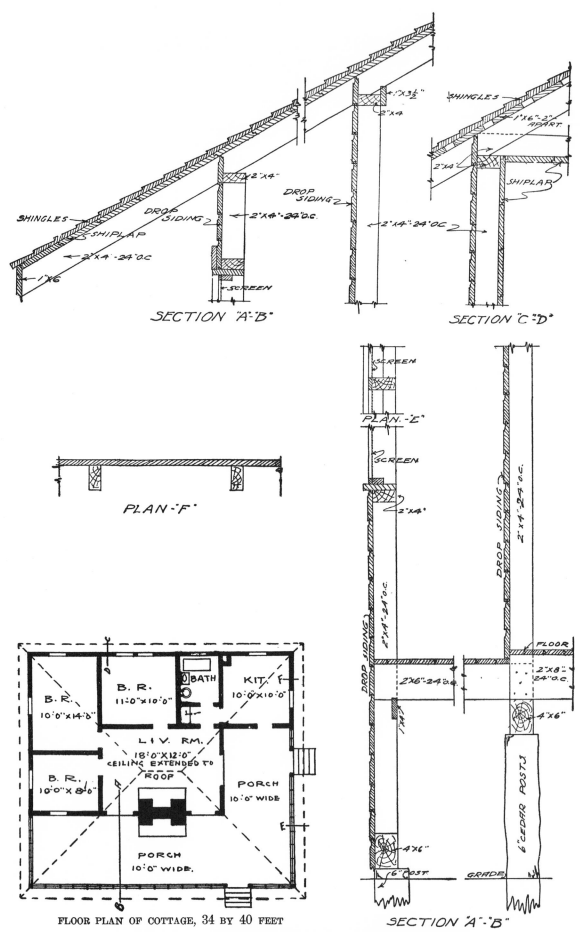

SECTION "A"-"B"

SECTION "C"-"D"

PLAN-"E"

PLAN-"F"

SECTION "A"-"B"

FLOOR PLAN OF COTTAGE, 34 BY 40 FEET

## PLATE 84—SUMMER COTTAGE CONSTRUCTION

Floor plan and complete details of construction of a typical summer cottage. Note that in this design the ridge of the hip roof comes exactly at the center of the living room so that an extra high ceiling is secured, formed by the "shiplap" roof boards, the rafters showing. Section "AB" is a view from foundation to roof through the porch including both inside porch wall and outside living room wall; section "CD," a bedroom outside wall. Cottage construction use does not need to be very tight. Cedar posts are the accepted foundation material. Drop siding is used alone without sheathing and building paper, and the inside face of the walls is left unceiled, except sometimes in bedrooms, bathrooms, etc., where "shiplap" or beaded ceiling is employed.

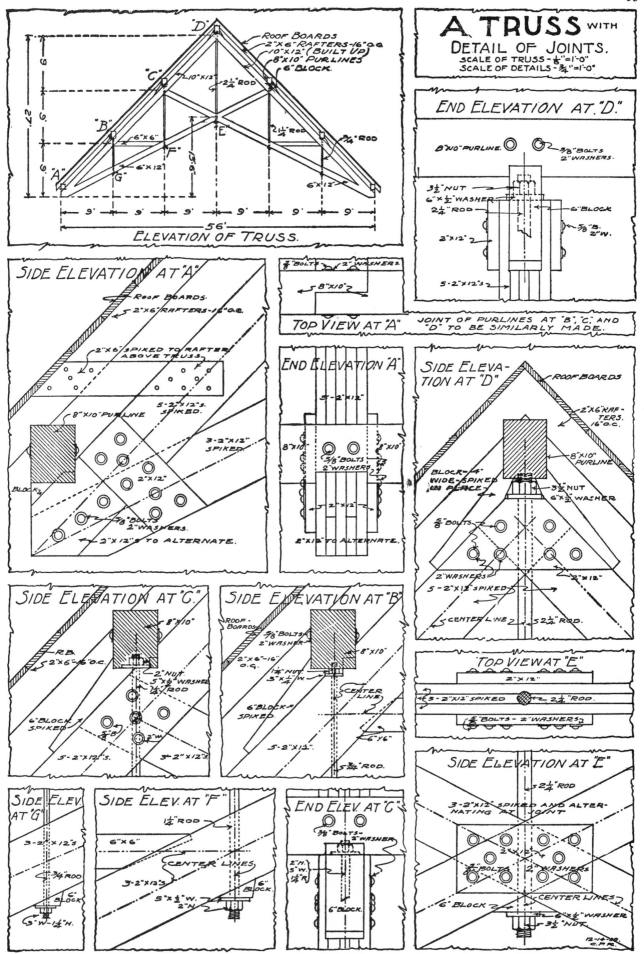

**PLATE 85—WOODEN ROOF TRUSS WITH DETAILS OF JOINTS**

A strong truss, giving a greater height in the center of a building than the ordinary truss with horizontal lower chord. The upper and lower chords are built up of 2 by 12 inch planks, thoroughly spiked together and bolted at the joints as shown. The constructive details are typical of many forms of wooden roof trusses. Note use of wood seat blocks in place of customary iron pads.

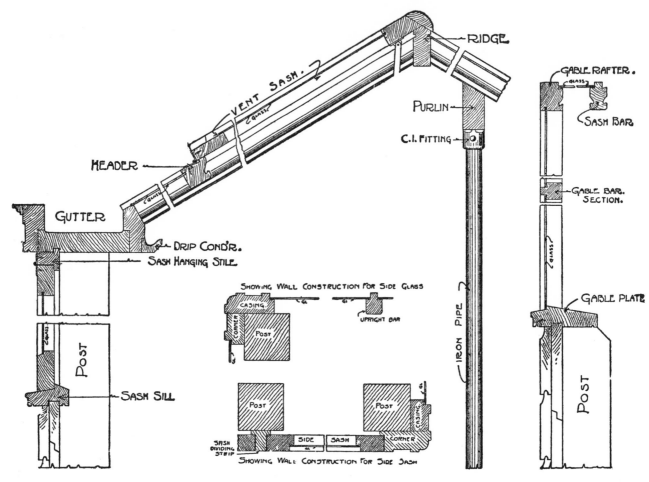

SECTION THROUGH WALL, EAVES AND RIDGE          SECTION THROUGH GABLE ENDS

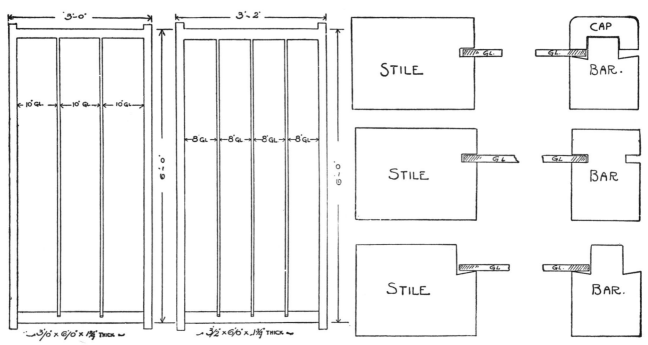

STATIONARY SASH FOR SIDES OR ROOF          METHODS OF SECURING GLASS

## PLATE 86—GREENHOUSE CONSTRUCTION

Details suitable for modern greenhouses of average size; red cypress to be used throughout where wood is called for. Wall and gutter support posts should be set in the ground at least three feet, all post footings to be surrounded with concrete. Purlin posts are of iron pipe resting on concrete footings. Proper ventilation is a very important factor in successful greenhouse work. Details show ventilating sash hinged near the eaves and with a storm-tight joint at the ridge. Unless continuous ventilation is desired there should be one stationary sash between each ventilating sash. A width of seven feet is about right for the ventilating sash.

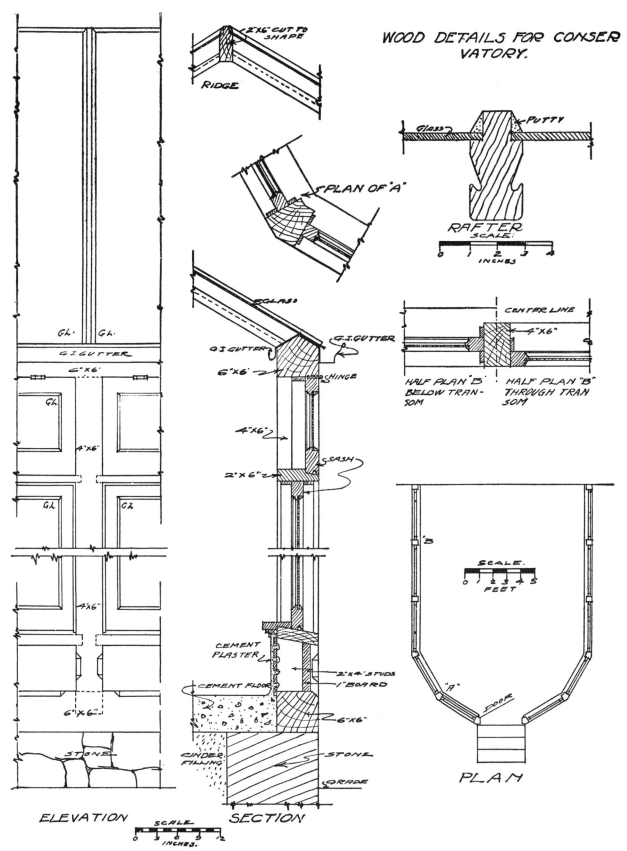

WOOD DETAILS FOR CONSER VATORY.

RIDGE

2"x6" CUT TO SHAPE

PLAN OF "A"

RAFTER
SCALE:

Glass          PUTTY

0   1   2   3   4
INCHES

GLASS

GL.   GL.

G.I. GUTTER

6"x6"

GL.

4"x6"

GL.   GL.

4"x6"

6"x6"

STONE

ELEVATION

SCALE
0   3   6   9   12
INCHES.

G.I. GUTTER

6"x6"

HINGE

4"x6"

SASH

2"x6"

CEMENT PLASTER

CEMENT FLOOR

CINDER FILLING

2"x4" STUDS
1" BOARD

6"x6"

STONE

GRADE

SECTION

CENTER LINE

4"x6"

HALF PLAN "B" BELOW TRANSOM

HALF PLAN "B" THROUGH TRANSOM

SCALE.
0   1   2   3   4   5
FEET

"B"

"A"

DOOR

PLAN

## PLATE 87—CONSERVATORY OR SUN ROOM FOR A RESIDENCE

Plan and complete details for sun room addition. Cement floor is made continuous with cement plaster side walls, with rounding corners so as to be easily washed out with hose. Lower sash are stationary; upper sash, above the transom bar, are hung on hinges so as to swing outward and upward to provide ventilation. The roof is made of ribbed sky-light glass. All woodwork should be of red cypress to resist decay. Note galvanized iron gutter to catch condensation drip from the under side of the roof glass. Screen can be substituted for lower sash in summer.

98

DESIGN OF AN ICE HOUSE HAVING A CAPACITY OF 200 TONS

SIDE ELEVATION

FRONT ELEVATION

DETAIL SHOWING CONSTRUCTION OF WALLS

DOOR FRAME

DOOR

DOOR

NOTE: ALL SHEATING MUST BE WELL MATCHED AND ALL JOINTS AIR TIGHT.

SOFT PINE SHEATHING
BLOCK MINERAL WOOL
PINE SHEATHING
AIR SPACE BETWEEN 2 X 4 STUDDING 16" APART
PINE SHEATHING
HAIR FELT 7/8" THICK
AIR SPACE BETWEEN 2 X 4 STUDDING 16" APART
PINE SHEATHING
BUILDING PAPER
MATCHED SIDING

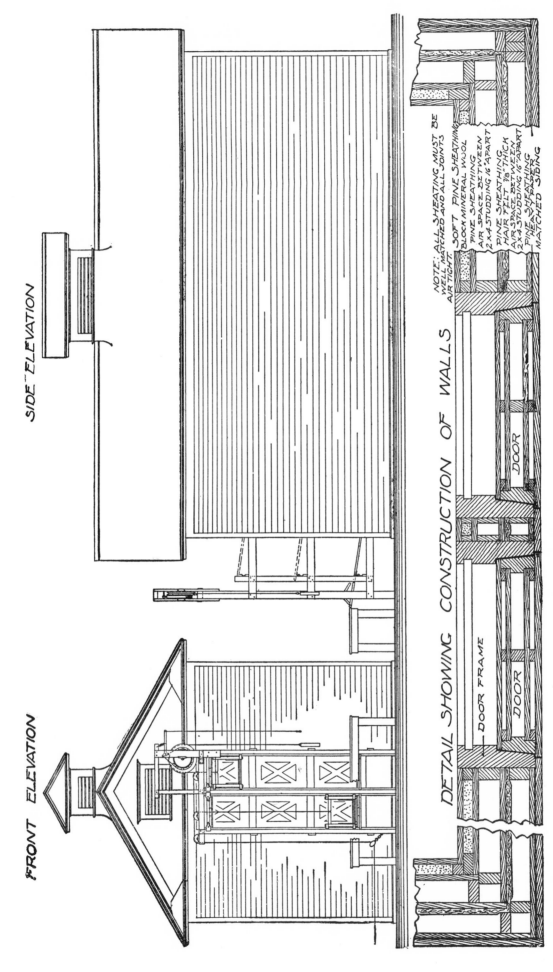

**PLATE 88—MODERN ICE HOUSE**

The walls of this ice house have two distinct and separate dead air spaces, besides insulating thicknesses of mineral wool, hair felt, matched boarding and heavy building paper. The construction illustrated is that in use by the leading packing, railroad and cold storage companies. The floor of the ice house is constructed of two inch planks, laid two inches apart on sleepers, laid two feet apart and embedded in crushed stone. The water from the melted ice will find its way through the crushed stone to the drain tile. Note the hoisting and lowering rig for ice. In the summer months the horse cable is detached and a friction brake controls the lowering of the ice and a counter-weight returns the elevator.

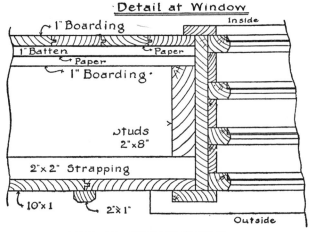

WALL AND WINDOW SECTION

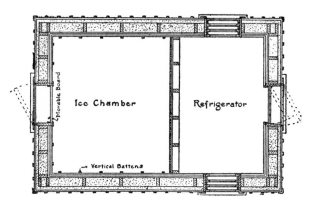

PLAN—SHOWING ALSO WALL CONSTRUCTION

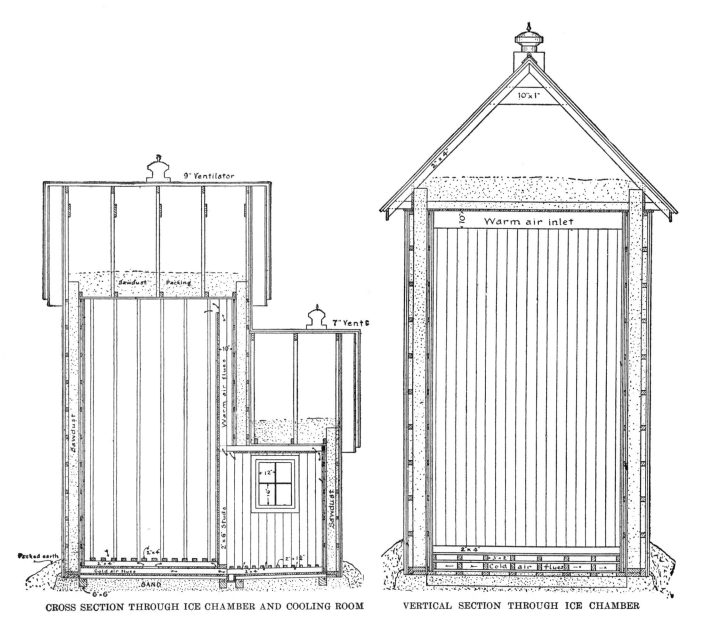

CROSS SECTION THROUGH ICE CHAMBER AND COOLING ROOM

VERTICAL SECTION THROUGH ICE CHAMBER

## PLATE 89—SMALL COLD STORAGE HOUSE

Floor plan, vertical sections showing complete details of construction and arrangement; also cross section view of wall showing insulated construction and four-ply cold storage windows. In this method of cold storage a current of air is passed over a mass of ice and thence into a separate chamber in which the food products are stored. From the natural law that warm air rises and cold air falls, a continuous circulation of cooled air passes through the refrigerating chamber back onto the surface of the ice in the ice chamber. This keeps the air in the food chamber in good condition. The average size for a small cold storage plant is 11 by 17 feet, the side wall studs to be 18 feet long for the ice chamber and 9 feet long for the refrigerating room.

100

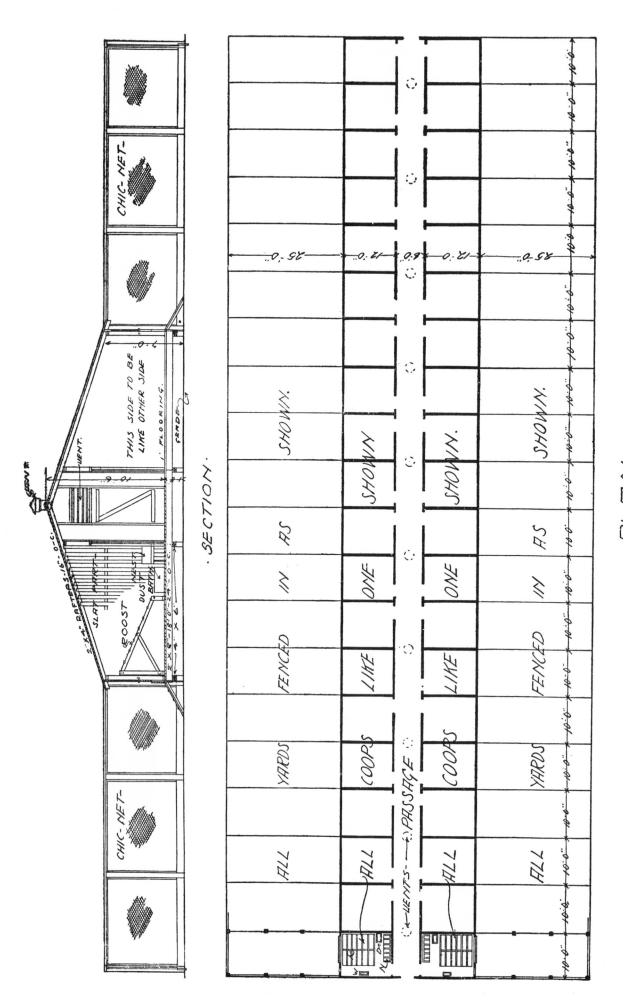

.SECTION.

.PLAN.

**PLATE 90—POULTRY HOUSE WITH OPEN YARDS**

Plan and cross section showing details of construction. This poultry establishment is made up of units; each unit consisting of a coop or shelter with an enclosed scratching yard without roof attached. This system can be extended to include as many of these units as are required.

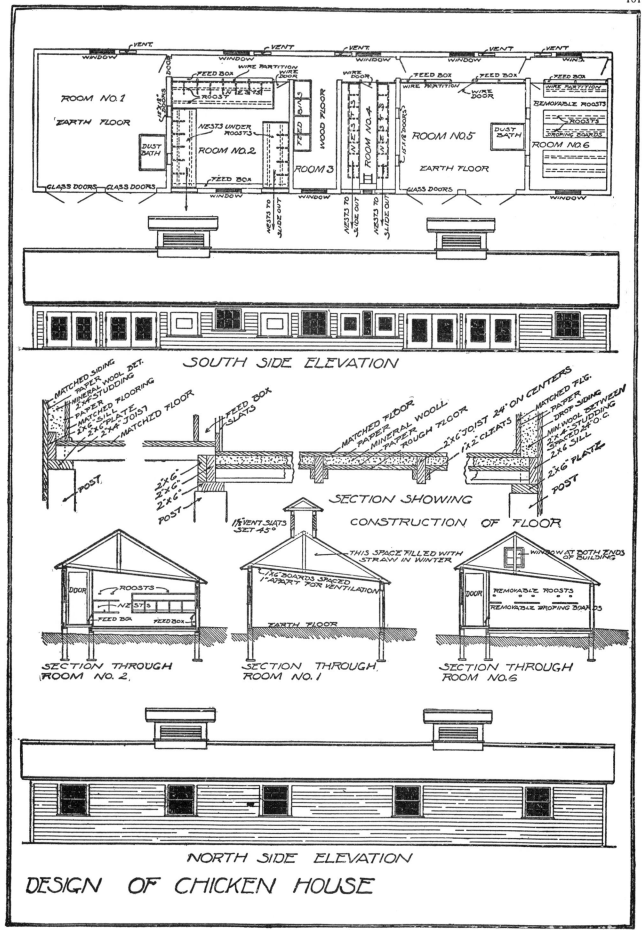

VENT WINDOW VENT VENT VENT VENT

ROOM NO.1
EARTH FLOOR

DUST BATH

GLASS DOORS   GLASS DOORS

WINDOW

FEED BOX   WIRE PARTITION   WIRE DOOR

ROOST   NESTS

NESTS UNDER ROOSTS

ROOM NO.2

FEED BOX

NESTS TO SLIDE OUT

WINDOW

FEED BINS

WOOD FLOOR

ROOM 3

NESTS TO SLIDE OUT

WINDOW

1"x6" 15 ×3   1"x6" 15 ×3

ROOM NO.4

NESTS TO SLIDE OUT

FEED BOX   FEED BOX   FEED BOX

WIRE PARTITION   WIRE DOOR

WIRE PARTITION
REMOVABLE ROOSTS
ROOSTS
DROPING BOARDS
ROOM NO.6

ROOM NO.5
EARTH FLOOR

DUST BATH

GLASS DOORS

WINDOW

WINDOW

**SOUTH SIDE ELEVATION**

MATCHED SIDING
PAPER WOOL BET.
MINERAL WOOL
2"x4" STUDDING
PAPER
MATCHED FLOORING
2"x6" SILL
2"x6" PLATE
2"x4" JOIST
MATCHED FLOOR

POST

FEED BOX SLATS

2"x6"
2"x6"
2"x6"

POST

MATCHED FLOOR
PAPER WOOL
MINERAL WOOL
PAPER
ROUGH FLOOR

1"x2" CLEATS

2"x6" JOIST 24" ON CENTERS

**SECTION SHOWING**

**CONSTRUCTION OF FLOOR**

MATCHED FLG.
PAPER
DROP SIDING
MIN. WOOL BETWEEN
2"x4" STUDDING
SPACED 24" O.C.
2"x6" SILL
2"x6" PLATE

POST

1½" VENT SLATS SET 45°

THIS SPACE FILLED WITH STRAW IN WINTER

DOOR   ROOSTS   NESTS

FEED BOX   FEED BOX

**SECTION THROUGH ROOM NO. 2**

1"x6" BOARDS SPACED 1" APART FOR VENTILATION

EARTH FLOOR

**SECTION THROUGH ROOM NO. 1**

WINDOW AT BOTH ENDS OF BUILDING

DOOR   REMOVABLE ROOSTS
REMOVABLE DROPING BOARDS

**SECTION THROUGH ROOM NO. 6**

**NORTH SIDE ELEVATION**

**DESIGN OF CHICKEN HOUSE**

## PLATE 91—POULTRY HOUSE WITH ENCLOSED RUN-WAYS

Design, plan and complete details of construction of a fine poultry establishment having scratching pens under cover. The house is thirty-four feet long by twelve feet wide.

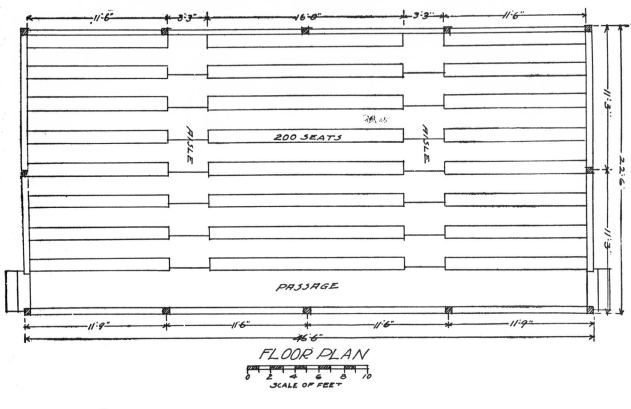

FLOOR PLAN

SCALE OF FEET

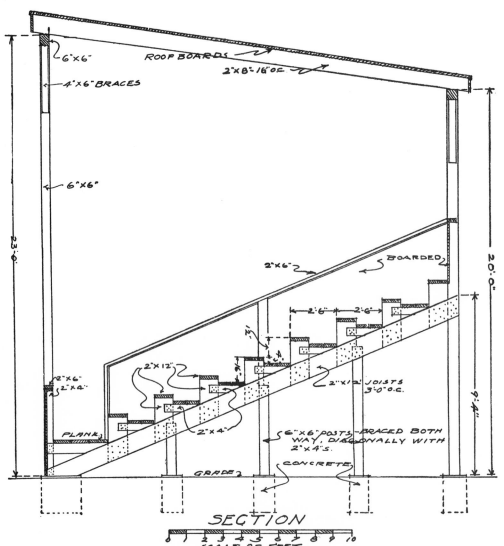

SECTION

SCALE OF FEET

## PLATE 92—SMALL GRAND STAND

Floor plan and cross section showing complete details of a grand stand for athletic grounds, to seat about 200 people. It is about as cheap as such a structure can be made, yet it is strong and makes a good appearance. It is well to nail wire netting over front of stand to keep out batted balls.

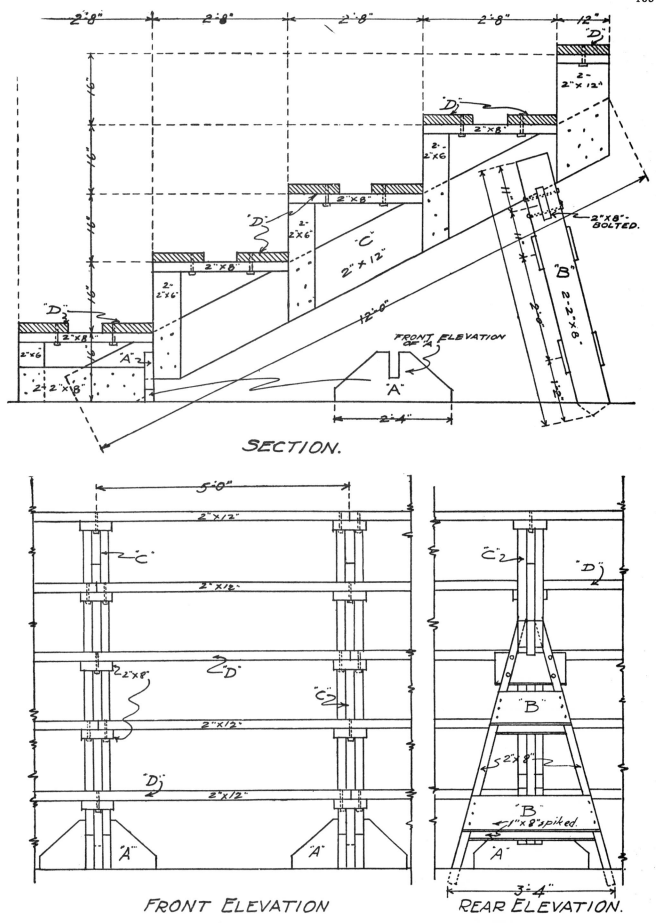

SECTION.

FRONT ELEVATION

REAR ELEVATION.

PLATE 93—PORTABLE KNOCK-DOWN "BLEACHERS"

Complete working drawings for portable bleachers for athletic grounds which can be "knocked down" for storage during the seasons when not in use. The structure consists of the main carriage, "C" and its supports, "B" and "A," and the seat planks, "D." The carriages are to be placed five feet apart, the 10-foot long seat planks alternating joints. The support, "B," extends into the ground a sufficient distance to prevent it from slipping. There should be a stake driven into the ground in front of each carriage to prevent it from slipping forward.

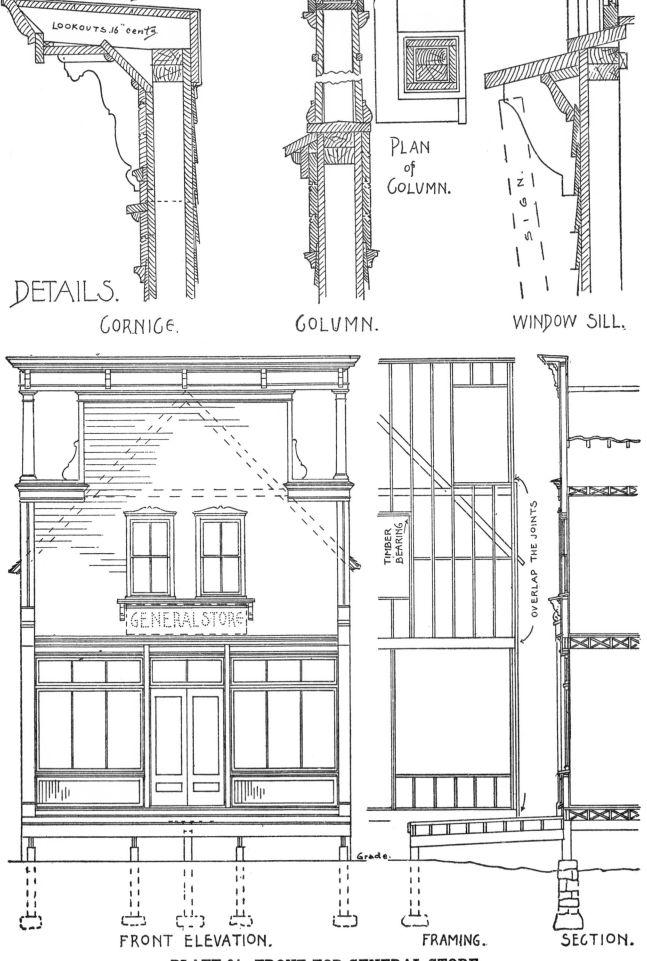

DETAILS.

CORNICE.        COLUMN.        WINDOW SILL.

FRONT ELEVATION.        FRAMING.        SECTION.

LOOKOUTS 16" cents.

PLAN of COLUMN.

SIGN.

GENERAL STORE

TIMBER BEARING

OVERLAP THE JOINTS

Grade.

**PLATE 94—FRONT FOR GENERAL STORE**

Design and details. This is a design that is neat and attractive in appearance and is easily constructed. It is an agreeable change from the billboard like fronts usually seen. The details show how the cornice should be framed to secure firmness; also how various parts of the building should be constructed. Note broad window sill ledge bracketed out to shelter the sign.

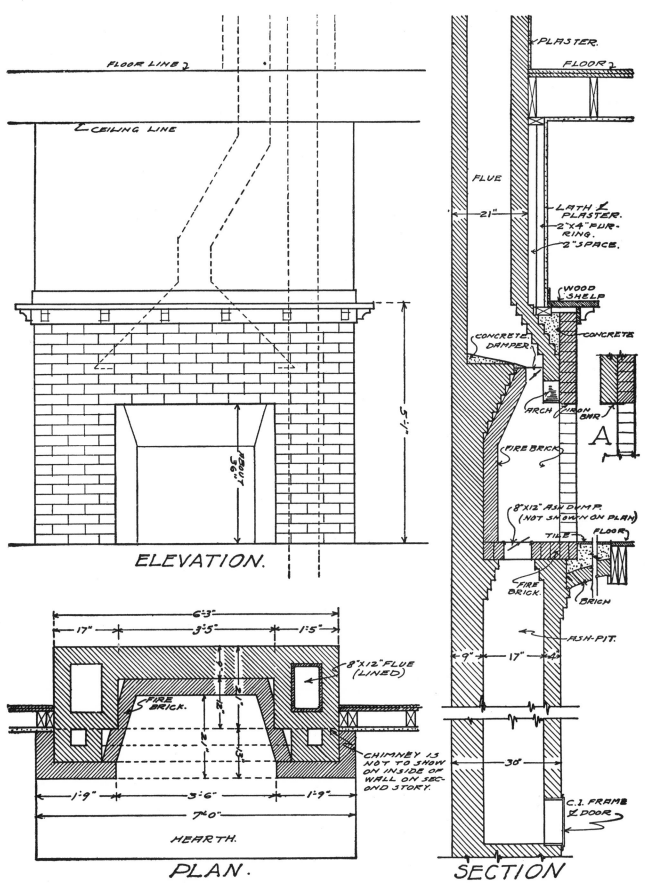

ELEVATION.

PLAN.

SECTION

## PLATE 95—FIRE PLACE CONSTRUCTION

Design for fire place with brick mantel, plan and elevation showing best construction and arrangement for an open fire place that will not smoke. At "A" is shown a form of construction for the arch above the fireplace that is sometimes used; but it cannot be recommended as it is apt to cause the fire place to smoke. Note air space between brick chimney and the wood framing. Dotted lines show the fire place flue carried across at an easy slant to be carried up along beside the furnace flue. These two flues must on no account be merged into one.

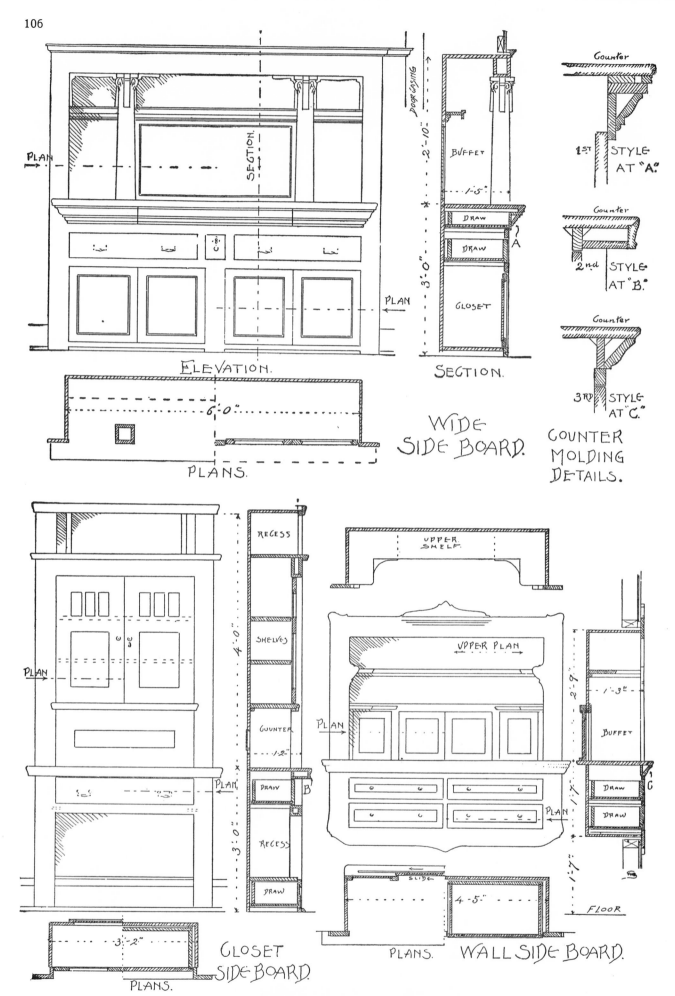

**PLATE 96—THREE BUILT-IN SIDE-BOARDS**

Designs and details for a wide sideboard, a closet sideboard and a wall sideboard. All of attractive appearance and suitable for fine dining room work.

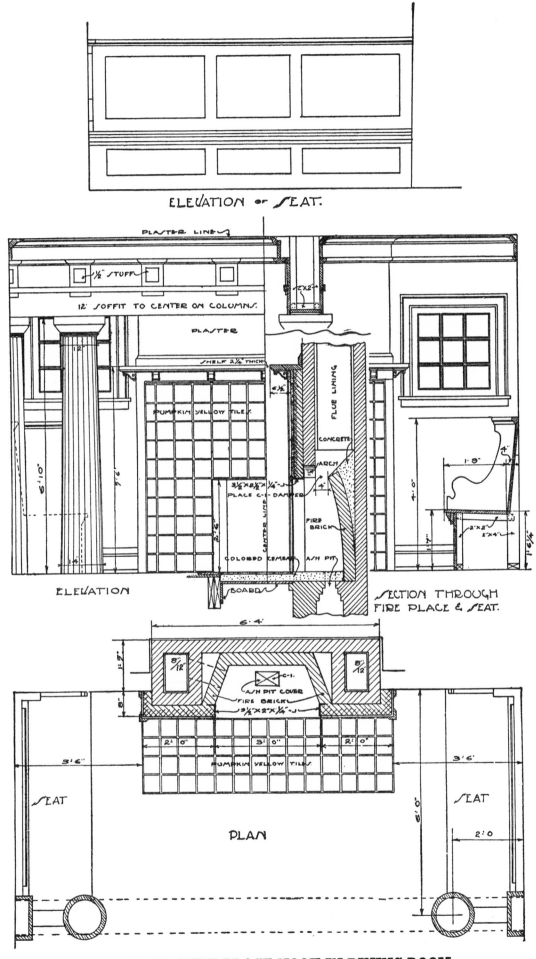

**PLATE 97—FIRE PLACE NOOK IN DINING ROOM**

Plan, elevations and sections of a very attractive, elaborate fire place nook for a living room. Hearth and mantel front are of square tile. Note construction and arrangement of built-in seats.

108

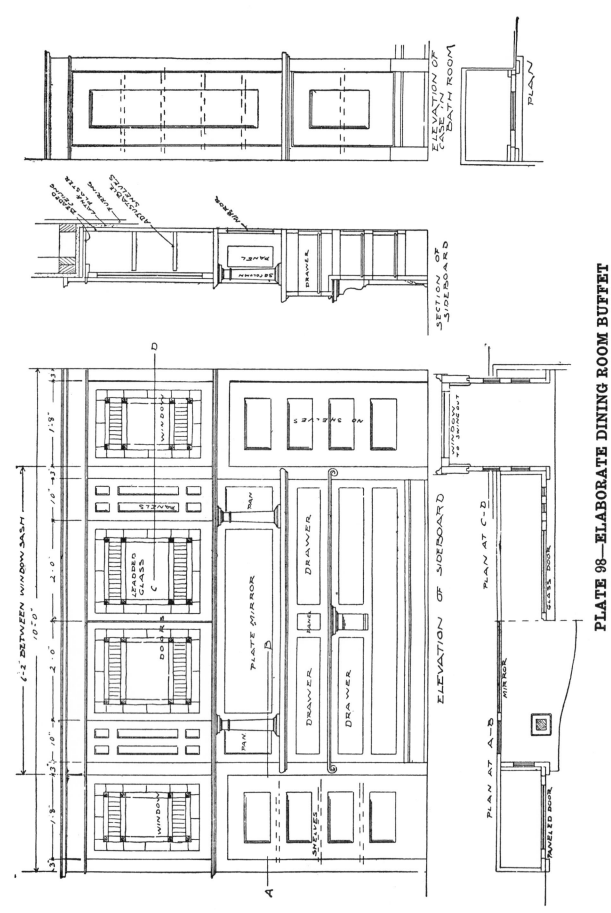

**PLATE 98—ELABORATE DINING ROOM BUFFET**

This is a large and striking design, using leaded art glass and plate mirror. A large amount of drawer room and shelving is provided. Plan and elevation for a full length bath room case are also shown in this plate.

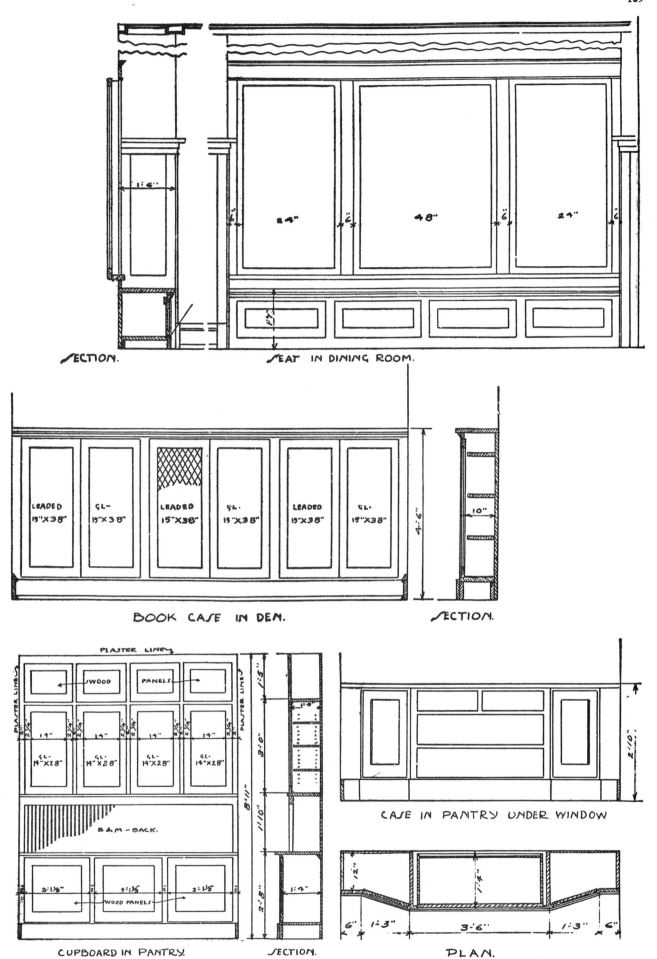

SECTION.

SEAT IN DINING ROOM.

BOOK CASE IN DEN.

SECTION.

CUPBOARD IN PANTRY.

SECTION.

CASE IN PANTRY UNDER WINDOW

PLAN.

### PLATE 99—BUILT-IN FEATURES OF INTERIOR TRIM

Elevation and section of built-in seat for paneled dining room bookcase for den or living room, cupboard for pantry or kitchen and case for pantry to go under window.

110

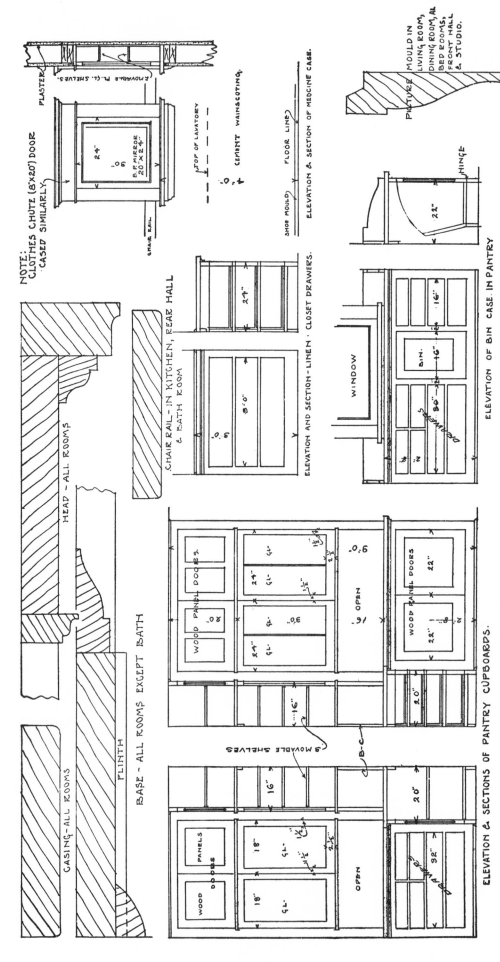

**PLATE 100—DETAILS OF INTERIOR FINISH**

Elevations and sections of pantry cupboards, of bin case in pantry, of linen closet and of medicine case; also base, casing and head trim of simple design popular in present-day work. See Plate 101 for additional details.

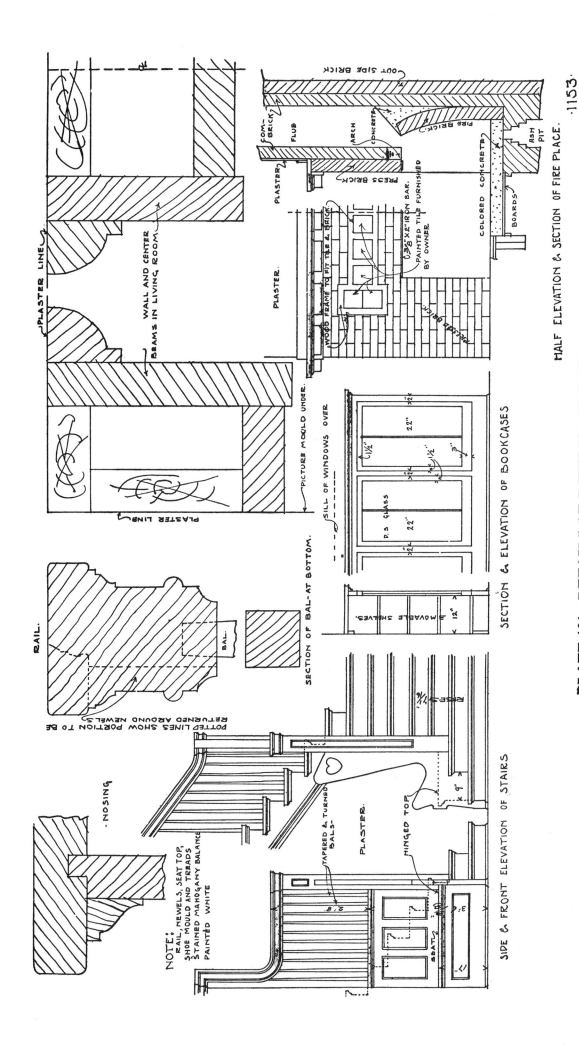

**PLATE 101—DETAILS OF INTERIOR FINISH**

Side and front elevations of stairs, section and elevation of book cases, half elevation and section of fire place and mantel showing construction; also details of ceiling beams. For additional details in this style see Plate 100.

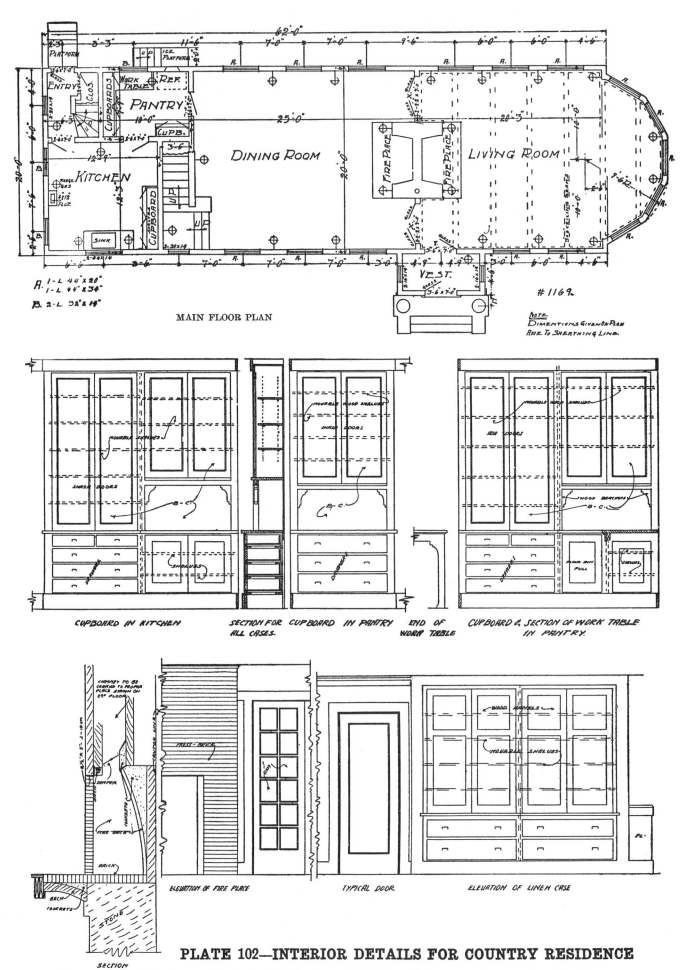

MAIN FLOOR PLAN

COPBOARD IN KITCHEN

SECTION FOR CUPBOARD IN PANTRY ALL CASES.

END OF WORK TABLE

CUPBOARD & SECTION OF WORK TABLE IN PANTRY.

SECTION

ELEVATION OF FIRE PLACE

TYPICAL DOOR

ELEVATION OF LINEN CASE

## PLATE 102—INTERIOR DETAILS FOR COUNTRY RESIDENCE

Floor plan and features of interior finish of an elaborate country place. Details show large central fire place with glass doors on either side; also kitchen cabinets, pantry cupboards, linen case, etc. For additional details of this house, see Plates 103, 104 and 105.

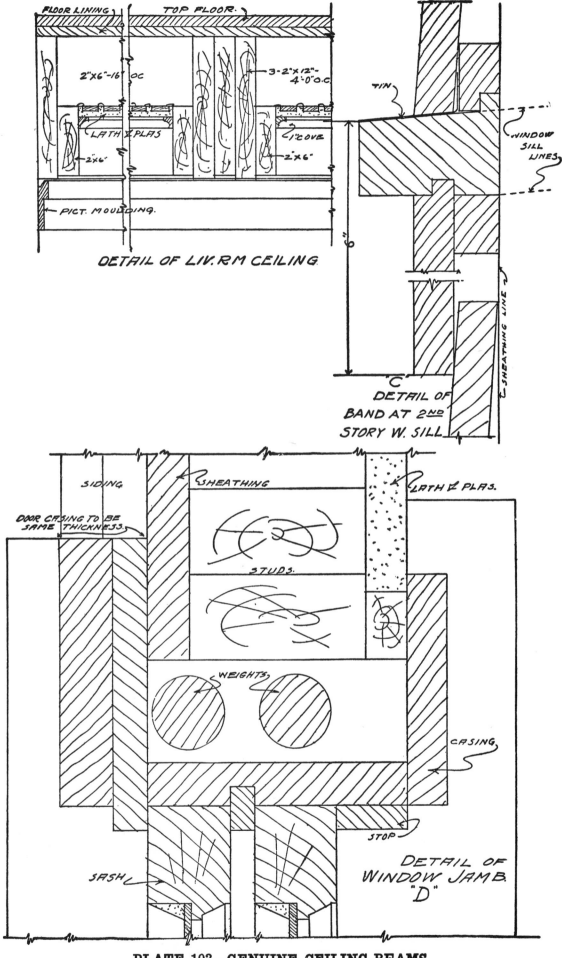

DETAIL OF LIV. RM CEILING.

FLOOR LINING
TOP FLOOR.
2"X6"-16" OC
3-2"X12"-4'-0" O.C.
LATH & PLAS.
2"X6"
1" COVE
2"X6"
PICT. MOULDING.

TIN
WINDOW SILL LINES
6"
"C"
DETAIL OF BAND AT 2ND STORY W. SILL
SHEATHING LINE

SIDING
SHEATHING
LATH & PLAS.
DOOR CASING TO BE SAME THICKNESS.
STUDS.
WEIGHTS
CASING
STOP
SASH
DETAIL OF WINDOW JAMB. "D"

**PLATE 103—GENUINE CEILING BEAMS**

Details showing construction of ceiling beams indicated in the floor plan sketch, Plate 102; the span for these beams is 20 feet. Three 2 by 12's are spiked together with the addition of a 2 by 6 spiked to both sides and added to give the necessary width for good appearance. The lath and plaster are applied at the top of these 2 by 6's, thus exposing to view a depth of about 5 inches between the plastered panels. Details are also shown in this Plate of outside-wall continuous band on a line with the second story window sills; also detail of second story window jambs.

114

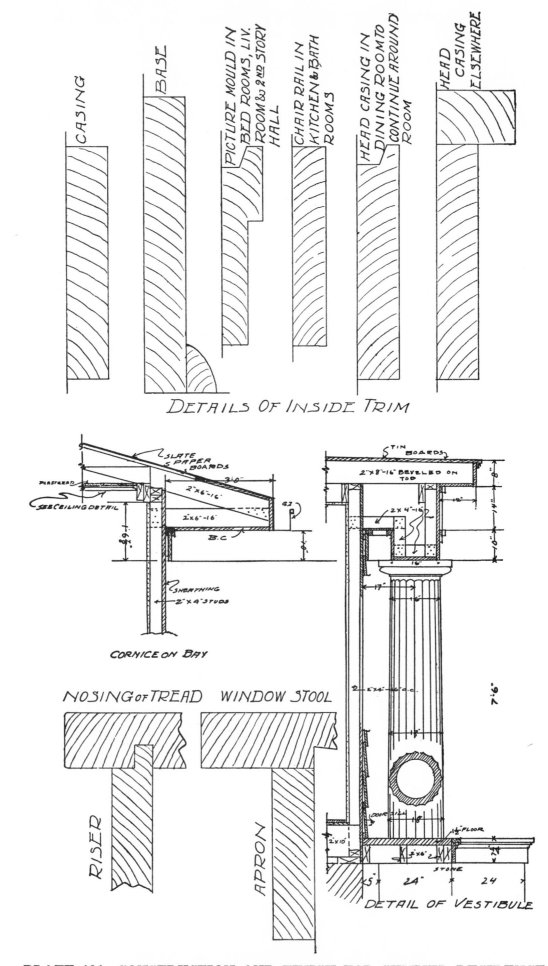

DETAILS OF INSIDE TRIM

CASING

BASE

PICTURE MOULD IN BED ROOMS, LIV. ROOM & 2ND STORY HALL

CHAIR RAIL IN KITCHEN & BATH ROOMS

HEAD CASING IN DINING ROOM TO CONTINUE AROUND ROOM

HEAD CASING ELSEWHERE

CORNICE ON BAY

NOSING of TREAD     WINDOW STOOL

RISER

APRON

DETAIL OF VESTIBULE

**PLATE 104—CONSTRUCTION AND FINISH FOR SUMMER RESIDENCE**

Complete details of interior trim; also details of classic porch shown on floor plan sketch, Plate
102.  For additional details of this house, see Plates 102, 103 and 105.

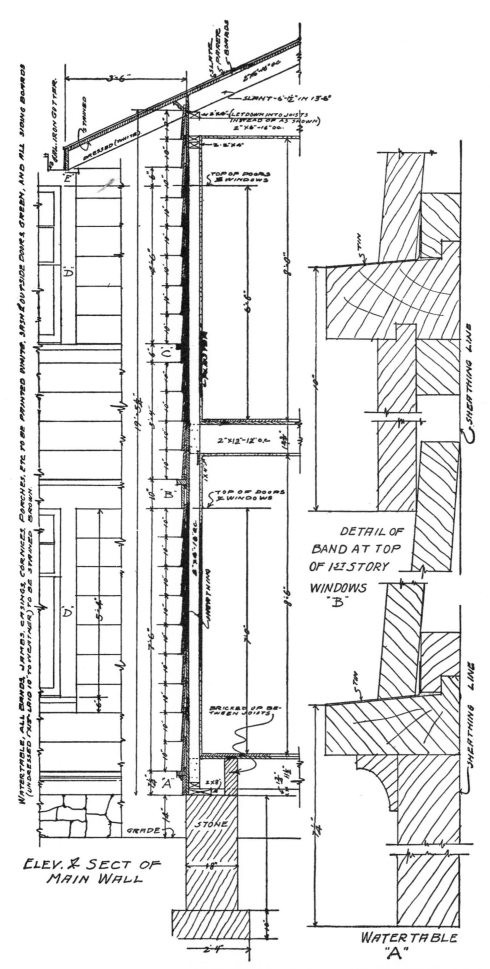

ELEV. & SECT OF
MAIN WALL

DETAIL OF
BAND AT TOP
OF 1ST STORY
WINDOWS
"B"

WATERTABLE
"A"

## PLATE 105—WALL SECTION AND CONSTRUCTION FOR SUMMER RESIDENCE

Details of exterior construction of large elaborate summer residence, main floor plan of which is
shown in Plate 102.  For additional details of this design see Plates 102, 103 and 104.

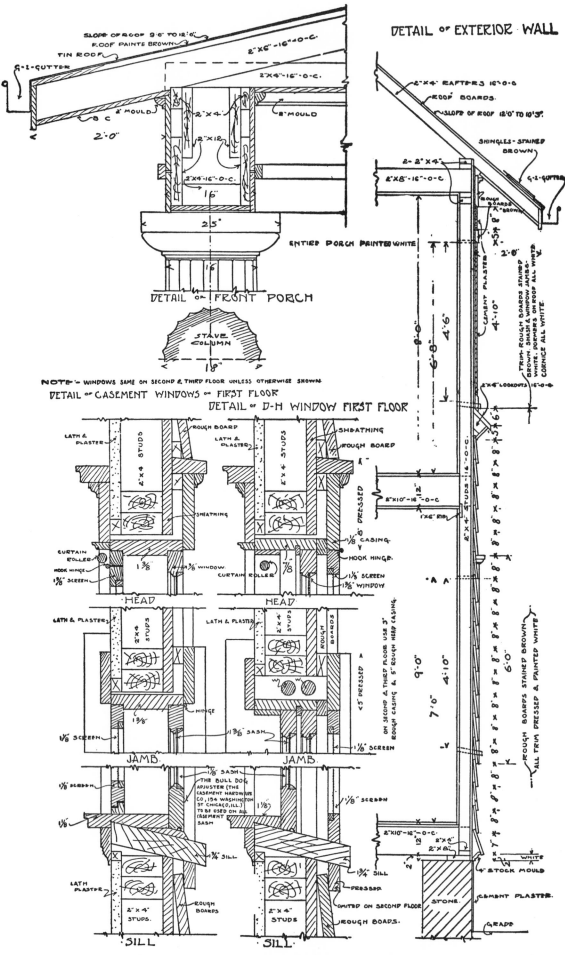

## PLATE 106—WALL, WINDOW AND PORCH DETAILS

Wall section shows use of rough boards laid eight inches to the weather for the first story up to the second story window sills, with cement plaster above. Working details of casement windows, also double hung windows. Details of porch cornice showing use of classic columns.

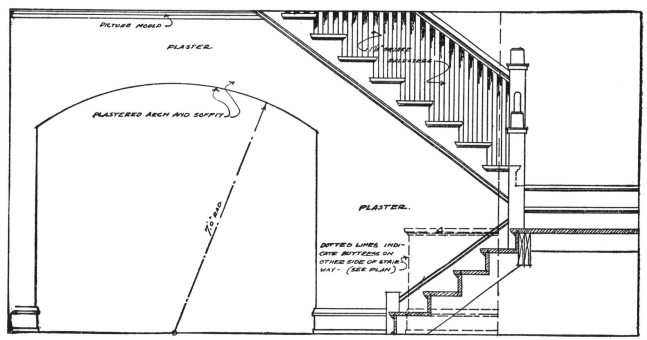

DETAIL OF MAIN STAIR HALL

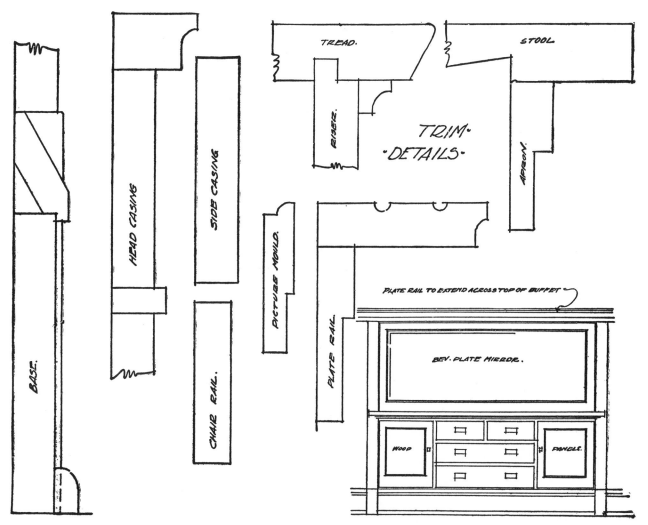

TRIM DETAILS

## PLATE 107—DETAILS OF HOUSE FINISH

Elevation and section of a simple platform stairway of beautiful lines, used in connection with a plastered arched opening; also design for dining room buffet and details of interior trim in the popular modern straight-line style. This finish is liked because it does not catch dust.

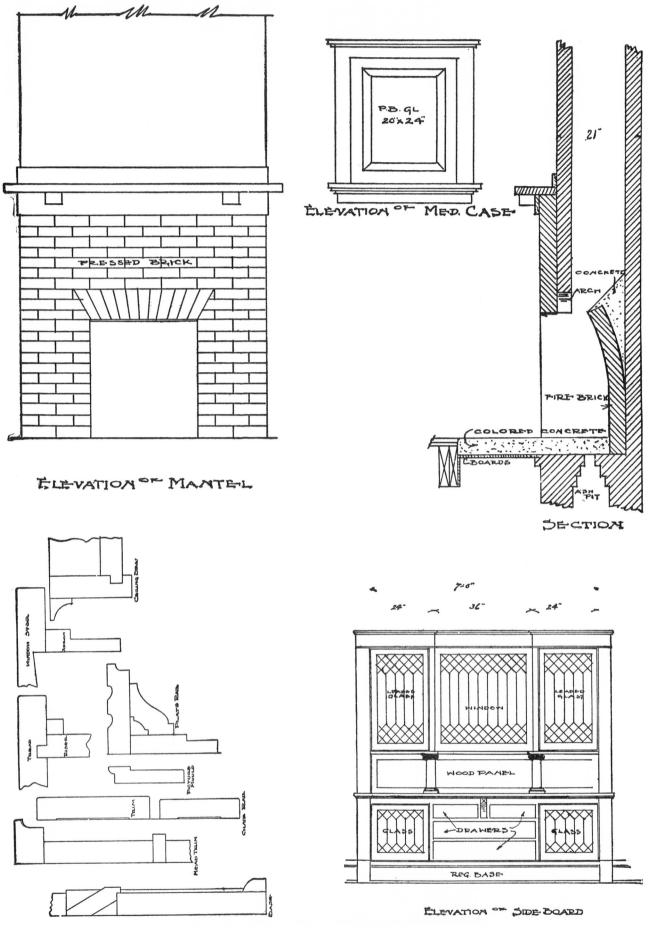

ELEVATION OF MED. CASE

P.B. GL
20"x24"

21"

CONCRETE ARCH

FIRE BRICK

COLORED CONCRETE

BOARDS

ASH PIT

SECTION

PRESSED BRICK

ELEVATION OF MANTEL

CEILING BEAM

WINDOW STOOL

APRON

PLATE RAIL

TREAD

RISER

PICTURE MOULD

TRIM

CHAIR RAIL

HEAD TRIM

BASE

7'-0"

24"    36"    24"

LEADED GLASS    WINDOW    LEADED GLASS

WOOD PANEL

GLASS    DRAWERS    GLASS

REG. BASE

ELEVATION OF SIDE-BOARD

## PLATE 108—MANTEL AND BUFFET DESIGNS

Simple, attractive designs for open fire place with brick mantel. Dining room buffet with leaded glass both in cupboard doors and for central window. Simple medicine case design. Complete details of interior trim of a simple pattern popular for modern work.

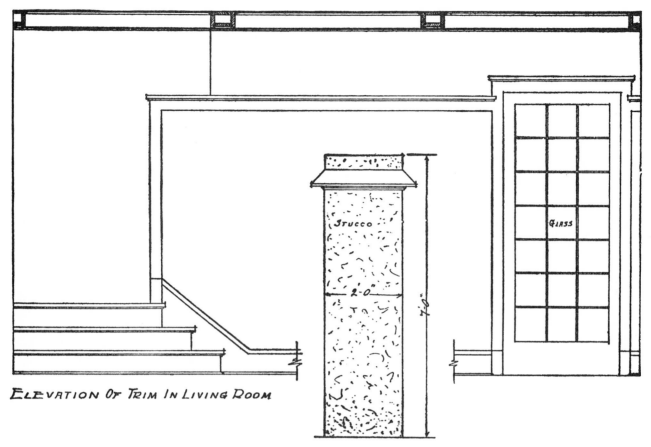

ELEVATION OF TRIM IN LIVING ROOM

ELEVATION OF GATE POST

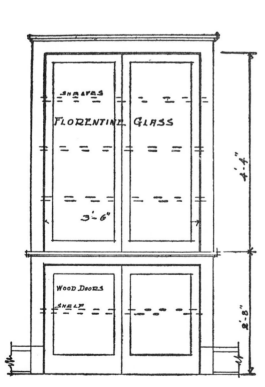

ELEVATION OF KITCHEN CASE.

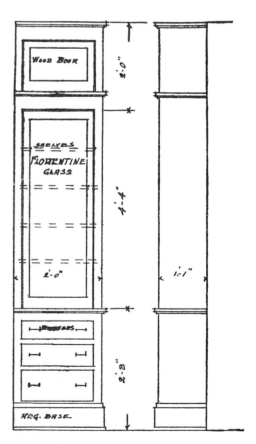

FRONT & SIDE ELEV. OF CUPBOARD
IN KITCHEN

## PLATE 109—DETAILS OF SPECIAL INTERIOR TRIM

Stairway landing in living room.  Full length glazed interior door;  Simple kitchen cabinet. Design for small kitchen cupboard.  Simple, attractive cement plaster gate post.

120

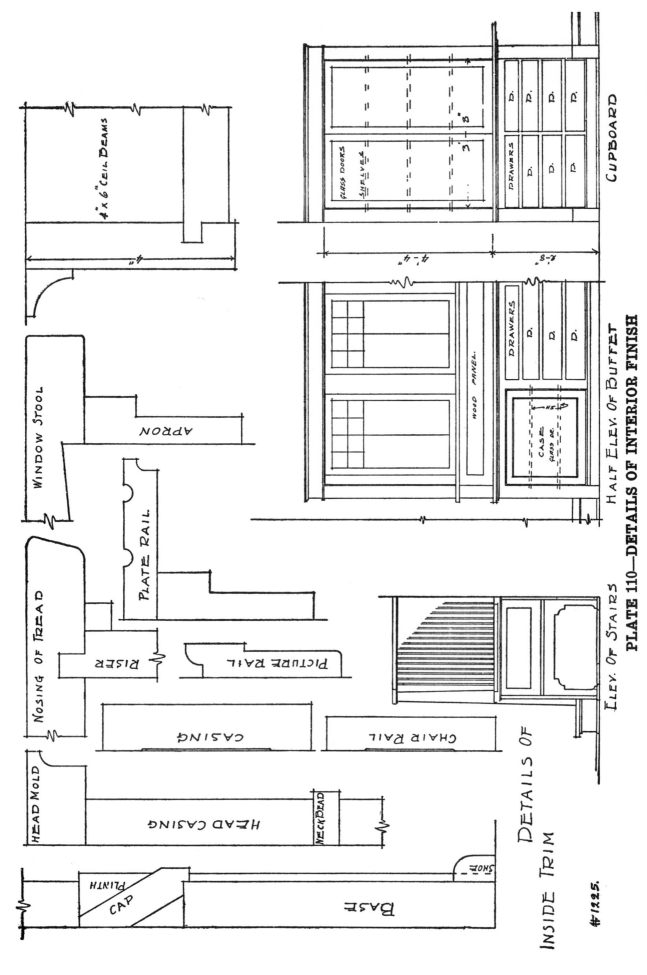

**PLATE 110—DETAILS OF INTERIOR FINISH**

Complete details for the interior trim of a modern residence to be finished in the popular, simple and sanitary style. Design for attractive dining room buffet, half elevation being shown. Design for practical kitchen cupboard. Attractive stairway landing in living room or hall, closed below and screened with spindle grille work above

Complete details for regular inside finish, including plate rail and ceiling beams. For additional details harmonizing with these, see Plate 111.

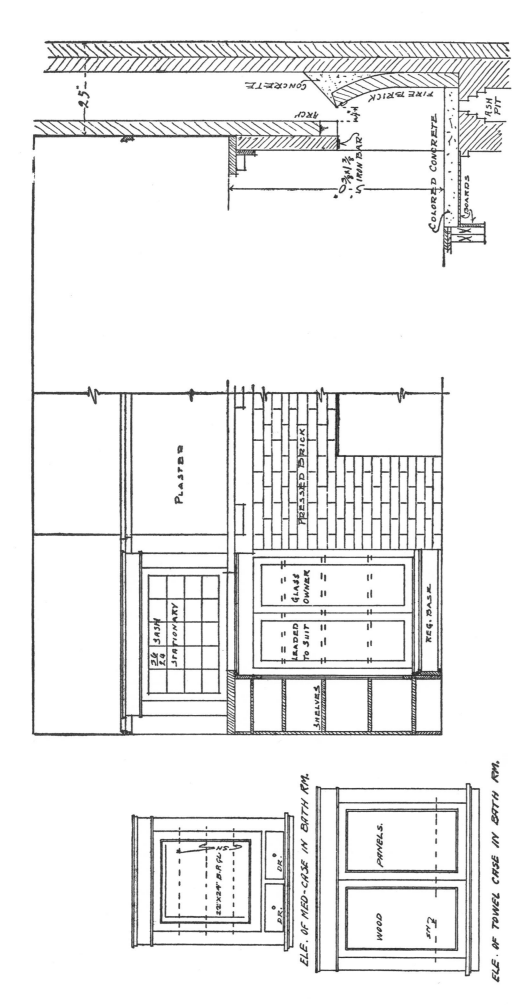

HALF ELEV. AND SECTION OF BRICK MANTEL
AND BOOK CASE IN LIVING ROOM

**PLATE 111—BRICK MANTEL AND BOOK CASE FOR LIVING ROOM**

A popular design, fully detailed, showing arrangement and construction for an open fire place with simple pressed brick mantel; built-in book case at one side having leaded doors. This book case is to be built into a corner of the room, the case on the end wall being shown in section in the drawing. A stationary leaded glass window above the book case furnishes good light. If desired the same sort of a book case arrangement could be used on the other side of the mantel. Details are also shown for a medicine case and towel cabinet for the bath room. For additional details harmonizing with these, see Plate 110.

ELE. OF MED-CASE IN BATH RM.

ELE. OF TOWEL CASE IN BATH RM.

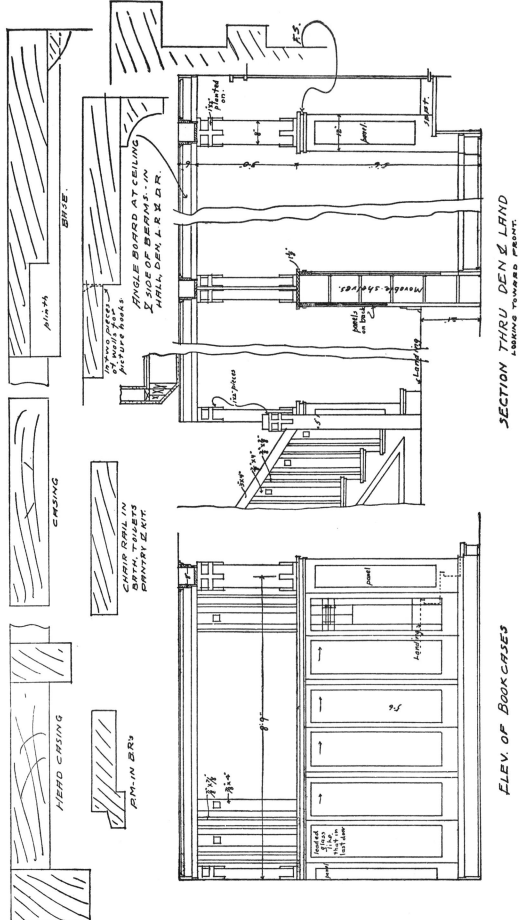

BASE.

plinth

CASING

HEAD CASING

CHAIR RAIL IN
BATH, TOILETS
PANTRY & KIT.

P.M.- IN B.R.'s

ANGLE BOARD AT CEILING
& SIDE OF BEAMS - IN
HALL, DEN, L.R. & D.R.

In two pieces
of walls for
picture hooks.

SECTION THRU DEN & LAND
LOOKING TOWARD FRONT.

ELEV. OF BOOKCASES

**PLATE 112—MODERN STAIRWAY FINISH WITH BOOK CASE**

Elevation, section and complete details for novel and attractive arrangement for stairway entrance out of living room, den, or hall. A paneled book case with leaded glass doors oc-cupies the lower part of the partition by the stairway, the upper half of the partition being an arrangement of decorated columns and slat spindles. Complete details for interior trim to match are also presented. This is the extreme straight line pattern with all square corners and without extra decorative members. For addi-tional harmonizing details, see Plate 113

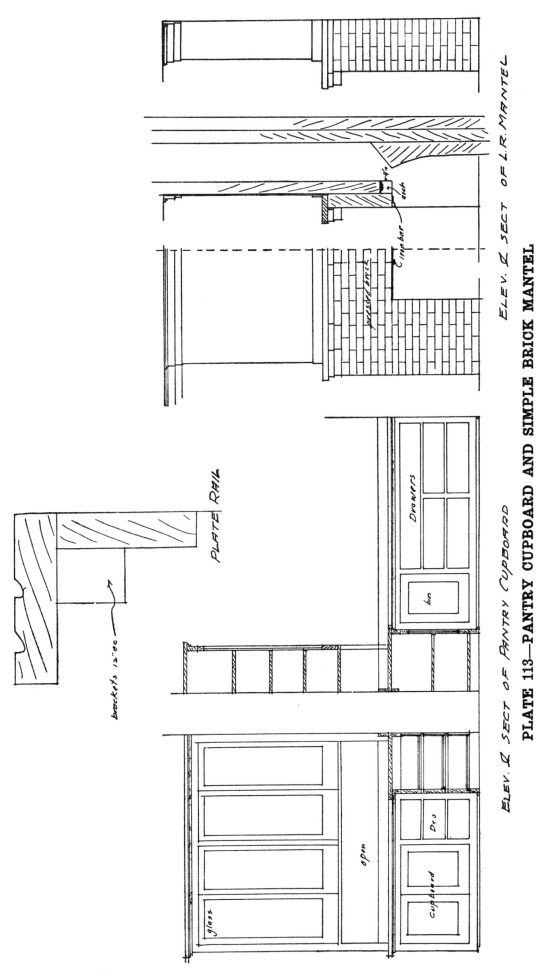

ELEV. & SECT. OF L.R. MANTEL

ELEV. & SECT OF PANTRY CUPBOARD

PLATE RAIL

brackets 12"o.c.

PLATE RAIL

Drawers

bin

Drs

open

Cupboard

glass

pressed brick

Cupboard

**PLATE 113—PANTRY CUPBOARD AND SIMPLE BRICK MANTEL**

Details of convenient pantry cupboard to occupy a corner, one side consisting of high shelves and the other side a working table with drawers and bin below. Also details of modern simple brick fireplace. For additional details harmonizing with these see Plate 112.

124

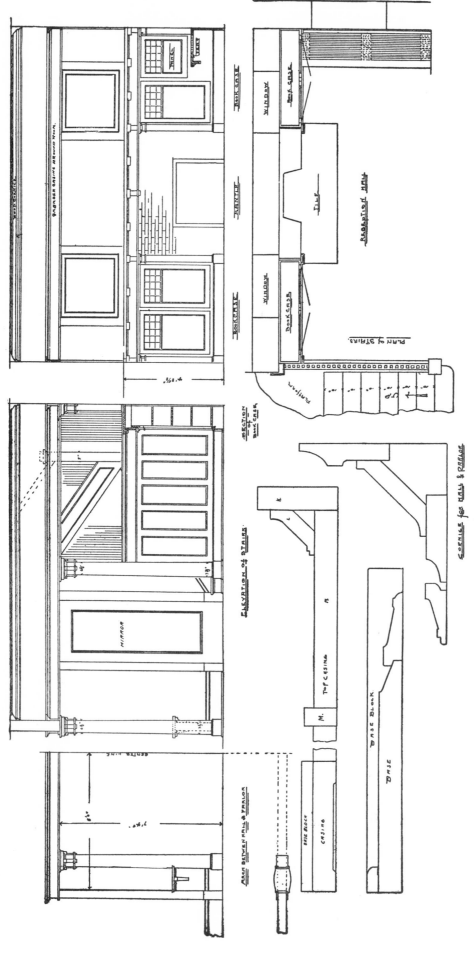

## PLATE 114—DETAILS OF RECEPTION HALL

Floor plan and two elevations, together with details, showing a very cozy and desirable reception hall, containing fire place, book cases and seat. The platform stairway is half open: square ornamented columns support the head casing beam. The doorway opening between reception hall and parlor is ten feet wide and has ornamental columns. Note also detail of cornice mould for hall and parlor. Cornice finish for the rooms of fine residences is becoming very popular. For additional details harmonizing with these, see Plate 115.

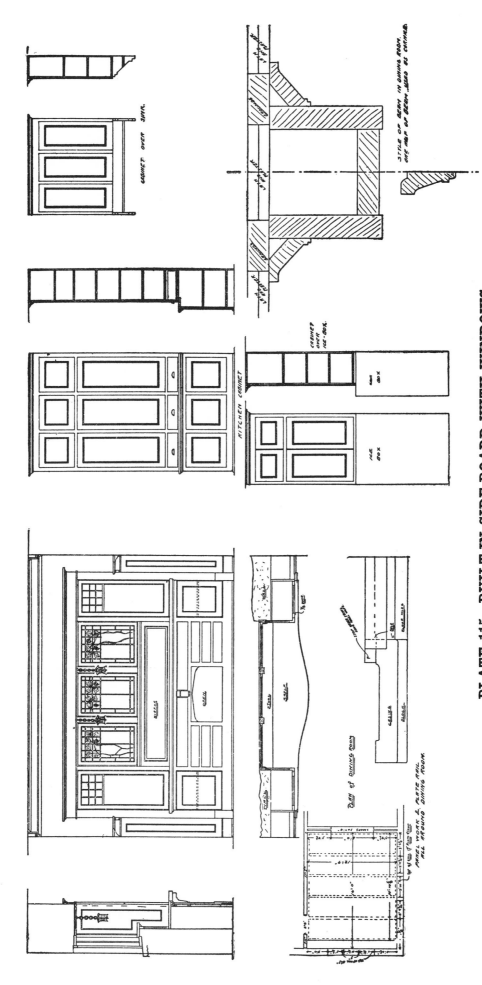

## PLATE 115—BUILT-IN SIDE-BOARD WITH WINDOWS

Elevation, plan and section of a very beautiful dining room buffet, built around and under three leaded, art-glass windows. Also useful designs for kitchen cabinet, ice-box with cabinet above, working detail of ceiling beams, etc. See Plate 114 for additional details.

125

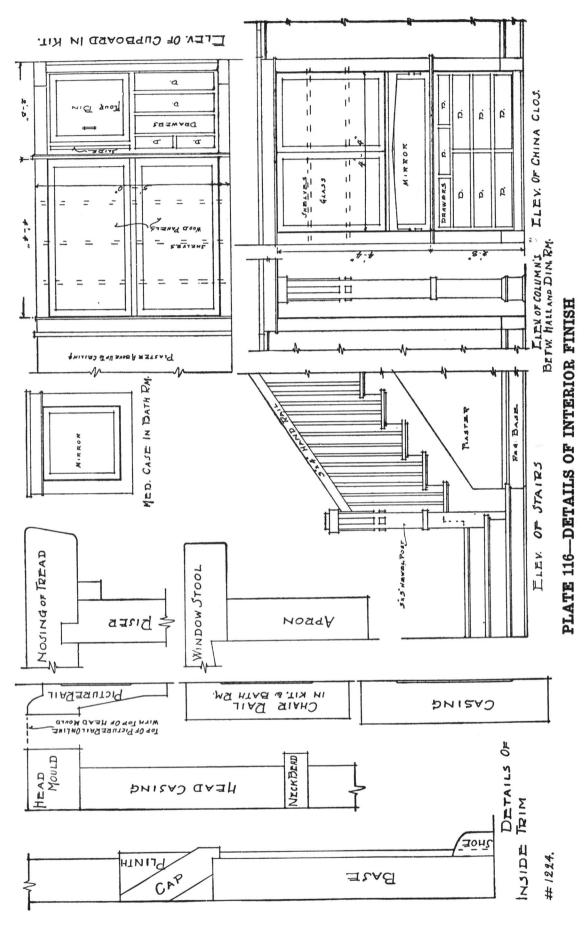

ELEV. OF CUPBOARD IN KIT.

ELEV. OF CHINA CLOS.

ELEV. OF COLUMN'S
BETW. HALL AND DIN. RM.

MED. CASE IN BATH RM.

ELEV. OF STAIRS

DETAILS OF INSIDE TRIM
#1244.

## PLATE 116—DETAILS OF INTERIOR FINISH

Neat design for a simple china closet. Kitchen cupboard with shelves, drawers and flour bin. Medicine case. Open platform stairway. Complete details of inside trim of a popular style.

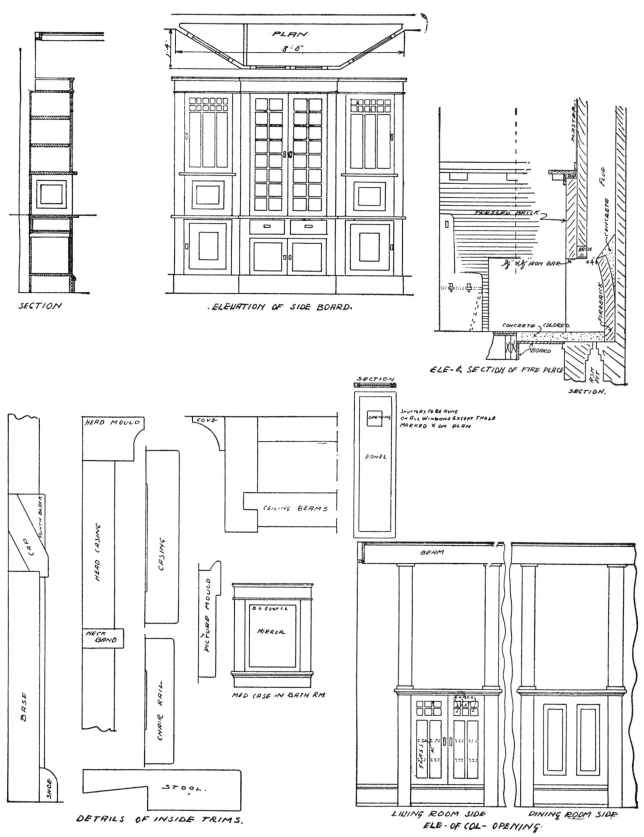

SECTION

.ELEVATION OF SIDE BOARD.

PRESSED BRICK

⅜"x¼" IRON BAR

PLASTER

FLUE

CONCRETE

ARCH

FIREBRICK

CONCRETE. COLORED.

BOARD

ASH PIT

SECTION.

ELE-& SECTION OF FIRE PLACE

HEAD MOULD

COVE

CEILING BEAMS

SECTION

SHUTTERS TO BE HUNG ON ALL WINDOWS EXCEPT THOSE MARKED X ON PLAN

OPENING

PANEL

TOOTH BLOCK

CAP

HEAD CASING

CASING

PICTURE MOULD

BEAM

NECK BAND

B.P. 20x26

MIRROR

BASE

CHAIR RAIL

SHOE

STOOL.

MED CASE IN BATH RM.

DETAILS OF INSIDE TRIMS.

GLASS

GLASS

LIVING ROOM SIDE

DINING ROOM SIDE

ELE - OF COL- OPENING

## PLATE 117—COLUMNED OPENING WITH BOOK CASE BUILT-IN

Useful and beautiful designs for attractive built-in features in the home. A columned opening to go between living room and dining room, the lower part utilized as a book case with glass doors on the living room side. Also beautiful side board design. Comfortable open fire place with built-in seat at one side. Complete details for interior trim for this house.

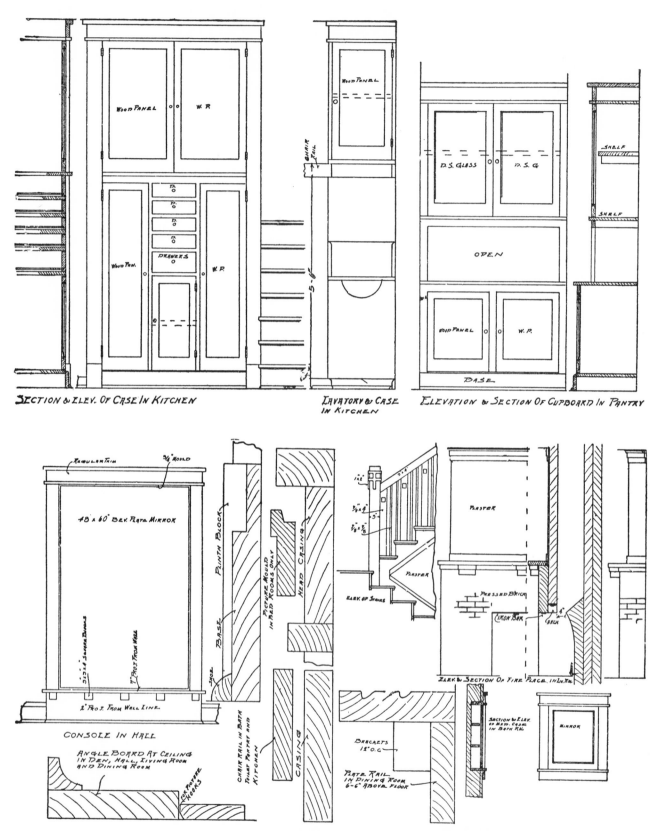

SECTION & ELEV. OF CASE IN KITCHEN

LAVATORY & CASE
IN KITCHEN

ELEVATION & SECTION OF CUPBOARD IN PANTRY

CONSOLE IN HALL

## PLATE 118—CONSOLE WITH BEVELED PLATE MIRROR

Design and details for beautiful console for the reception hall, a feature which is in great demand at the present time.  Also good ideas for cases and cupboards for kitchen and pantry.  Brick mantel design.  Open platform stairway.  Complete details of straight line interior trim.

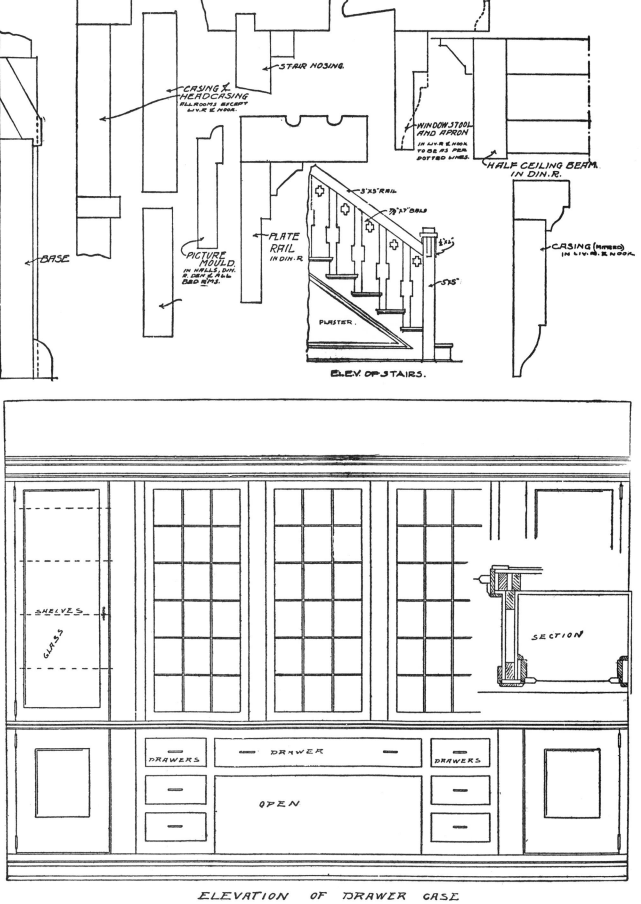

*ELEVATION OF DRAWER CASE*

## PLATE 119—LARGE BUILT-IN SIDE-BOARD

Idea for dining room buffet, lighted centrally by three casement windows, outward opening. Also details of popular interior finish including novel stairway treatment with ornamental balusters. These are standard details for houses of the Western bungalow order.

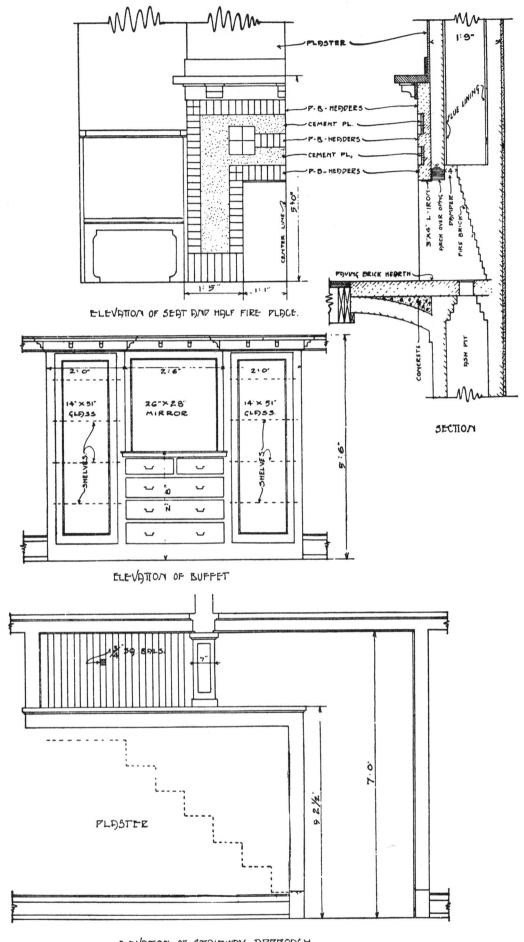

ELEVATION OF SEAT AND HALF FIRE PLACE.

SECTION

ELEVATION OF BUFFET

ELEVATION OF STAIRWAY APPROACH

## PLATE 120—DETAILS OF INTERIOR TRIM

Design and construction for a beautiful art mantel and fireplace, using a combination of cement plaster and paving bricks. Elevation of dining room buffet of a simple, attractive design.

Elevation of novel stairway approach as viewed from fireplace nook in living room. For large size details of interior trim, harmonizing with these special features, see Plate 121.

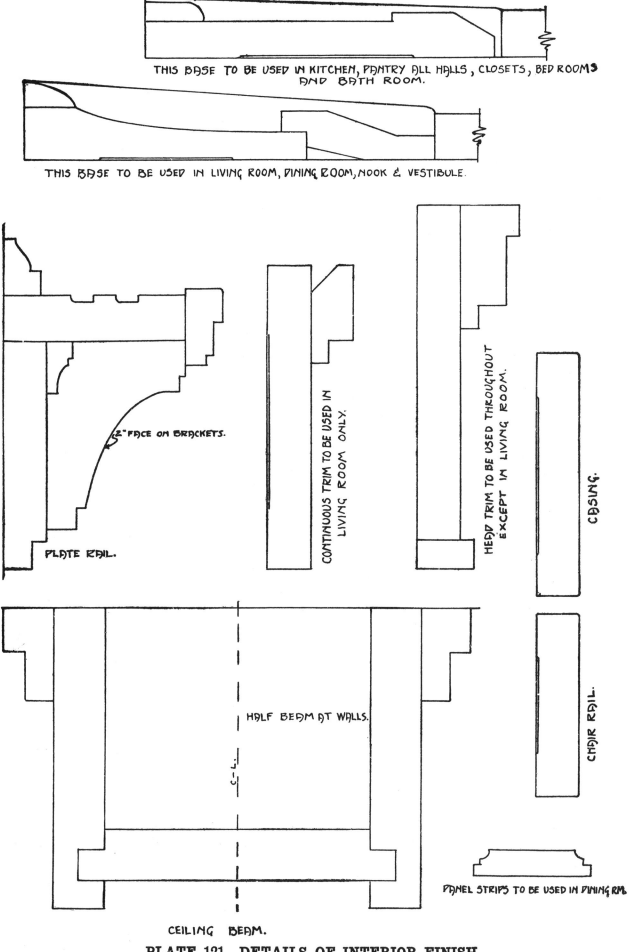

THIS BASE TO BE USED IN KITCHEN, PANTRY ALL HALLS, CLOSETS, BED ROOMS AND BATH ROOM.

THIS BASE TO BE USED IN LIVING ROOM, DINING ROOM, NOOK & VESTIBULE.

2" FACE ON BRACKETS.

PLATE RAIL.

CONTINUOUS TRIM TO BE USED IN LIVING ROOM ONLY.

HEAD TRIM TO BE USED THROUGHOUT EXCEPT IN LIVING ROOM.

CASING.

CHAIR RAIL.

HALF BEAM AT WALLS.

C - L.

PANEL STRIPS TO BE USED IN DINING RM.

CEILING BEAM.

## PLATE 121—DETAILS OF INTERIOR FINISH

Large size details for interior trim of special pattern for a modern residence. Note construction of ceiling beams, plate rail with brackets, continuous head trim for living room, strips for dining room paneling, etc. For special built-in features to harmonize with these, see Plate 120.

132

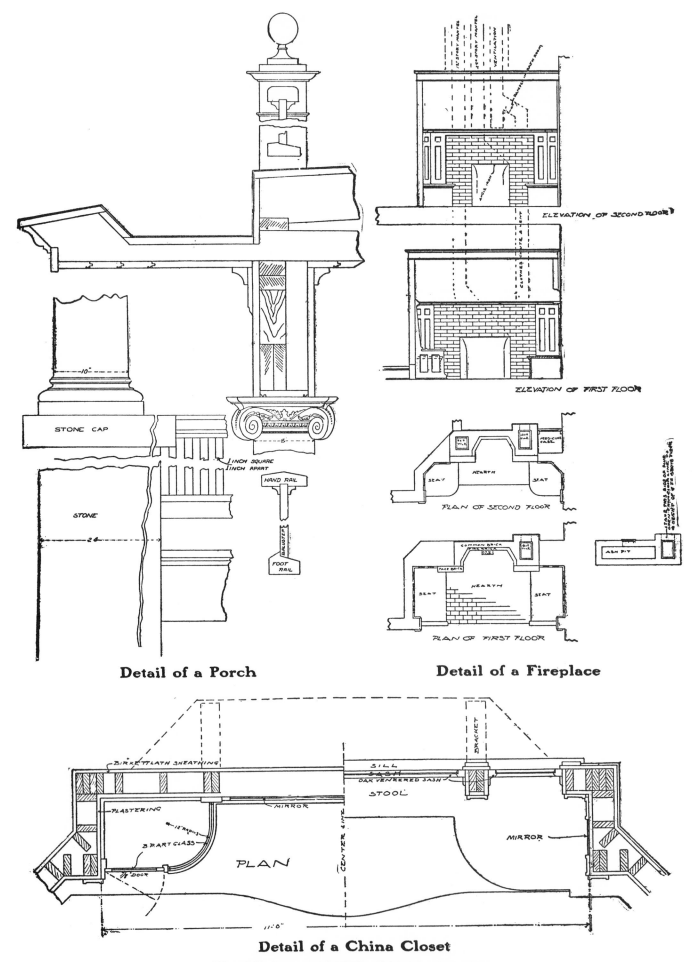

Detail of a Porch

Detail of a Fireplace

Detail of a China Closet

## PLATE 122—CORNER CHINA CLOSET

Plan and section showing construction of a nicely arranged china closet to be built in the corner of a room. Also detail showing the arrangement of open fire places on first and second floor, together with method of running the flues. Porch details, showing proper relation between the various members. Note that soffit and balcony rail are centered over porch columns.

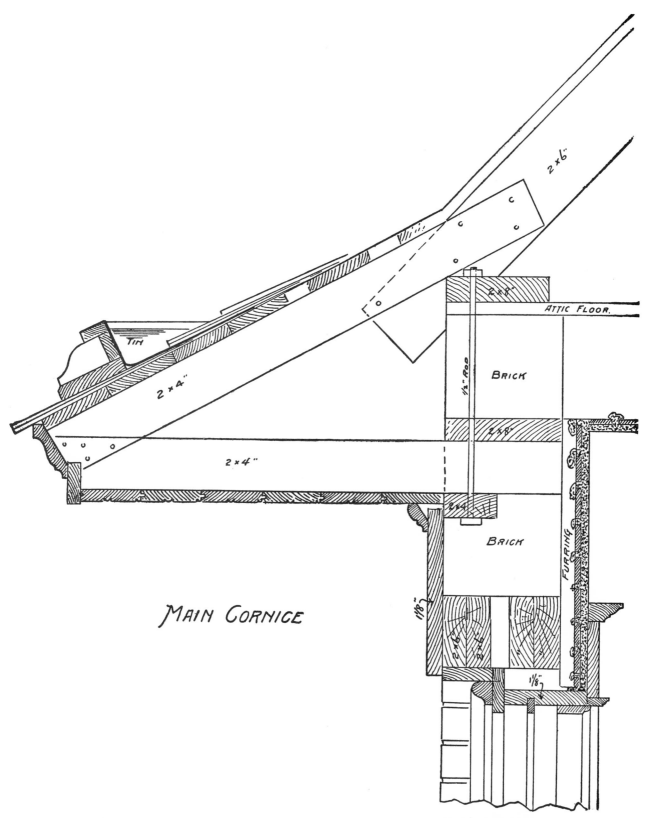

2 x 6"

ATTIC FLOOR.

BRICK

½" ROD

TIN

2 x 4"

2 x 4"

MAIN CORNICE

FURRING

BRICK

1⅛"

2 x 6"   2 x 4"

1⅛"

## PLATE 123—DETAIL OF MAIN CORNICE ON BRICK HOUSE

Substantial cornice construction for a brick house. The cornice is of the wide extending box type, the roof being given a perceptible flare at the eaves by means of two by four pieces nailed onto the rafter ends. Note method of securely tying together the members which constitute the plate and of supporting the cornice by means of ½-inch iron rods.

134

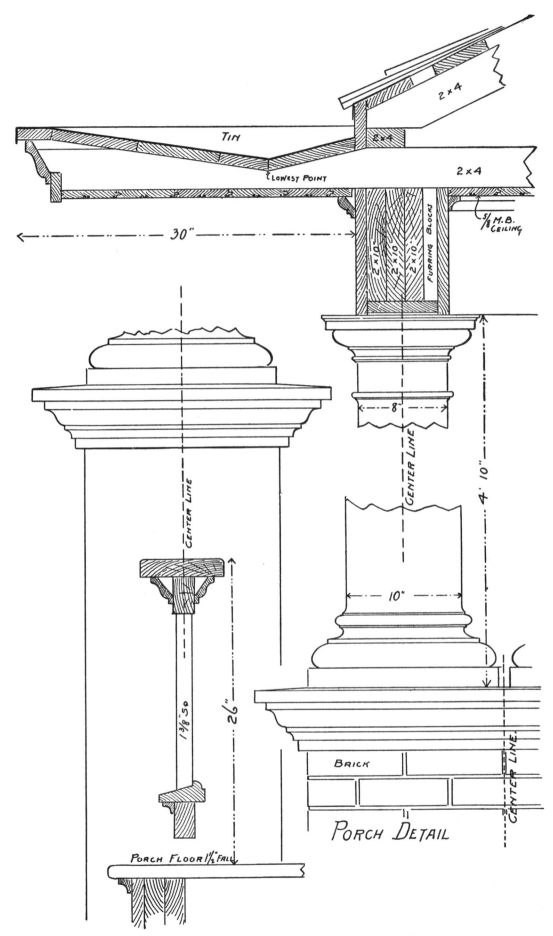

**PLATE 124—DETAILS OF PORCH CONSTRUCTION**

Working drawings showing the design and construction of a porch with classic columns resting on a brick and stone base. Note novel method of constructing porch cornice to make the eaves trough invisible. Special attention is called to the fact that all the members of the porch system, balustrade, columns and architrave, are arranged on the same center line.

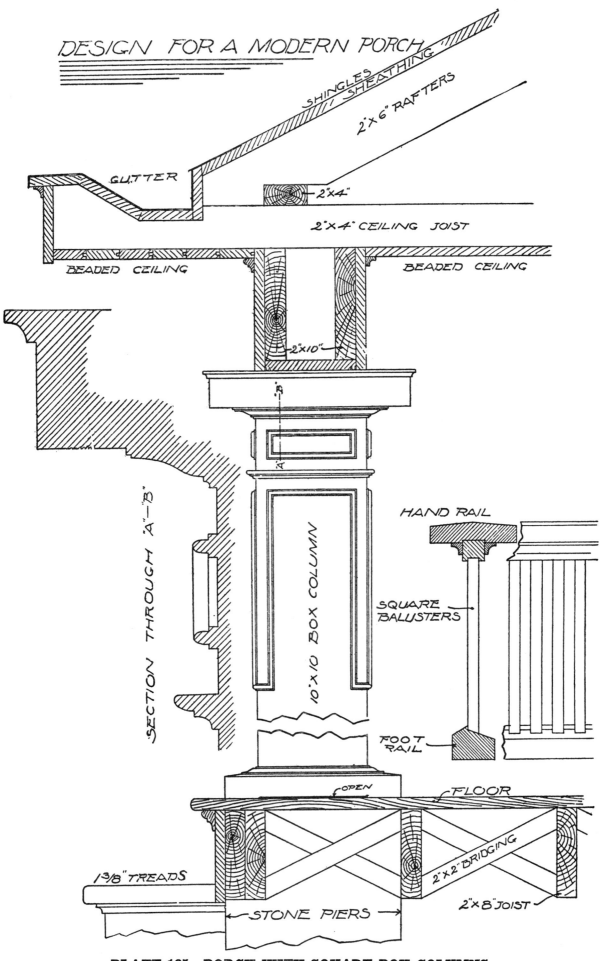

DESIGN FOR A MODERN PORCH

SHINGLES
SHEATHING
2"X6" RAFTERS
GUTTER
2"X4"
2"X4" CEILING JOIST
BEADED CEILING
BEADED CEILING
2"X10"
"B"
SECTION THROUGH "A"-"B"
10"X10 BOX COLUMN
"A"
HAND RAIL
SQUARE BALUSTERS
FOOT RAIL
OPEN
FLOOR
1 3/8" TREADS
2"X2" BRIDGING
STONE PIERS
2"X8" JOIST

## PLATE 125—PORCH WITH SQUARE BOX COLUMNS

Design and complete details showing construction of a modern porch, consisting of 10 by 10 inch box columns, ornamented, simple square balusters and broad hand rail. This is a dignified design well worked out. Note the method of seating the porch rafters; also concealed gutter.

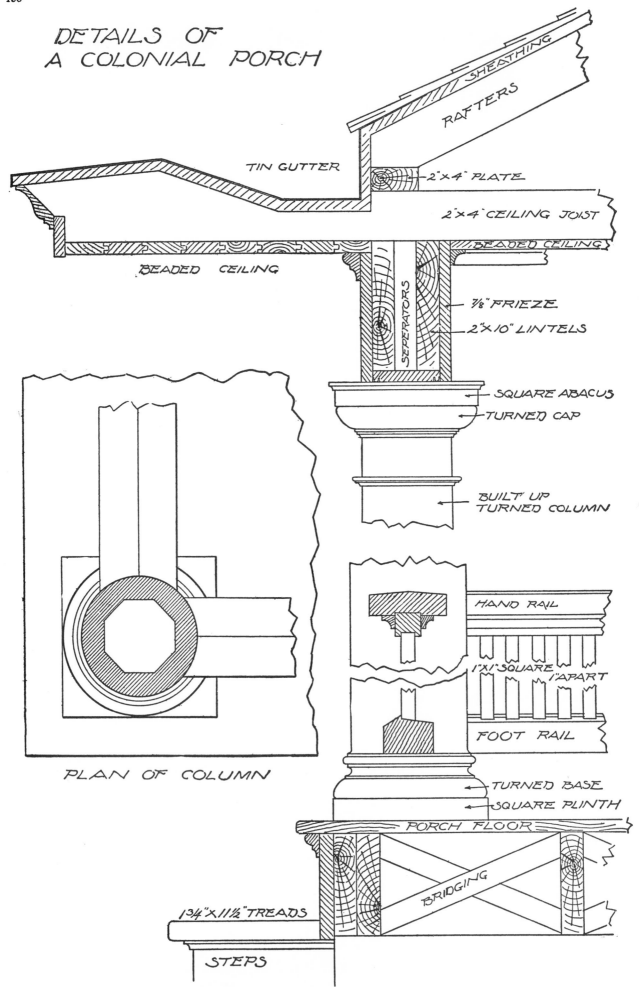

DETAILS OF
A COLONIAL PORCH

SHEATHING

RAFTERS

TIN GUTTER

2"X4" PLATE

2"X4" CEILING JOIST

BEADED CEILING

BEADED CEILING

SEPERATORS

7/8" FRIEZE

2"X10" LINTELS

SQUARE ABACUS

TURNED CAP

BUILT UP
TURNED COLUMN

HAND RAIL

1"X1" SQUARE
1" APART

FOOT RAIL

PLAN OF COLUMN

TURNED BASE

SQUARE PLINTH

PORCH FLOOR

BRIDGING

1¾"X11½" TREADS

STEPS

## PLATE 126—DESIGN AND DETAILS FOR COLONIAL PORCH

The Colonial porch composed of neat turned columns and simple hand rail is very popular, both for new and remodeling work. This is a conservative design of very good lines. A wide cornice with concealed eaves gutter is used. Note shape of foot rail of balustrade.

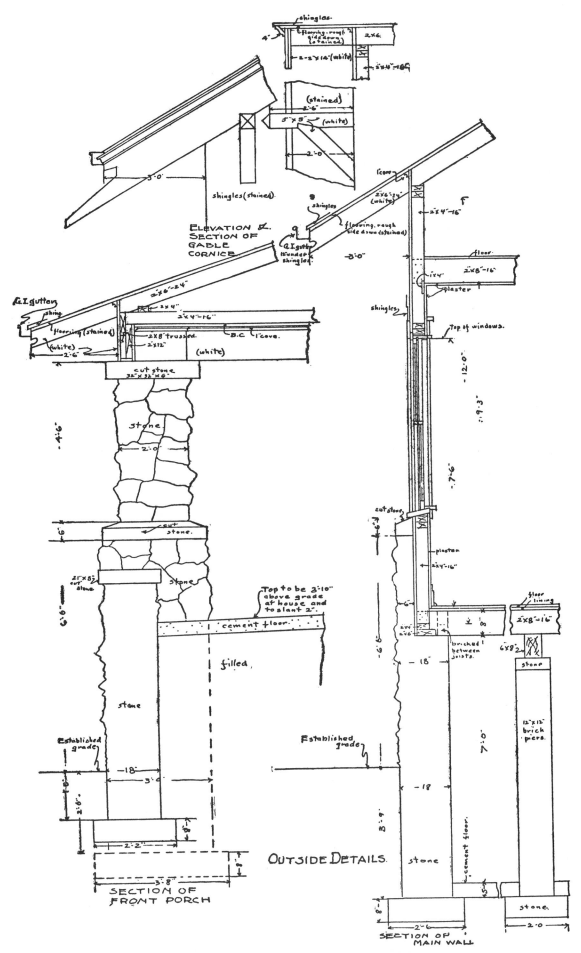

ELEVATION &.
SECTION OF
GABLE
CORNICE

OUTSIDE DETAILS.

SECTION OF
FRONT PORCH

SECTION OF
MAIN WALL

## PLATE 127—ROUGH STONE WORK

Details showing design and arrangement for porch and wall construction; also bracketed cornice with exposed rafters, all to be used in connection with rough stone masonry. Work of this kind is very popular for bungalows and country places. The details show both the design and proper construction for this kind of work. Space under cement porch floor is filled.

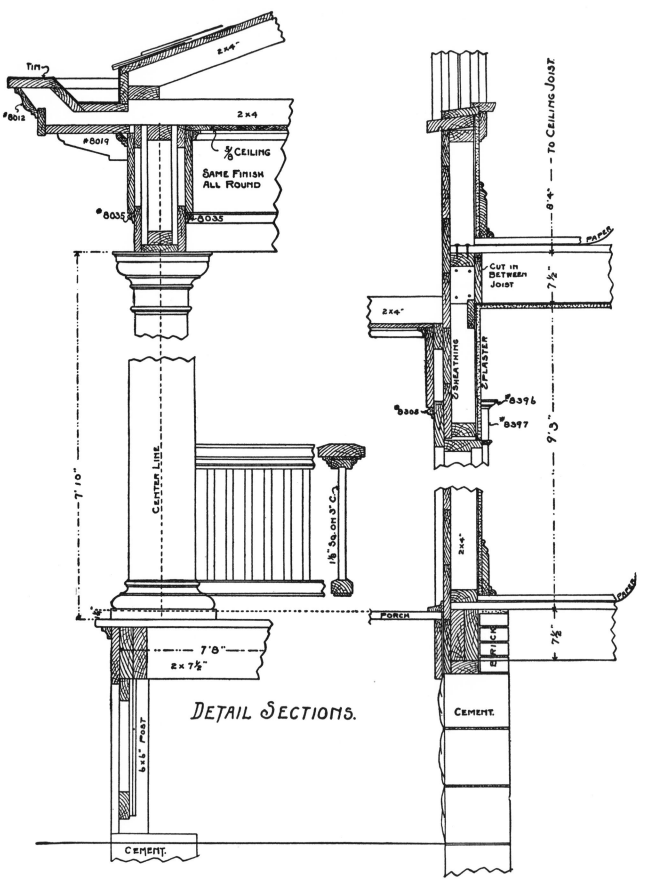

Tin

#8012

#8019

2x4"

2x4

⅝ CEILING
SAME FINISH
ALL ROUND

#8035

#8035

CENTER LINE

7'10"

1⅛" SQ. ON 3" C.

7'8"

2 x 7½"

6x6" POST

DETAIL SECTIONS.

CEMENT.

TO CEILING JOIST

8'4"

PAPER

CUT IN
BETWEEN
JOIST

2x4"

7½"

SHEATHING

PLASTER

#8305

#8396

#8397

9'3"

2x4"

PORCH

PAPER

BRICK

7½"

CEMENT.

**PLATE 128—DETAILS OF PORCH CONSTRUCTION**

Sections through porch cornice and also through main wall of house showing how porch joins on. Approved method of construction for this work. Note brick wind-stop built in between main joists as part of the sill construction; note also wind and fire stop, two by fours, nailed in just above second floor joists. This should be done both in outside walls and main partition walls running continuously from first floor to roof. Stock mouldings of appropriate designs are indicated for the finish of the various parts, the numbers being from "Universal" moulding book.

139

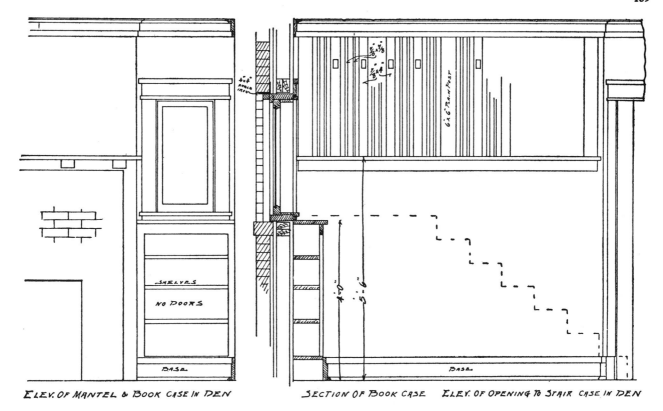

ELEV. OF MANTEL & BOOK CASE IN DEN     SECTION OF BOOK CASE  ELEV. OF OPENING TO STAIR CASE IN DEN

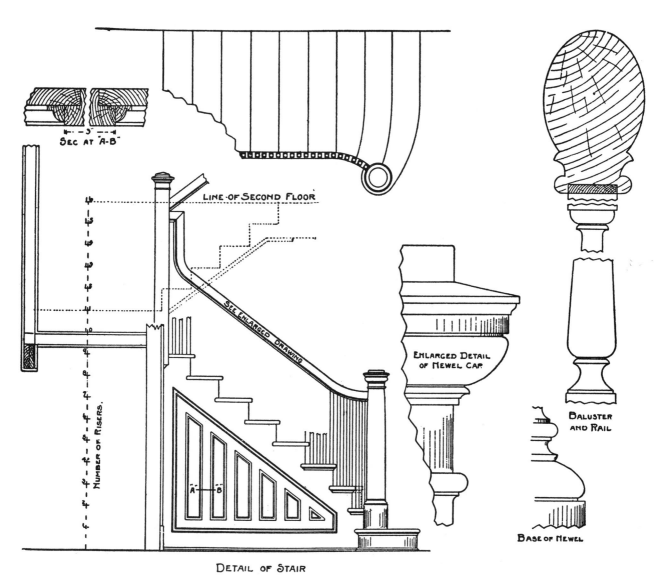

SEC AT "A-B"

LINE OF SECOND FLOOR

SEE ENLARGED DRAWING

NUMBER OF RISERS.

ENLARGED DETAIL OF NEWEL CAP.

BALUSTER AND RAIL

BASE OF NEWEL

DETAIL OF STAIR

**PLATE 129—STAIRWAY DETAILS**

140

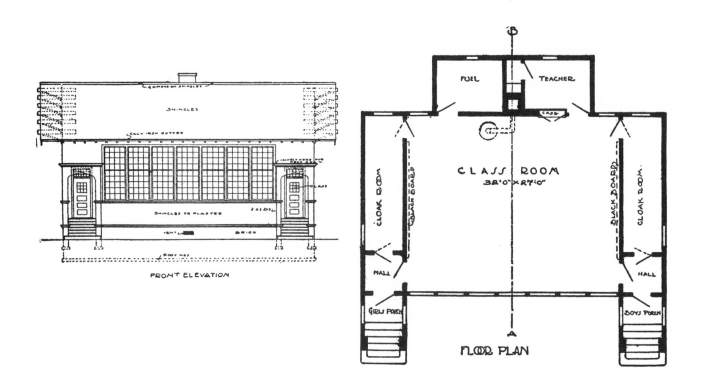

FRONT ELEVATION

FLOOR PLAN

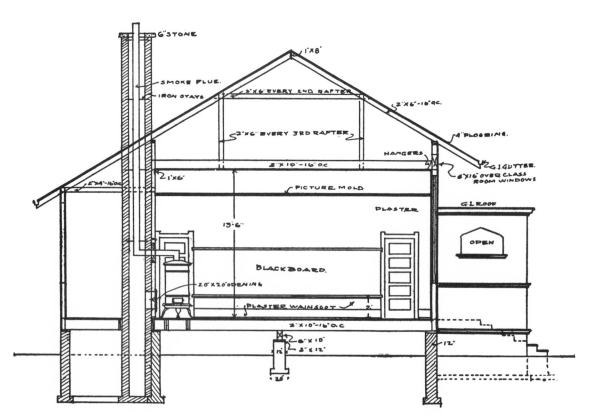

CROSS SECTION ON LINE A-B.

**PLATE 130—WISCONSIN'S MODEL COUNTRY SCHOOL**

Front elevation, floor plan and cross section showing improved ventilation scheme and details of construction of one of the model school designs recommended by the Wisconsin State School Department. Normal capacity of school, 50 pupils; cost, not including stove, blackboards and furnishings, $1,650. The steel stack leading from the stove attaches to a ventilating duct leading from the floor, so that the room can be cleared of foul air in fifteen minutes. The room is very well lighted, yet all the light comes from one side. Additional details are given in Plate 87.

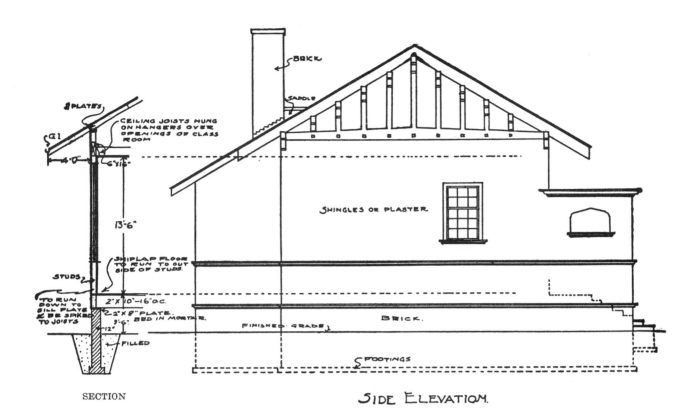

SECTION     SIDE ELEVATION.

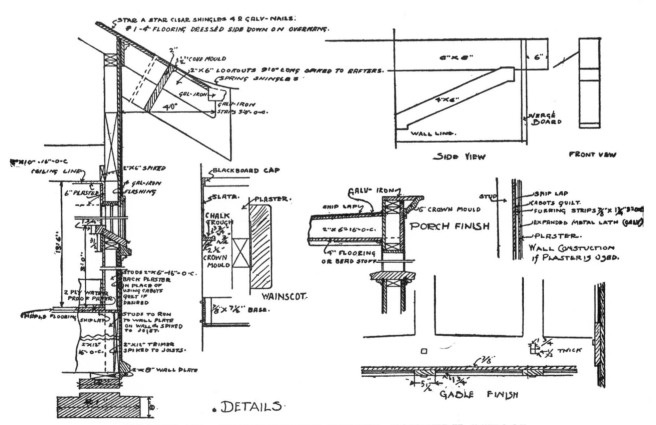

. DETAILS .

## PLATE 131—WISCONSIN'S MODEL COUNTRY SCHOOL

Side elevation and complete details of construction. Specifications call for trusses over all openings more than four feet wide. Sills are to be 2″ by 8″, laid flat, bedded in cement mortar. Floor joists to be 2″ by 12″, spaced 16″ on centers, ceiling joists 2″ by 10″, 16″ on centers; headers and trimmers 2″ by 12″, double and triple; plates 2″ by 4″ and 2″ by 6″; studs 2″ by 4″, spaced 16″; rafters 2″ by 6″, 16″ on centers; porch joists 2″ by 8″.

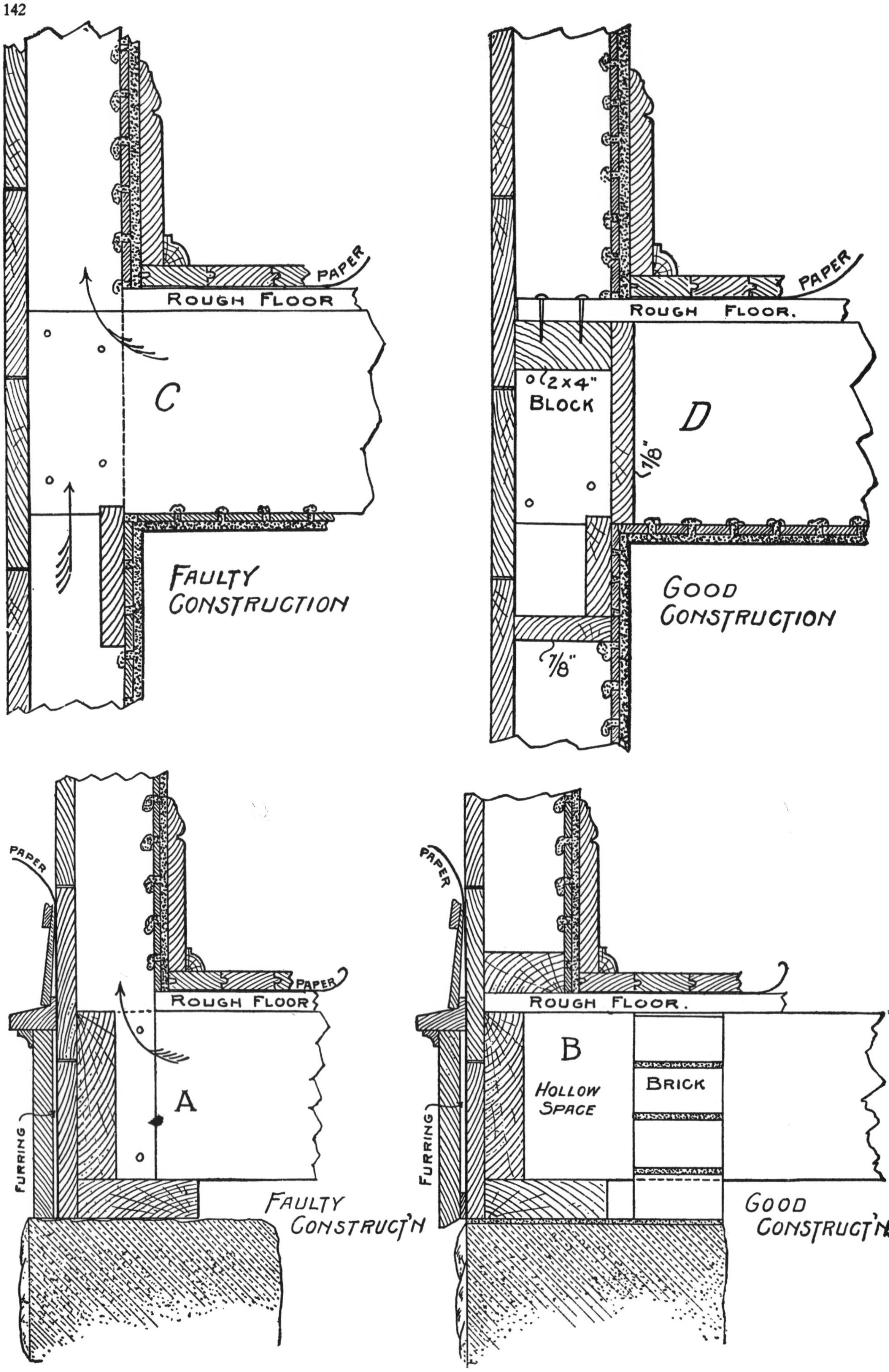

142

**PLATE 132—FAULTY VS. GOOD CONSTRUCTION**

At "A" and "B" are shown methods of sill construction. At "A" the masonry projects beyond the base-board—conducive to dampness; studding are weakened and there are no fire nor wind stops. At "C" and "D" are shown forms of construction at the bearing of the second floor joists. "C" is the usual method of construction. At "D" is better construction, providing stops.

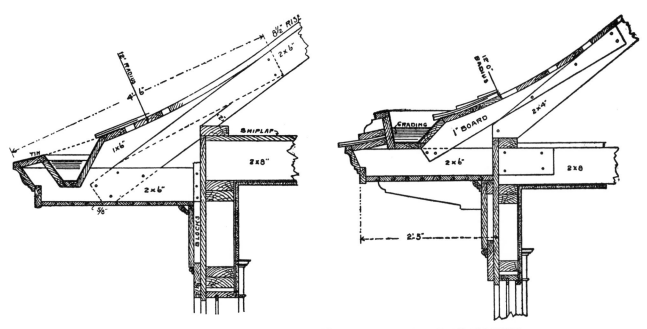

## PLATE 133 B—CONSTRUCTION FOR CURVING EAVES

Two methods are illustrated for producing the curve or flare at the eaves. Often the tendency in such roofs is not to allow enough radius for the curve, thus making the roof too flat at the eaves. A 12-foot radius is here illustrated. Note that the horizontal lookouts are dropped below the plate line. One inch boards sawed to the curve are nailed to the rafter ends.

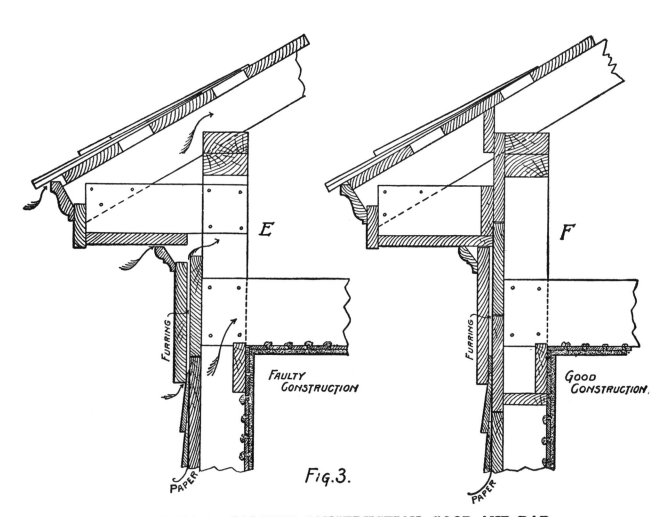

Fig. 3.

## PLATE 133 A—CORNICE CONSTRUCTION, GOOD AND BAD

At "E" is illustrated the usual method of cornice construction for cottages where the ceiling is lower than the plate. The spaces between the studding are left open and the cold winds circulate freely. The result is a cold house. At "F" is shown how these defects can be easily remedied at a very small extra expense. All cracks should be closed up and wind stops put in.

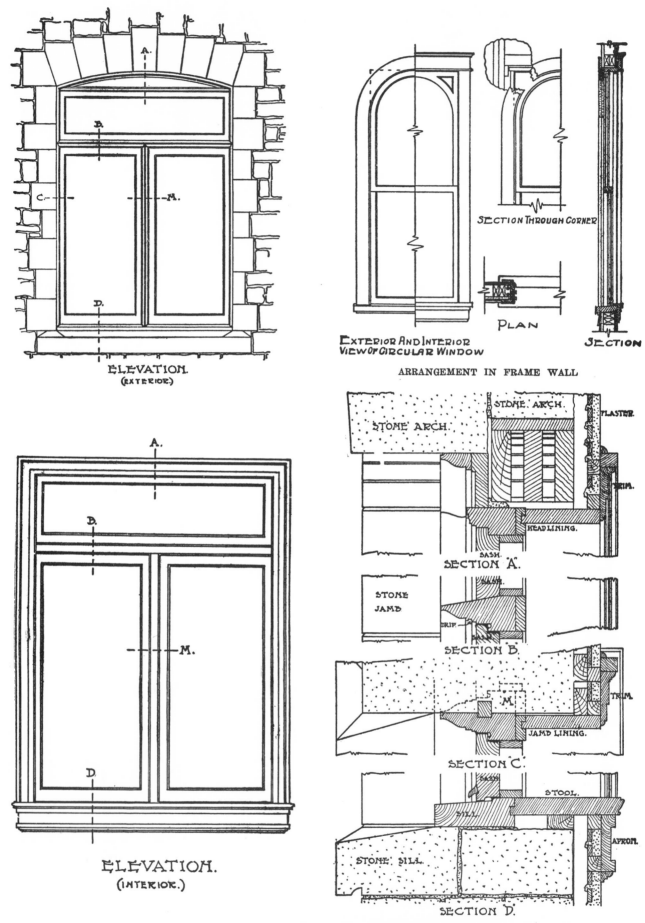

**ELEVATION.**
(EXTERIOR)

**ELEVATION.**
(INTERIOR.)

SECTION THROUGH CORNER

PLAN

SECTION

EXTERIOR AND INTERIOR
VIEW OF CIRCULAR WINDOW

ARRANGEMENT IN FRAME WALL

STONE ARCH.

STONE ARCH.

PLASTER.

TRIM.

HEAD LINING.

SASH.

SECTION "A."

STONE JAMB

SASH.

DRIP.

SECTION B.

TRIM.

M

JAMB LINING.

SECTION C.

SASH.

STOOL.

SILL.

STONE SILL.

APRON.

SECTION D.

## PLATE 134—CIRCLE HEAD WINDOW FINISHED SQUARE INSIDE

Interior and exterior elevations and details of construction of a segmental head window finished with a square soffit inside. In this window the sash are of the outward opening casement type and the transom is stationary. The letters on the elevations indicate the positions of the various sections. The details in the upper right-hand corner show the arrangement for a double hung window with circle head and square interior finish arranged in ordinary frame wall.

# PART IV. "THE HANDY MAN'S FRIEND"—HOW TO MAKE A THOUSAND AND ONE USEFUL THINGS

___

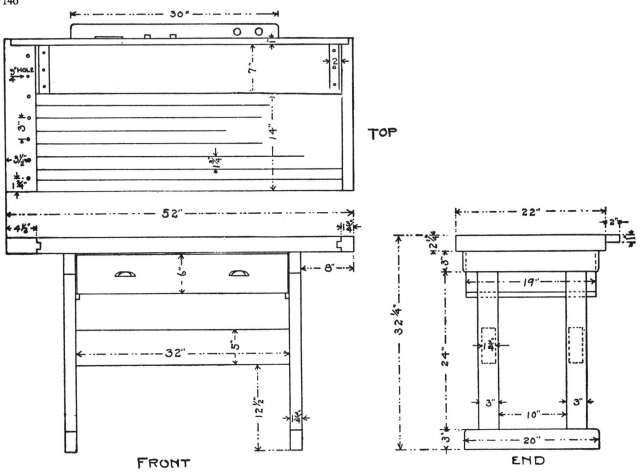

## PLATE 135 B—HOW TO MAKE A WOODWORKER'S BENCH

### Material Required

4 horizontals (frame), 1¾ by 3 by 20½ inches.  
2 horizontals (frame), 1¾ by 5 by 32½ inches.  
2 horizontals (frame), ¾ by 1¾ by 19½ inches.  
4 verticals (frame), 1¾ by 3 by 30 inches, S-4-S.  
1 piece (top), 2⅜ by 5 by 22½ inches, S-4-S.  
1 piece (top), 2⅜ by 2¼ by 22½ inches, S-4-S.  
8 pieces (top), 2⅜ by 1⅞ by 46¼ inches, S-4-S.

1 piece (top), 1 by 8 by 46¼ inches, S-2-S.  
1 piece (top), 1 by 2¼ by 52 inches, S-4-S.  
1 piece (top), 1 by 2 by 30 inches, S-4-S.  
2 pieces (top), 1¼ by 2 by 7½ inches, S-4-S.  
2 pieces (drawer), ⅞ by 6¼ by 32½ inches.  
2 pieces (drawer), ⅞ by 6¼ by 19½ inches.  
1 piece (drawer), ⅜ by 22 by 32 inches, S-2-S.

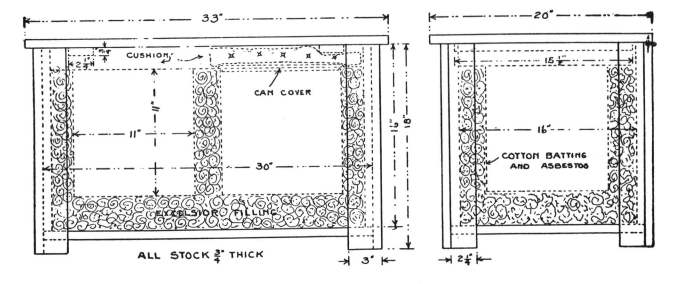

## PLATE 135 A—HOW TO MAKE A FIRELESS COOKER

### Material Required

Lid, 1 piece, ¾ by 20½ by 33½ inches, S-2-S.  
Sides, 2 pieces, ¾ by 16½ by 30½ inches, S-2-S.  
Ends, 2 pieces, ¾ by 16½ by 16½ inches, S-2-S.  
Bottom, 1 piece, ¾ by 18 by 30½ inches, S-2-S.

Posts, 4 pieces, ¾ by 2½ by 18½ inches, S-2-S.  
Posts, 4 pieces, ¾ by 3¼ by 18½ inches, S-2-S.  
Cleats, 2 pieces, ¾ by 2½ by 16 inches, S-2-S.

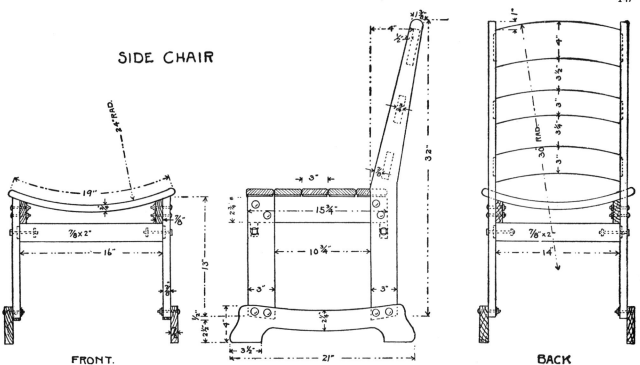

SIDE CHAIR

FRONT.

BACK

## PLATE 136 B—HOW TO MAKE A PORCH CHAIR

### Material Required

Front verticals, 2 pieces, ⅞ by 3 by 14 inches, inches, S-4-S.

Back verticals, 2 pieces, ⅞ by 6 by 33 inches, S-4-S.

Bases, 2 pieces, ⅞ by 4½ by 21½ inches, S-4-S.

Side rails, 2 pieces, ⅞ by 2¾ by 16 inches, S-4-S.

Front rail, 1 piece, ⅞ by 2 by 17 inches, S-4-S.

Back rail, 1 piece, ⅞ by 2 by 15 inches, S-4-S.

Back rail, 2 pieces, ¾ by 5 by 15 inches, S-2-S.

Back rail, 1 piece, ¾ by 6 by 15 inches, S-2-S.

Seat, 5 pieces, ¾ by 3 by 20 inches, S-4-S.

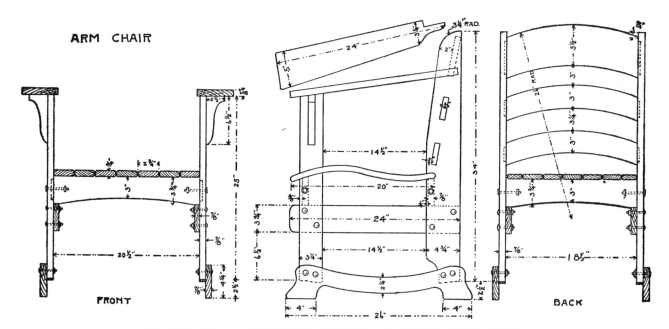

ARM CHAIR

FRONT

BACK

## PLATE 136 A—HOW TO MAKE A PORCH ARM CHAIR

### Material Required

Front verticals, 2 pieces, ⅞ by 3¼ by 27½ inches, S-4-S.

Back verticals, 2 pieces, ⅞ by 4¾ by 34½ inches, S-4-S.

Bases, 2 pieces, ⅞ by 4¼ by 26½ inches, S-4-S.

Side rails, 2 pieces, ⅞ by 3¾ by 24½ inches, S-4-S.

Front rail, 1 piece, ⅞ by 3¾ by 21½ inches, S-4-S.

Back rail, 1 piece, ⅞ by 3¾ by 19½ inches, S-4-S.

Back rails, 2 pieces, ¾ by 5 by 19½ inches, S-2-S.

Back rails, 1 piece, ¾ by 7½ by 19½ inches, S-2-S.

Arms, 2 pieces, ⅞ by 5¼ by 25 inches, S-2-S.

Braces under arms, 2 pieces, ⅞ by 2½ by 7 inches, S-4-S.

Seat, 7 pieces, ¾ by 2¾ by 20½ inches, S-4-S.

Cleats, 2 pieces, ⅞ by ⅞ by 21 inches, S-4-S.

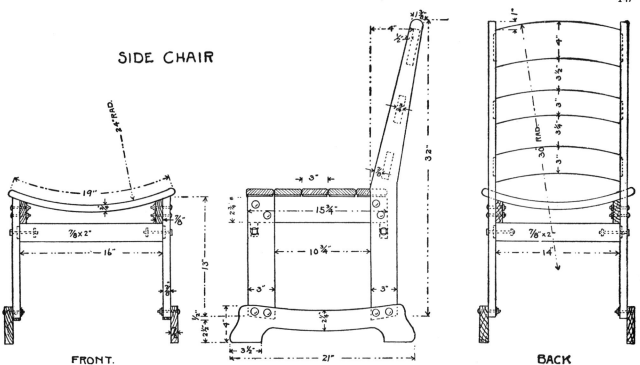

147

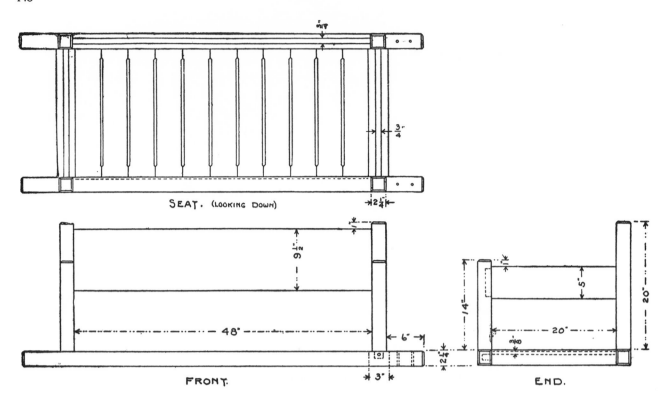

## PLATE 137 B—HOW TO MAKE A PORCH SWING

### Material Required

Seat, 2 pieces, 2¼ by 2¼ by 66 inches, S-4-S.
Seat, 2 pieces, 2¼ by 3 by 23 inches, S-4-S.
Posts, 2 pieces, 2¼ by 2¼ by 15 inches, S-4-S.
Posts, 2 pieces, 2¼ by 2¼ by 21 inches, S-4-S.

Arms, 2 pieces, ¾ by 5½ inches by 22 inches, S-2-S.
Back, 1 piece, ¾ by 10 by 51 inches, S-2-S.
Slats, 11 pieces, ⅜ by 4½ inches, S-2-S.

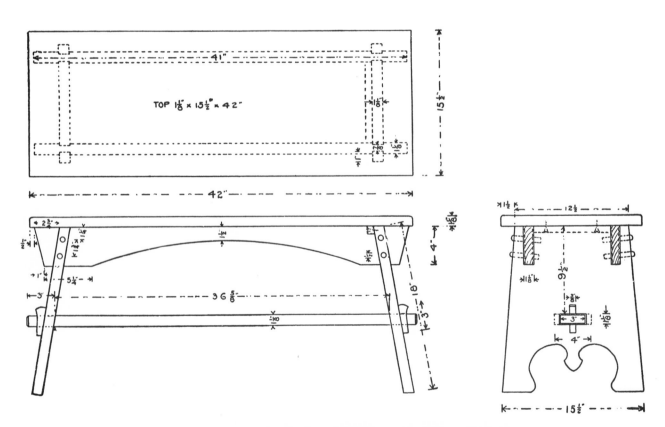

## PLATE 137 A—HOW TO MAKE A PIANO BENCH

### Material Required

Top, 1 piece, 1⅛ by 16 by 43 inches.
Legs, 2 pieces, 1⅛ by 16 by 18½ inches.
Rails, 2 pieces, 1⅛ by 4¼ by 41½ inches.

Stretcher, 1 piece, 1⅛ by 4¼ by 43 inches.
Keys, 2 pieces, ¾ by 1½ by 3½ inches.
Cleats, 2 pieces, ¾ by ¾ by 9 inches.

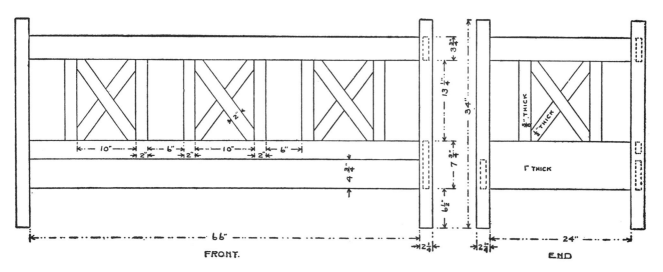

## PLATE 138 B—HOW TO MAKE A SETTEE
### Material Required

Posts, 4 pieces, 2¼ by 2¼ by 34½ inches, S-4-S.
Front rail, 1 piece, 1 by 4¾ by 68 inches, S-4-S.
Back rail, 1 piece, 1 by 7¾ by 68 inches, S-4-S.
Back rail, 1 piece, 1 by 3¾ by 68 inches, S-4-S.
End rails, 2 pieces, 1 by 7¾ by 26 inches, S-4-S.
End rails, 2 pieces, 1 by 3¾ by 26 inches, S-4-S.

Verticals, 10 pieces, ⅝ by 2 by 14 inches, S-4-S.
Diagonals, 10 pieces, ½ by 2 by 18 inches, S-4-S.
Seat cleats, 2 pieces, ½ by 3¾ by 67 inches, S-4-S.
Seat slats, 12 pieces, ⅜ by 3 by 26 inches, S-4-S.

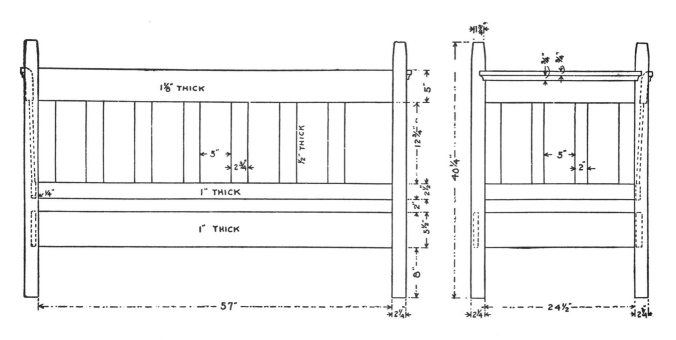

## PLATE 138 A—HOW TO MAKE A MISSION SETTLE
### Material Required

Front and back rails, 2 pieces, 1 by 5½ by 59 inches, S-4-S.
Back rail, 1 piece, 1⅛ by 3½ by 59 inches, S-4-S.
Back rail, top of, 1 piece, ¾ by 1½ by 59 inches, S-4-S.
Moulding under top, 1 piece, ½-inch cove, 59 inches.
Back rail, 1 piece, 1 by 2½ by 59 inches, S-4-S.
Side rails, 2 pieces, 1 by 5½ by 26½ inches, S-4-S.
Side rails, 2 pieces, 1⅛ by 3½ by 26½ inches, S-4-S.

Side rails, top of, 2 pieces, ¾ by 1½ by 26½ inches, S-4-S.
Moulding under top, 2 pieces, ½-inch cove, 26½ inches.
Side rails, 2 pieces, 1 by 2½ by 26½ inches, S-4-S.
Slats for back and sides, 13 pieces, ½ by 5 by 13¾ inches, S-4-S.
Seat frame, 2 pieces, 1½ by 2½ by 58 inches, S-4-S.
Seat frame, 2 pieces, 1½ by 2½ by 25 inches, S-4-S.
Posts, 4 pieces, 2¼ by 2¼ by 40½ inches, S-4-S.

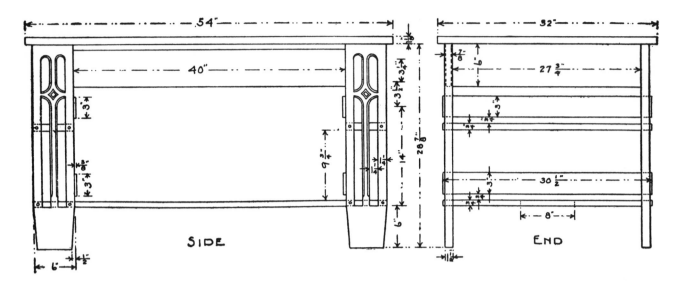

## PLATE 139 B—LIBRARY TABLE WITH BOOK SHELVES

### Material Required

Top, 1 piece, 1⅛ by 32½ by 54½ inches, S-2-S.
Side rails, 2 pieces, ⅞ by 6¼ by 42 inches, S-2-S.
End rails, 2 pieces, ⅞ by 6¼ by 30 inches, S-2-S.
Legs, 4 pieces, 1⅛ by 6¼ by 28½ inches, S-2-S.
Shelves, 4 pieces, ¾ by 6¼ by 31 inches, S-2-S.

Backs for shelves, 4 pieces, ⅜ by 3¼ by 31 inches, S-2-S.
Stretcher, 1 piece, ¼ by 8¼ by 42 inches, S-2-S.
Moulding, 2 pieces, ⅛ by 1¼ by 40½ inches, S-2-S.

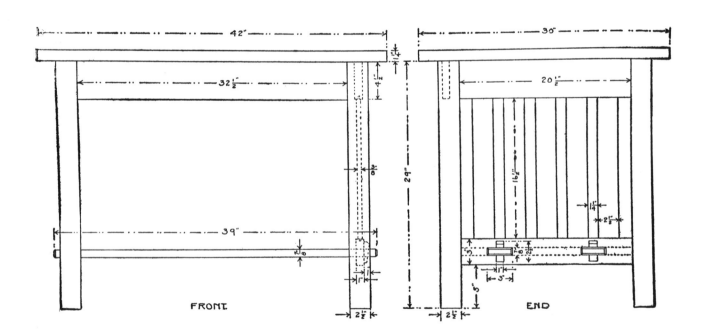

## PLATE 139 A—HOW TO MAKE A MISSION TABLE

### Material Required

Top, 1 piece, 1¼ by 30½ by 42½ inches, S-2-S.
Legs, 4 pieces, 2½ by 2½ by 29½ inches, S-4-S.
Side rails, 2 pieces, ⅞ by 4½ by 35 inches, S-4-S.
End rails, 2 pieces, ⅞ by 4½ by 23½ inches, S-4-S.

Stretchers, 2 pieces, 1 by 3 by 23½ inches, S-4-S.
Shelf, 1 piece, ⅞ by 22 by 39 inches, S-2-S.
Slats, 10 pieces, ⅜ by 2½ by 17½ inches, S-4-S.
Keys, 4 pieces, ¾ by 1 by 3 inches, S-2-S.

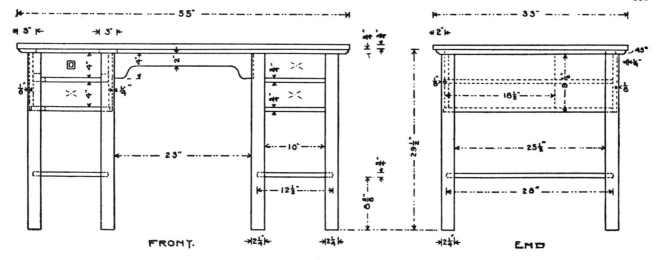

**PLATE 140 B—HOW TO MAKE A LIBRARY TABLE**

### Material Required

Top, 1 piece, ¾ by 34 by 56 inches, S-2-S.
Posts, 4 pieces, 2¼ by 2¼ by 30 inches, S-4-S.
Shelves, 2 pieces, ¾ by 13 by 28½ inches, S-2-S.
Ends, 4 pieces, ¾ by 10 by 28 inches, S-2-S.
Backs, 2 pieces, ¾ by 10 by 12 inches, S-2-S.
Facings, 2 pieces, ¾ by 4¼ by 24 inches, S-2-S.
Frame, 2 pieces, ¾ by 2¼ by 56 inches, S-2-S.
Frame, 4 pieces, ¾ by 3¼ by 34 inches, S-2-S.
Drawer supports, 8 pieces, ¾ by 2½ by 28 inches, S-2-S.

Drawer supports, 8 pieces, ¾ by 3 by 15 inches.
Drawer supports, 8 pieces, ¾ by 1¼ by 19 inches, S-2-S.
Drawers, fronts, 4 pieces, ¾ by 4¼ by 10½ inches, S-2-S.
Drawers, sides, 8 pieces, ⅜ by 4¼ by 19 inches.
Drawers, backs, 4 pieces, ⅜ by 4 by 10 inches, S-2-S.
Drawers, bottoms, 4 pieces, ⅜ by 18½ by 10 inches, S-2-S.

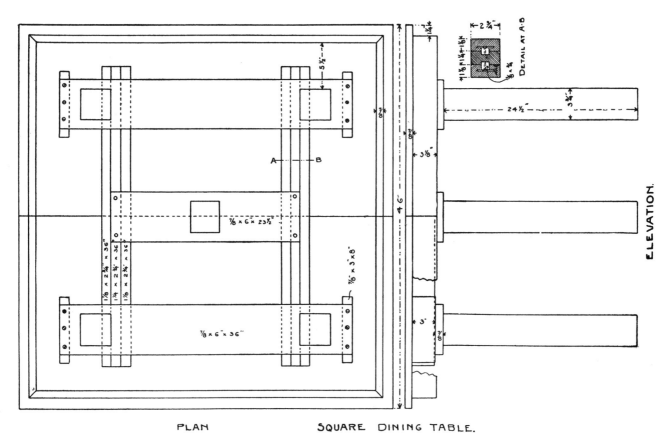

**PLATE 140 A—HOW TO MAKE A SQUARE DINING TABLE**

### Material Required

Top, 2 pieces, ⅞ by 24 by 48 inches, S-2-S, oak.
Leaves, 4 pieces, ⅞ by 12 by 48 inches, S-2-S.
Facings, 4 pieces, ⅞ by 3½ by 48 inches, S-2-S.
Slides, 4 pieces, ⅝ by 3 by 37 inches, S-2-S hard maple.
Slides, 8 pieces, ⅜ by 1¼ by 37 inches, S-2-S, hard maple.
Slides, 2 pieces, ⅝ by ¾ by 37 inches, S-2-S, hard maple.

Slides, 2 pieces, 1¼ by 3 by 37 inches, S-2-S, hard maple.
Blocks, 4 pieces, ⅞ by 3¼ by 8½ inches, S-2-S.
Leg supports, 3 pieces, ⅞ by 6¼ by 37 inches, S-2-S, hard maple.
Legs, 10 pieces, ¾ by 4 by 25 inches, S-2-S, oak.
Legs, 10 pieces, ¾ by 2½ by 25 inches, S-2-S.
Leg blocks, 10 pieces, 2½ by 2½ by 5 inches, S-4-S, oak.

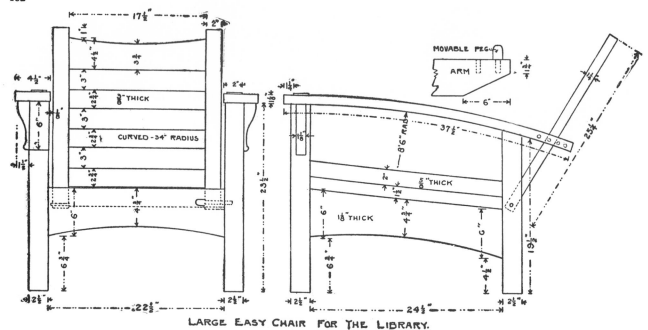

LARGE EASY CHAIR FOR THE LIBRARY.

## PLATE 141 B—HOW TO MAKE A BIG EASY CHAIR

### Material Required

Posts, 4 pieces, 2½ by 2½ by 25 inches, S-4-S.

Front and back rails, 2 pieces, 1⅛ by 6¼ by 25 inches, S-2-S.

Side rails, 2 pieces, 1⅛ by 6¼ by 27 inches, S-2-S.

Side rails, 2 pieces, ⅝ by 2 by 27 inches, S-4-S.

Arms, 2 pieces, 1⅛ by 4¾ by 38 inches, S-2-S.

Braces, 2 pieces, 1⅛ by 1¾ by 6½ inches, S-2-S.

Back verticals, 2 pieces, 1¼ by 2 by 26 inches, S-4-S.

Back horizontals, 3 pieces, ⅜ by 2¾ by 20 inches, S-4-S.

Back horizontal, 1 piece, ⅜ by 4¾ by 20 inches, S-2-S.

Seat frame, 4 pieces, 1⅛ by 2½ by 23 inches.

Pins, 4 pieces, 1¼ by 1¼ by 5 inches, S-4-S.

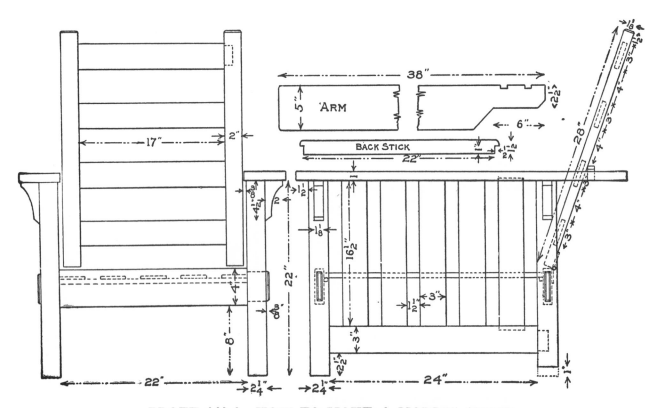

## PLATE 141 A—HOW TO MAKE A MORRIS CHAIR

### Material Required

Posts, 4 pieces, 2¼ by 2¼ by 22½ inches, S-4-S.

Front and back rails, 2 pieces, 1 by 4 by 28 inches, S-4-S.

Side rails, 2 pieces, 1 by 3 by 27 inches, S-4-S.

Side slats, 10 pieces, ½ by 3 by 17½ inches, S-4-S.

Arms, 2 pieces, 1 by 5 by 38½ inches, S-4-S.

Brackets, 4 pieces, 1⅛ by 2¼ by 5 inches, S-2-S.

Cleats, 2 pieces, 1 by 1 by 22½ inches, S-4-S.

Seats slats, 5 pieces, ⅜ by 3 by 26 inches, S-4-S.

Back verticals, 2 pieces, 1⅛ by 2 by 28½ inches, S-4-S.

Back horizontals, 4 pieces, ⅝ by 2½ by 19½ inches, S-4-S.

Back stick, 1 piece, ¾ by 1½ by 24½ inches. S-4-S.

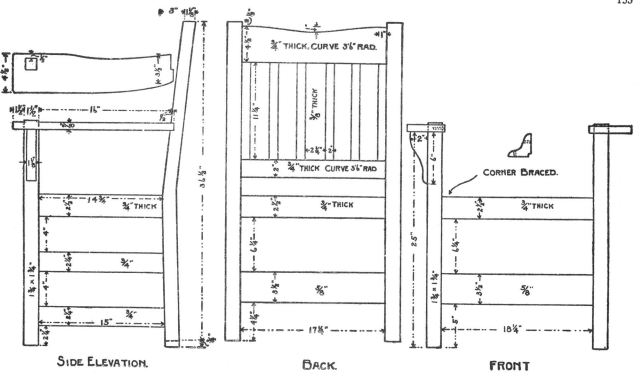

SIDE ELEVATION.        BACK.        FRONT

## PLATE 142 A—SIMPLE MORRIS CHAIR DESIGN

### Material Required

Posts, 4 pieces, 2¼ by 2¼ by 21½ inches, S-4-S.

Side rails, 2 pieces, ⅞ by 5 by 21 inches, S-4-S.

Front and back rails, 2 pieces, ⅞ by 5 by 26 inches, S-4-S.

Arms, 2 pieces, 1¼ by 5½ by 36½ inches, S-2-S.

Back horizontals, 2 pieces, ½ by 2½ by 19½ inches, S-4-S.

Back horizontals, 2 pieces, ¼ by 2½ by 19½ inches, S-4-S.

Cleats, 2 pieces, ⅞ by 2 by 24 inches, S-4-S.

Slats, 5 pieces, ⅜ by 3 by 20½ inches, S-4-S.

Pegs, 2 pieces, 1 inch dowel, 2½ inches long, each.

Pegs, 2 pieces ⅝ inch dowel, 2½ inches long.

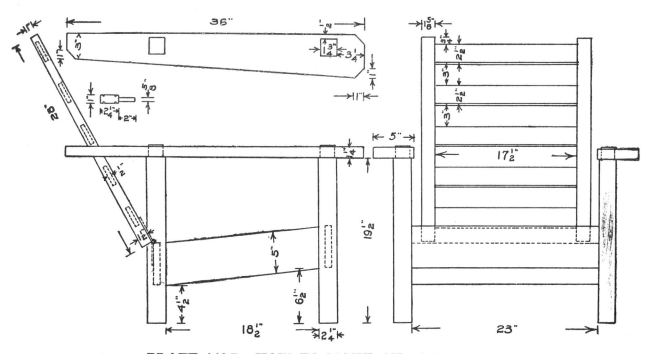

## PLATE 142 B—HOW TO MAKE AN ARM CHAIR

### Material Required

Front posts, 2 pieces, 1¾ by 1¾ by 27 inches.

Back posts, 1 piece, 6½ by 1¾ by 38 inches.

Front horizontal, 1 piece, ¾ by 2½ by 20¾″.

Front horizontal, 1 piece, ⅝ by 3½ by 20¾″.

Back horizontal, 1 piece, ¾ by 4½ by 20½″.

Back horizontal, 1 piece, ¾ by 2 by 20½ inches.

Back horizontal, 1 piece, ¾ by 2½ by 19¾ inches.

Back horizontal, 1 piece, ⅝ by 3½ by 19¾″.

Side horizontal, 2 pieces, ¾ by 2½ by 17⅛″.

Side horizontal, 2 pieces, ¾ by 2¼ by 17¼″.

Side horizontal, 2 pieces, ¾ by 2¼ by 17½″.

Back slats, 5 pieces, ⅜ by 2¼ by 12¼ inches.

Arms, 2 pieces, ⅞ by 4½ by 20 inches.

Braces, 2 pieces, 1⅛ by 2¼ by 6½ inches.

Braces, 4 pieces, ⅞ by 3 by 3 inches.

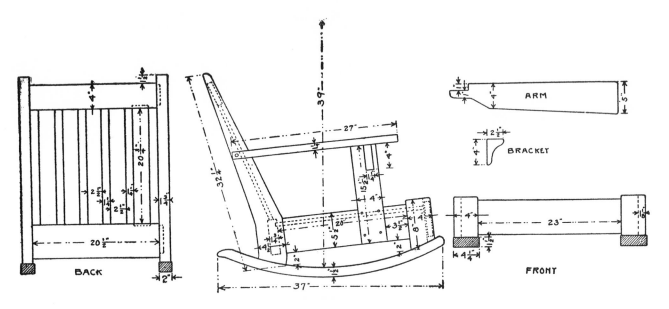

## PLATE 143 B—HOW TO MAKE A BIG EASY ROCKER

### Material Required

Back posts, 1 piece, 1¾ by 8 by 34 inches, S-2-S.
Back rail, 1 piece, 1¾ by 5½ by 22 inches, S-4-S.
Back rail, 1 piece, ⅞ by 4 by 22 inches, S-4-S.
Back slats, 5 pieces, ⅜ by 2½ by 30¾ inches, S-4-S.
Brackets, 2 pieces, 1¼ by 2¾ by 4½ inches, S-2-S.
Arm supports, 2 pieces, ⅞ by 4 by 16 inches, S-4-S.

Arms, 2 pieces, 1¼ by 5¼ by 27½ inches, S-2-S.
Front rail, 1 piece, ⅞ by 5½ by 25 inches, S-4-S.
Side rails, 2 pieces, ⅞ by 5½ by 22 inches, S-2-S.
Front posts, 2 pieces, 1⅛ by 3¼ by 8½ inches, S-2-S.
Front posts, 2 pieces, 1⅛ by 4¼ by 8½ inches, S-2-S.
Rockers, 2 pieces, 1½ by 4½ by 39 inches, S-2-S.

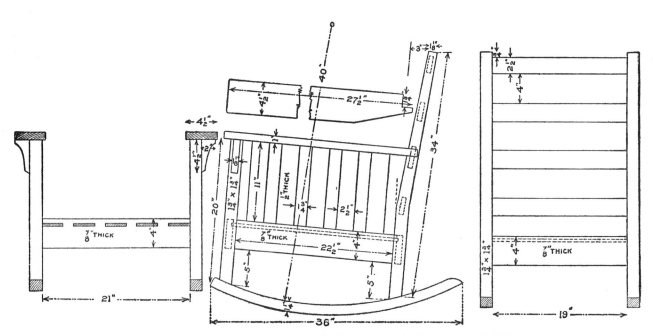

## PLATE 143 A—HOW TO MAKE A MISSION ROCKER

### Material Required

Front posts, 2 pieces, 1¾ by 1¾ by 21 inches, S-4-S.
Back posts, 1 piece, 1¾ by 6 by 35 inches, S-2-S.
Front rail, 1 piece, ⅞ by 4 by 23 inches, S-4-S.
Back rail, 1 piece, ⅞ by 4 by 22 inches, S-4-S.
Back rails, 4 pieces, ⅝ by 2½ by 22 inches. S-4-S.

Side rails, 2 pieces, ⅞ by 4 by 25½ inches, S-4-S.
Side slats, 10 pieces, ½ by 2½ by 12 inches, S-4-S.
Brackets, 2 pieces, 1⅛ by 2¼ by 5 inches, S-2-S.
Arms, 2 pieces, 1 by 4½ by 27½ inches, S-4-S.
Seat slats, 5 pieces, ⅜ by 3 by 25 inches, S-4-S.
Rockers, 1 piece, 1¾ by 6½ by 36½ inches, S-2-S.

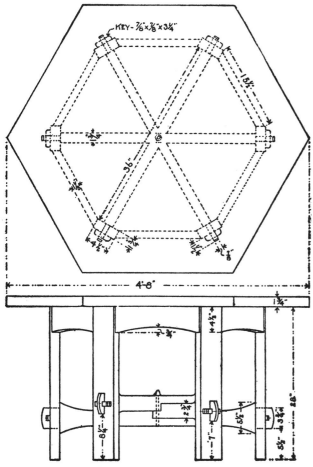

## SIX-SIDED DINING ROOM TABLE

Top, 1 piece, 1¾ by 51 by 60 inches.
Legs, 6 pieces, 1¾ by 4½ by 29 inches.
Stretcher, 3 pieces, 1¾ by 5½ by 44 inches.
Rails, 6 pieces, 1⅛ by 4½ by 16½ inches.
Keys, 6 pieces, ⅞ by ⅞ by 3¼ inches.

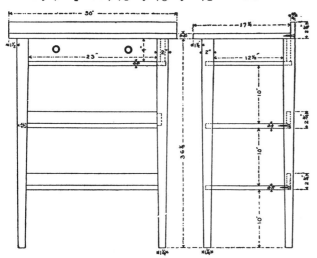

## DINING ROOM SERVING TABLE

Legs, 4 pieces, 2 by 2 by 36½ inches, S-4-S.
Top, 1 piece, ⅞ by 18 by 30½ inches, S-2-S.
Shelves, 2 pieces, ¾ by 16 by 27 inches, S-2-S.
Backs, 2 pieces, ¾ by 3 by 27 inches, S-2-S.
Back, 1 piece, ¾ by 3 by 30½ inches, S-2-S.
Back rail, 1 piece, ¾ by 4¼ by 27 inches, S-2-S.
Side rails, 2 pieces, ¾ by 4¼ by 14½ inches.
Drawer support, 1 piece, ⅝ by 16 by 27 inches.
Drawer front, 1 piece, ¾ by 4¼ by 23½ inches.
Drawer back, 1 piece, ⅜ by 4 by 23½ inches, S-2-S, poplar.
Drawer sides, 2 pieces, ⅜ by 4¼ by 14½ inches, S-2-S, poplar.
Drawer bottom, 1 piece, ⅜ by 14½ by 23½ inches, S-2-S, poplar.
Drawer guides, 2 pieces, ⅝ by 1 by 13 inches.

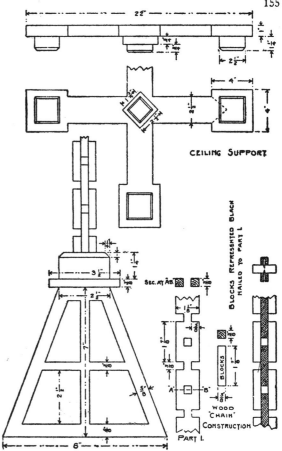

CEILING SUPPORT

## DINING ROOM DROP SHADE

Support, 2 pieces, 1 by 4 by 22½ inches, S-4-S.
4 pieces, 1¼ by 2½ by 3 inches, S-4-S.
1 piece, ¾ by 2½ by 3 inches, S-4-S.
1 piece, ¾ by 1¾ by 2 inches, S-4-S.
Chains, 4 pieces, ⅜ by 1⅛ by 36 inches, S-4-S.
8 pieces, ⅜ by ⅜ by 36 inches, S-4-S.
Shades, 4 pieces, 1¼ by 2½ by 3 inches, S-4-S.
4 pieces, ⅜ by 3½ by 4 inches, S-4-S.
32 pieces, 3/16 by ⅞ by 8½ inches, S-2-S.
16 pieces, 3/16 by ⅞ by 3½ inches, S-2-S.
16 pieces, 3/16 by ⅞ by 8½ inches, S-2-S.
16 pieces, 3/16 by ⅝ by 6 inches, S-2-S.
16 pieces, 3/16 by ⅝ by 7½ inches, S-2-S.

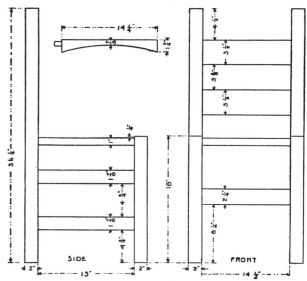

## SOLID DINING ROOM CHAIR

Posts, pieces, 2 by 2 by 18½ inches, S-4-S.
Posts, 2 pieces, 2 by 2 by 36¾ inches, S-4-S.
Side rails, 4 pieces, ⅞ by 1⅞ by 14 inches, S-4-S.
Front and back rails, 2 pieces, ⅞ by 2¼ by 15¼".
Back rails, 2 pieces, 1¾ by 3½ by 15¼ inches.
Seat rails, 2 pieces, 1 by 1½ by 14 inches, S-4-S.
Seat rails, 2 pieces, 1 by 1½ by 15¼ inches.

## PLATE 144—HANDCRAFT DINING ROOM FURNITURE

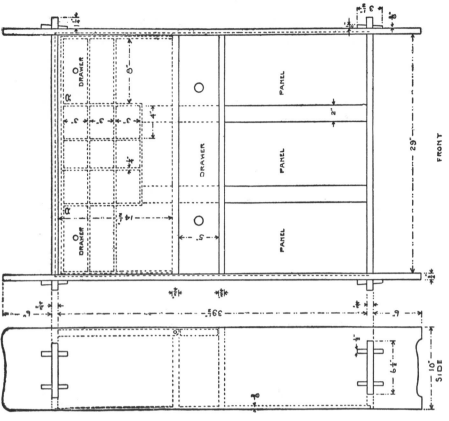

WRITING DESK.

Pigeon-holes, verticals, 12 pieces, ¼ by 8 by 3½ inches, S-4-S, Yellow Poplar.
Pigeon-holes, horizontals, 3 pieces, ¼ by 8 by 29 inches, S-4-S, Yellow Poplar.
Drawers, fronts, 2 pieces, ⅜ by 3 by 8½ inches, S-4-S, Oak.
Drawers, sides, 4 pieces, ¼ by 3 by 8 inches, S-4-S, Yellow Poplar.
Drawers, backs, 2 pieces, ¼ by 3 by 8 inches, S-4-S, Yellow Poplar.
Drawers, bottoms, 2 pieces, ¼ by 8 by 8 inches, S-4-S, Yellow Poplar.

**PLATE 145—TABORET AND WRITING DESK**

## HOW TO MAKE A TABORET
### Material Required

Top, 1 piece, ⅞ by 12½ inches, S-2-S.
Posts, 4 pieces, 1⅝ by 1⅝ by 20½ inches, S-4-S.
Stretchers, 4 pieces, ¾ by 2 by 14 inches, S-2-S.

## HOW TO MAKE A WRITING DESK
### Material Required

Sides, 2 pieces, ¾ by 10 by 52 inches, S-4-S, Oak.
Top and bottom shelves, 2 pieces, ¾ by 10 by 34 inches, S-4-S, Oak.
Middle shelf, 1 piece, ¾ by 9⅝ by 30 inches, S-4-S, Oak.
Drawer support frame, 2 pieces, ¾ by 2½ by 30 inches, S-4-S, Oak.
Drawer support frame, 2 pieces, ¾ by 2½ by 6 inches, S-4-S, Oak.
Lid, 1 piece, ¾ by 15 by 29½ inches, S-4-S, Oak.
Back, 3 pieces, ⅜ by 10 by 41 inches, S-2-S, Oak.
Back, 2 pieces, ⅜ by 2 by 40 inches, S-4-S, Oak.
Drawer, front, 1 piece, ¾ by 5 by 29½ inches, S-4-S, Oak.
Drawer, sides, 2 pieces, ⅜ by 5 by 10 inches, S-4-S, Yellow Poplar.
Drawer, back, 1 piece, ⅜ by 5 by 29 inches, S-4-S, Yellow Poplar.
Drawer, bottom, 1 piece, ⅜ by 10 by 29 inches, S-4-S, Yellow Poplar.
Keys for tenons, 8 pieces, ½ by ½ by 4 inches, S-2-S, Oak.
Pigeon-holes, verticals, 2 pieces, ¼ by 8 by 14½ inches, S-4-S, Yellow Poplar.

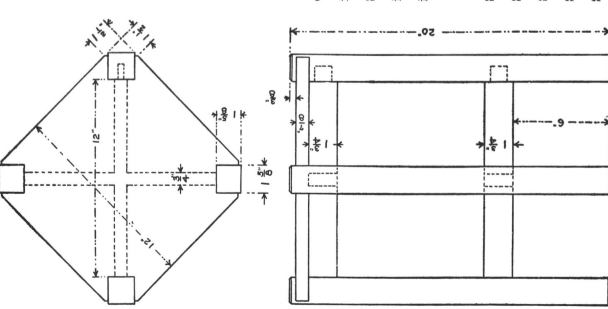

TABORET.

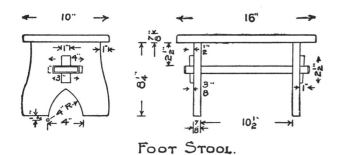

FOOT STOOL.

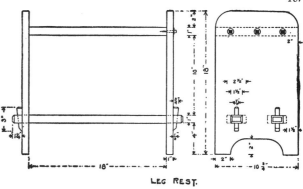

LEG REST.

## HOW TO MAKE A FOOT STOOL

### Material Required

Top, 1 piece, ⅞ by 10 by 16½ inches, S-4-S.
Legs, 2 pieces, ⅞ by 10½ by 8½ inches, S-2-S.
Stretcher, 1 piece, ⅞ by 4 by 15 inches, S-4-S.
Keys, 2 pieces, 1 by ¾ by 3 inches, S-2-S.
Cleats, 2 pieces, ¾ by ¾ by 7 inches, S-4-S.

## HOW TO MAKE A LEG-REST

### Material Required

Sides, 2 pieces, 1 by 10¾ by 18½ inches, S-4-S.
Top, 1 piece, 1 by 10¾ by 18½ inches, S-4-S.
Stretchers, 2 pieces, 1 by 2½ by 23 inches, S-4-S.
Keys, 1 piece, ½ by ¾ by 12½ inches, S-4-S.

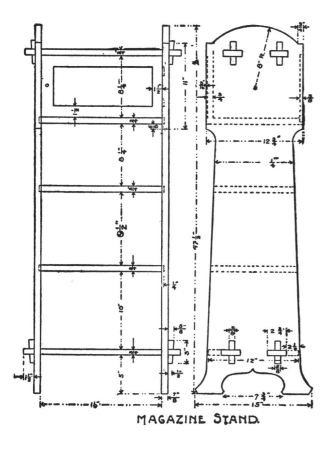

MAGAZINE STAND.

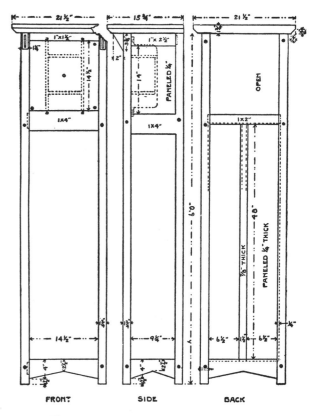

FRONT          SIDE          BACK

## HOW TO MAKE A HALL CLOCK

### Material Required

4 posts, 1¾ by 1¾ inches by 6 feet 1 inch, S-4-S.
3 rails, 1 by 4 by 15¾ inches, S-4-S.
4 rails, 1 by 4 by 10½ inches, S-4-S.
1 rail, 1 by 2 by 15¾ inches, S-4-S.
1 rail, 1 by 1½ by 15¾ inches, S-4-S.
2 rails, 1 by 2½ by 10½ inches, S-4-S.
1 stile, ⅞ by 1½ by 48¾ inches, S-4-S.
2 panels, ¼ by 7 by 48¾ inches, S-4-S.
2 panels, ¼ by 9¾ by 14¾ inches, S-4-S.
1 panel, ¼ by 14¾ by 14¾ inches, S-4-S.
1 top, 1¾ by 16 by 22 inches, S-2-S.
2 brackets, 1¼ by 2¼ by 4 inches, S-2-S.
Movement box, 2 pieces, ½ by 6 by 16½ inches, yellow poplar, S-2-S.
Movement box, 2 pieces, ½ by 6 by 7 inches, yellow poplar, S-2-S.
Movement box, 1 piece, ½ by 8 by 8 inches, yellow poplar, S-2-S.

## DESIGN FOR MAGAZINE STAND

### Material Required

Sides, 2 pieces, ⅞ by 15½ inches by 48 inches, S-2-S.
Top and bottom shelves, 2 pieces, ¾ by 13 by 21 inches, S-2-S.
Middle shelves, 1 piece, ¾ by 13 by 17 inches, S-2-S.
Middle shelves, 2 pieces, ¾ by 12 by 17 inches, S-2-S.
Door, 2 pieces, ¾ by 1¾ by 16½ inches, S-2-S.
Door, 2 pieces, ¾ by 1¾ by 8½ inches, S-2-S.
Door, 1 piece, 5-16 by 6 by 14 inches, S-2-S.
Backing, enough to cover one square foot of space, ⅜ inch, matched and beaded.
Keys, 8 pieces, ⅝ by ¾ by 3½ inches, S-2-S.

**PLATE 146—WORK FOR THE HOME SHOP**

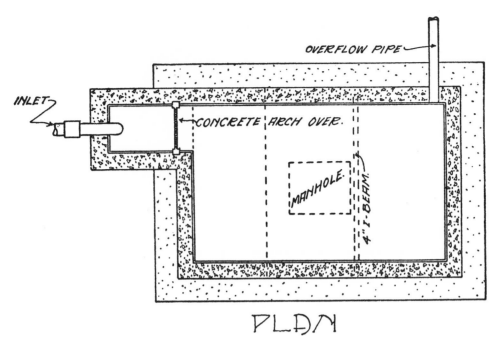

PLAN

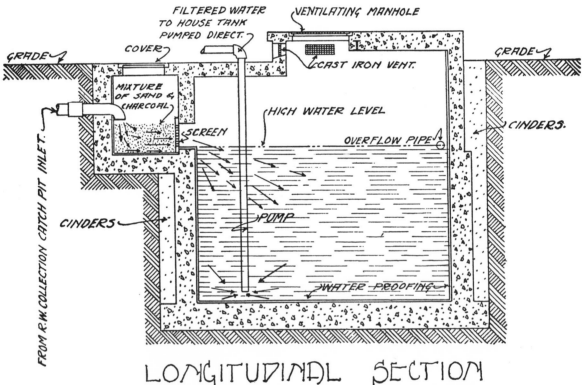

LONGITUDINAL SECTION

**PLATE 147—CEMENT CISTERN FOR DRINKING WATER**

Plan and cross section showing details of construction of a concrete cistern with filtering compartment, for the storage of rain water for drinking purposes. For work of this kind, the sand and gravel used for the concrete should be clean and free from clayey matter which, dissolving out slowly from the concrete, would discolor the water. The filter is made of alternate layers of sand and charcoal, all about one foot in thickness. This filter is contained in a small compartment at one side of the cistern proper, and through this the water is conducted into the main tank. A filter of this kind needs to be renewed occasionally, or it will itself become a source of pollution to the water. The concrete arch covering the cistern may be built up over a sand core, though this means considerable labor in shoveling out the sand through the manhole after the concrete has set. A flat slab four inches thick and strongly reinforced with steel rods or reinforcing fabric makes a good cistern covering. Such a slab can be moulded at one side and then placed as a whole over the cistern top. A 4 inch I-beam spans the cistern to support the slab.

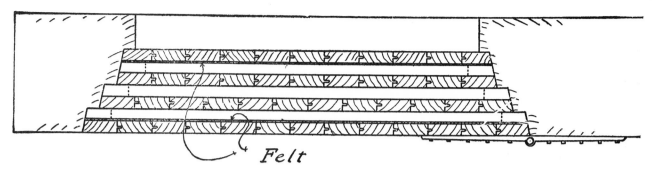

DETAIL OF INSULATED DOOR FOR COLD STORAGE

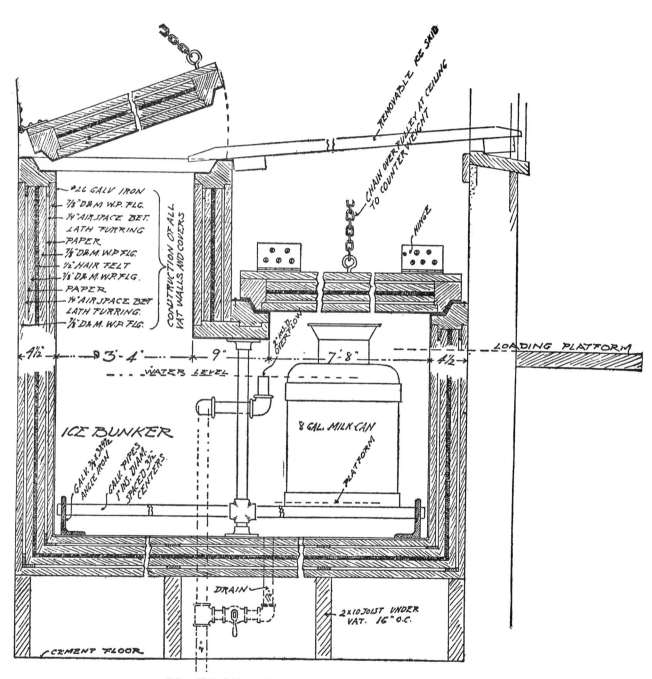

**PLATE 148—ICE CHEST AND MILK COOLER**

Cross section showing details of construction of a very efficient milk cooler for dairies, creameries and milk shipping stations. The insulated walls are built up with four thicknesses of ⅞ inch flooring, two quarter inch air spaces, one half inch of hair felt and two thicknesses of insulating paper. The overflow drain pipe is so arranged that the milk cans stand immersed in ice water.

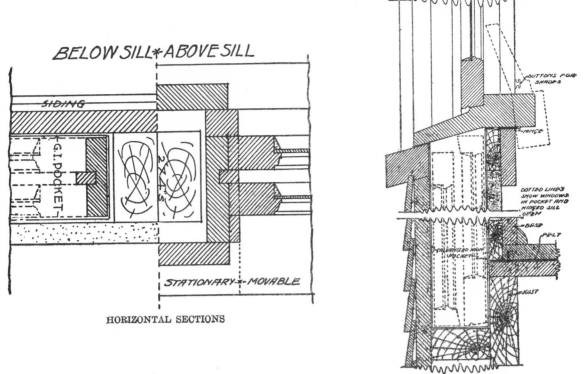

*BELOW SILL * ABOVE SILL*

SIDING

G.I. POCKET

STATIONARY—x—MOVABLE

**HORIZONTAL SECTIONS**

BUTTONS FOR SNAPS

HINGE

DOTTED LINES SHOW WINDOWS IN POCKET AND HINGED SILL OPEN

HASP

GALVANIZED IRON POCKET

JOIST

**VERTICAL SECTION THROUGH STORM-PROOF SILL AND WINDOW BOX**

## PLATE 149 B—WINDOW DETAILS FOR SECOND-FLOOR OPEN AIR ROOM

Frequently open air sleeping rooms are desired on the second floor above important first floor rooms. It then becomes necessary that the windows and flooring be made thoroughly water-proof, since rain at times is sure to come in. Details show double hung windows for this purpose. Both sash drop down out of sight into a galvanized iron box; the sill is hinged.

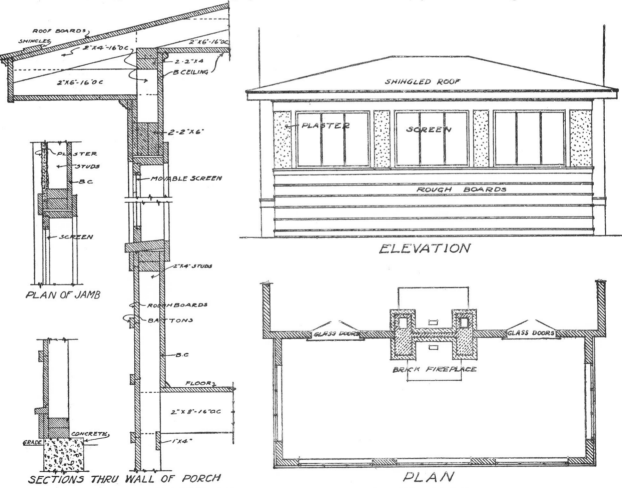

ROOF BOARDS
SHINGLES
2"x4"-16"0C
2"x6"-16"0C
2-2"x4"
B CEILING
2"x6"-16"0C

PLASTER
STUDS
B.C.
SCREEN

**PLAN OF JAMB**

2-2"x6"
MOVABLE SCREEN
2"x4" STUDS
ROUGH BOARDS
BATTONS
B.C.
FLOOR
2"x8"-16"0C
1"x4"

CONCRETE
GRADE

**SECTIONS THRU WALL OF PORCH**

SHINGLED ROOF
PLASTER     SCREEN
ROUGH   BOARDS

**ELEVATION**

GLASS DOORS          GLASS DOORS
BRICK FIREPLACE

**PLAN**

### PLATE 149 A—"OUTDOOR" LIVING ROOM

Elevation, plan and details of construction of the popular type open air living room or screened porch formed in a single story, hip-roof addition. Movable screens are fitted into the windows for the warm weather season and glazed sash are substituted for these during the winter. The room is finished with beaded ceiling, which does very well for inexpensive work. The flooring is of cypress.

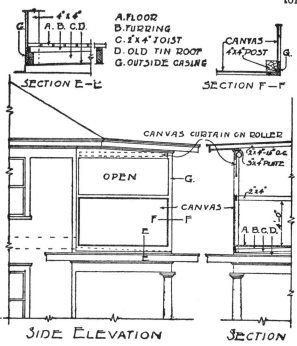

Section E-E

A. FLOOR
B. FURRING
C. 2"x4" JOIST
D. OLD TIN ROOF
G. OUTSIDE CASING

Section F—F

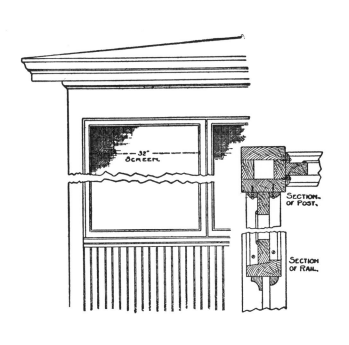

DETAIL OF FASTENING FOR SCREENS OR SASH

ARRANGEMENT OF SLEEPING PORCH ON PIAZZA ROOF

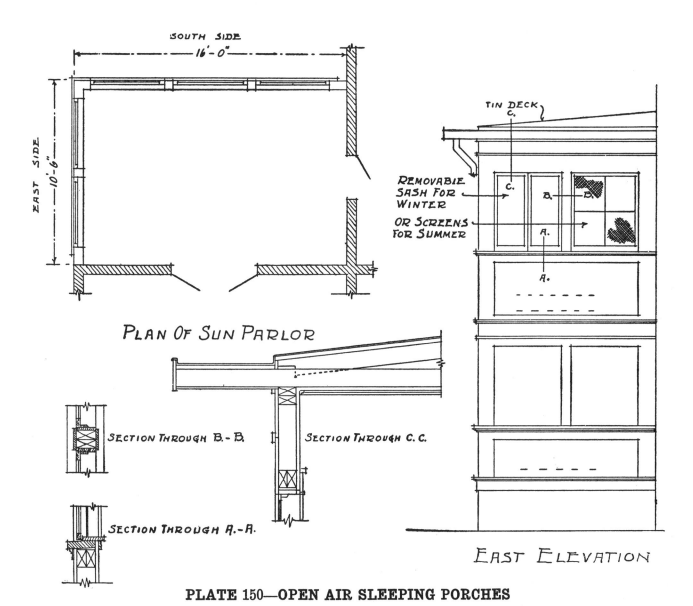

PLAN OF SUN PARLOR

SECTION THROUGH B.-B.

SECTION THROUGH C. C.

SECTION THROUGH A.-A.

EAST ELEVATION

## PLATE 150—OPEN AIR SLEEPING PORCHES

Arrangement, design and details of construction of several inexpensive open air sleeping porches. A sleeping porch can be built very nicely in an inside corner of a house, either upstairs or down. Fitted with screens for the summer and with removable sash for the winter, they serve both as healthful sleeping rooms, outdoor living rooms and sun parlors. One of the arrangements here illustrated is intended to be built on a piazza roof and has been erected for $60.

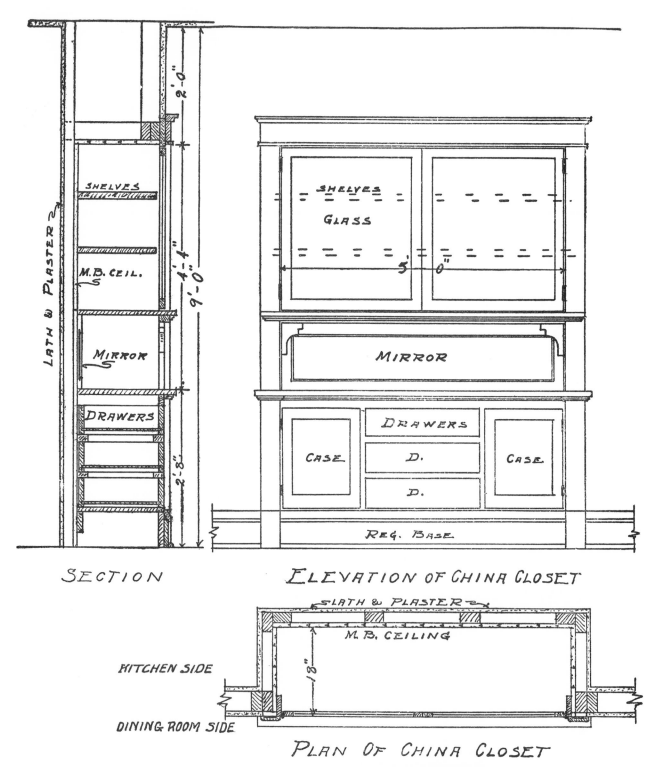

SECTION

ELEVATION OF CHINA CLOSET

PLAN OF CHINA CLOSET

## PLATE 151—CHINA CLOSET IN PARTITION

Plan, elevation and cross section showing design and method of construction of a neat china closet or built-in sideboard, the face flush with the partition wall of the dining room side and the back projecting into the kitchen. This is a desirable solution of a problem often encountered in remodeling work. The back may be opened to allow food to be passed through from the kitchen.

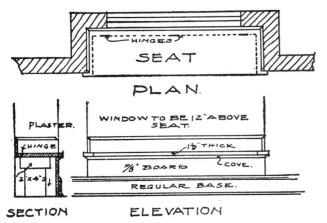

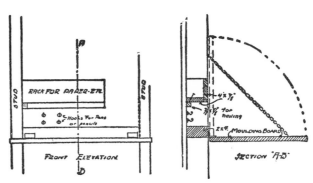

## WRITING DESK FOR SUMMER COTTAGE

A convenient and easily constructed writing desk for a summer cottage is shown in elevation and section. The 2 by 4 nailed in between the studding forms the foundation for the desk and an ordinary moulding board hinged to it is held in the proper position by a small chain. Racks for paper, envelopes, etc., can be easily arranged as indicated, or in any other way desired.

## BUILT-IN WINDOW SEAT

Working details for seat to be built into window recess; very simple trim is used. The seat is hinged to raise up. The seat should be 17 inches above the floor and the window sill about 12 inches above the seat.

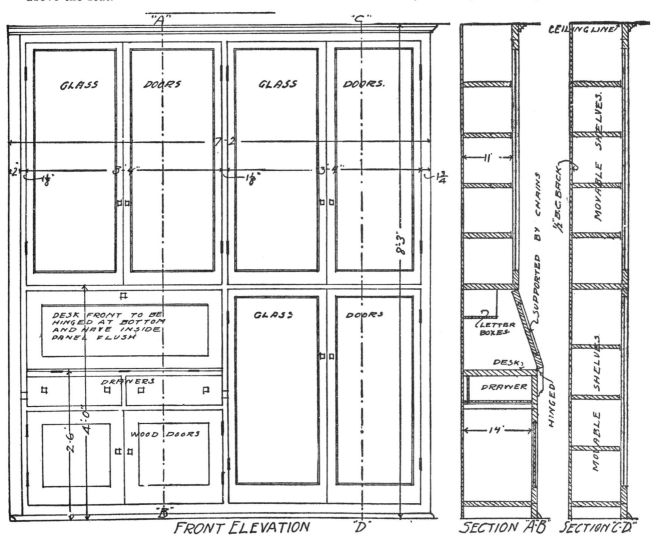

## PLATE 152—BUILT-IN BOOK CASE WITH WRITING DESK

Elevation and sections showing the design and method of construction of a large combination book case and writing desk to go clear to the ceiling. The desk section consists of a hinged cover supported by chains when let down and serving as the writing board. Inside are pigeon holes for paper, envelopes, etc. The book case is in three sections, with swinging glass doors. The shelves should be movable so that they may be adjusted to suit the various heights of books. Small metal lugs may be obtained for supporting such movable shelves.

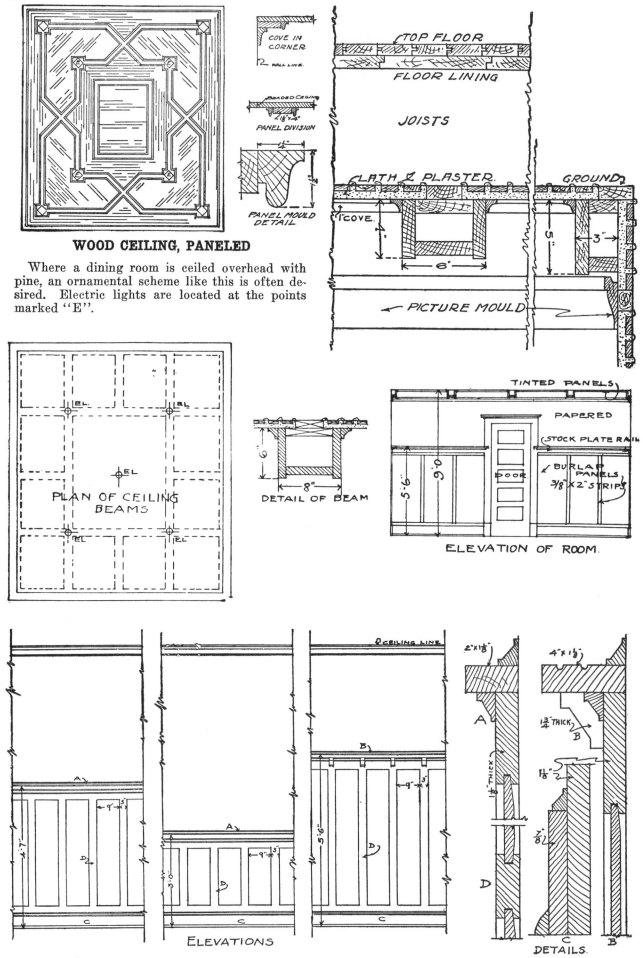

## WOOD CEILING, PANELED

Where a dining room is ceiled overhead with pine, an ornamental scheme like this is often desired. Electric lights are located at the points marked "E".

## PLATE 153—PANELED CEILINGS AND SIDE WALLS

Designs and details for several types of ornamental ceiling and side wall paneling. Paneled wainscoting for reception halls should be three feet high, or for more elaborate work four feet seven inches. Dining room paneled wainscoting is usually five feet six inches high and is topped with a plate rail. A beamed ceiling should go with paneled wainscoting. Details showing design and construction for these beams are given. Details of wood paneled wainscots with top rails.

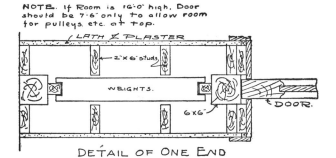

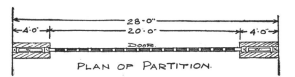

### DOORS TO WORK UP AND DOWN

Wide doors or partitions to work up and down are often required for churches. They are operated like windows hung on weights, sliding up in the double partition. The drawings show details of this arrangement.

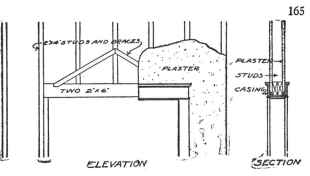

### FRAMING FOR CASED OPENING

A simple form of trussing for door openings that are not too wide. Two 2 by 6's braced with 2 by 4's as shown are amply strong.

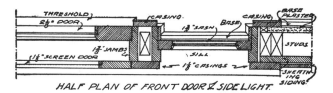

### FRONT DOOR WITH SIDE LIGHTS

The entire frame for a door with full length side lights is made in one piece rather than as three separate frames. Jambs are rabbeted for doors and sash and stops are inserted to secure the sash.

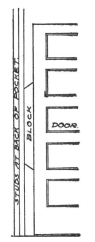

### BUMPER FOR SLIDING DOOR

A bumper of sufficient width should be fixed at the back end of the pocket and arranged to strike the middle of the door.

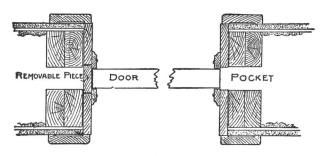

### SINGLE SLIDING DOOR

Cross section showing details of construction for a single door to slide one way. A removable bumping piece closes the pocket on one side. This piece is the thickness of the jamb; and the joints are concealed with the stop mouldings as shown.

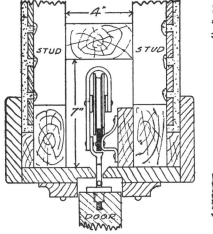

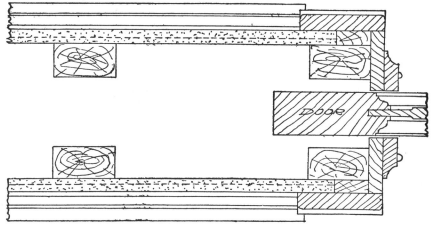

### PLATE 154—DETAILS OF SPECIAL DOOR CONSTRUCTION

Working drawings of sliding door showing details of partition studding and of door hanger and rail. Details are also shown for several other special doors and door openings.

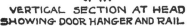

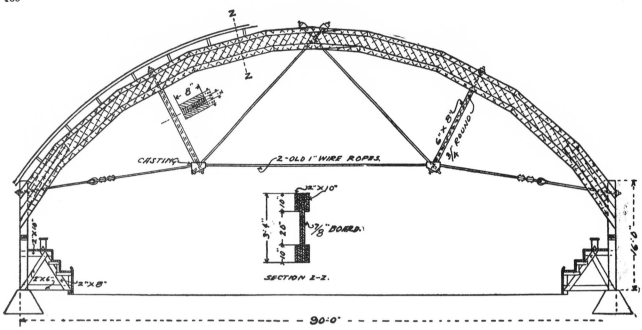

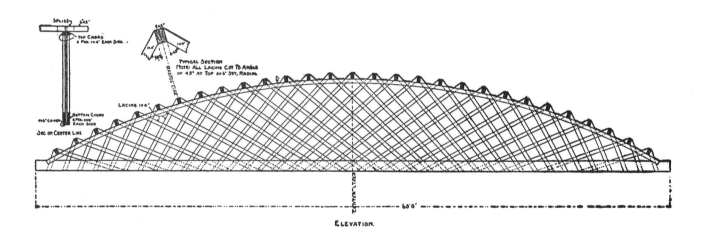

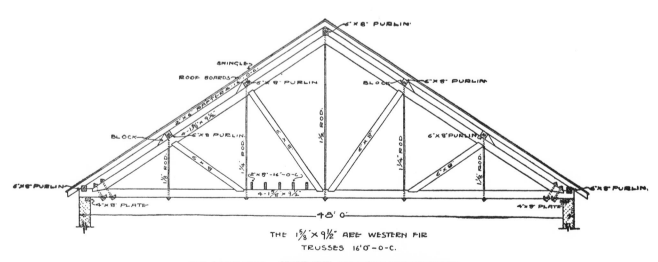

## PLATE 155—THREE WOOD TRUSSES

Design and method of construction for three valuable types of wood trusses. The upper illustration shows a built-up arch truss. The arch has a single vertical web made up of two solid courses of crossed diagonal 7/8 inch boards nailed together, and nailed to four 2 by 10 inch pieces to form top and bottom flanges. The struts are built up of 2 by 8 inch planks and the tension members are one inch wire ropes. The middle illustration shows a light lattice truss. This is a strong inexpensive truss, very popular for garages, rinks, etc. The lower illustration is of a very useful truss. Correct arrangement and proportioning of parts is shown.

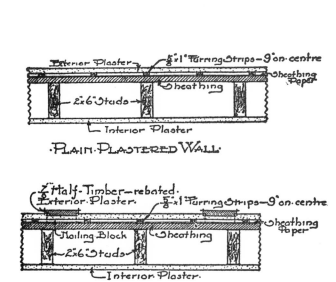

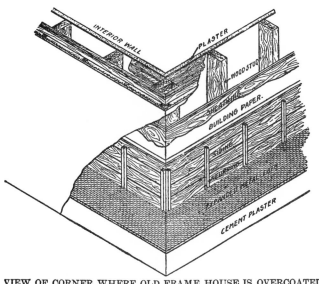

PLAIN-PLASTERED-WALL

HALF-TIMBERED-WALL

TYPICAL WALL SECTIONS FOR CEMENT PLASTER HOUSES

VIEW OF CORNER WHERE OLD FRAME HOUSE IS OVERCOATED
WITH CEMENT PLASTER

SECTION

RECOMMENDED HOUSE CONSTRUCTION USING
CONCRETE BLOCKS

PLAN

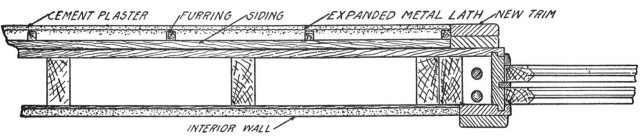

SECTION SHOWING LATH AND PLASTER PUT ON OVER SIDING AND NEW TRIM ADDED

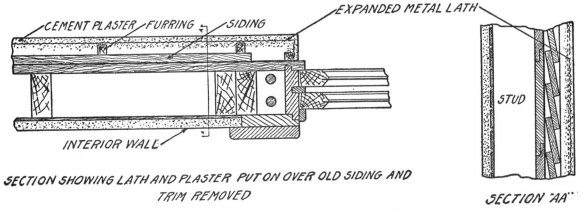

SECTION SHOWING LATH AND PLASTER PUT ON OVER OLD SIDING AND
TRIM REMOVED

SECTION "AA"

## PLATE 156—CEMENT PLASTER SIDING

Wall sections showing method of arrangement where old frame houses are overcoated with cement plaster on expanded metal lath. Approved construction is also illustrated for cement stucco work, both plain and with the half timber paneling. Recommended construction using blocks.

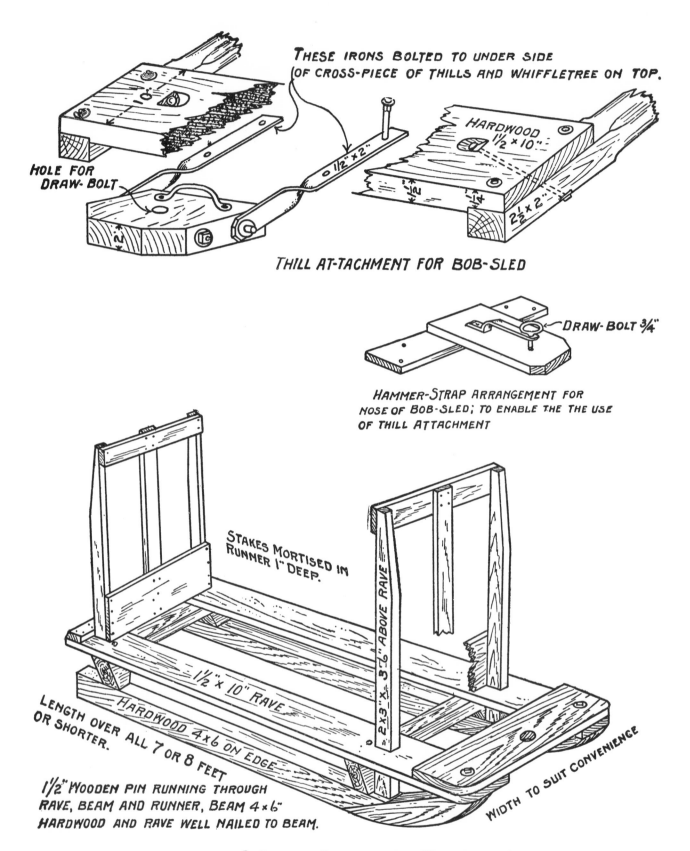

THESE IRONS BOLTED TO UNDER SIDE OF CROSS-PIECE OF THILLS AND WHIFFLETREE ON TOP.

HOLE FOR DRAW-BOLT

HARDWOOD 1½ x 10"

1½ x 2"

2½ x 2"

THILL AT-TACHMENT FOR BOB-SLED

DRAW-BOLT ¾"

HAMMER-STRAP ARRANGEMENT FOR NOSE OF BOB-SLED; TO ENABLE THE THE USE OF THILL ATTACHMENT

STAKES MORTISED IN RUNNER 1" DEEP.

2x3" x 3'-6" ABOVE RAVE

1½" x 10" RAVE

LENGTH OVER ALL 7 OR 8 FEET OR SHORTER.

HARDWOOD 4x6 ON EDGE

WIDTH TO SUIT CONVENIENCE

1½" WOODEN PIN RUNNING THROUGH RAVE, BEAM AND RUNNER, BEAM 4 x 6" HARDWOOD AND RAVE WELL NAILED TO BEAM.

A CHEAPLY CONSTRUCTED BOB-SLED. CAN BE USED WITH CHAIN AND WHIFFLETREE, OR THILL ATTACH' PROVIDED

### PLATE 157—CHEAP AND SERVICEABLE DRAY SLED

A design of great strength and simplicity containing very little iron work and consequently inexpensive. If the runners are constructed as shown, no shoes are needed. Each runner is made of two hardwood pieces; and for the lower or long portion, a piece should be selected that is slightly cross-grained; and care should be taken that the wood fibre points backward and downward. It will then wear smoothly and last a long time.

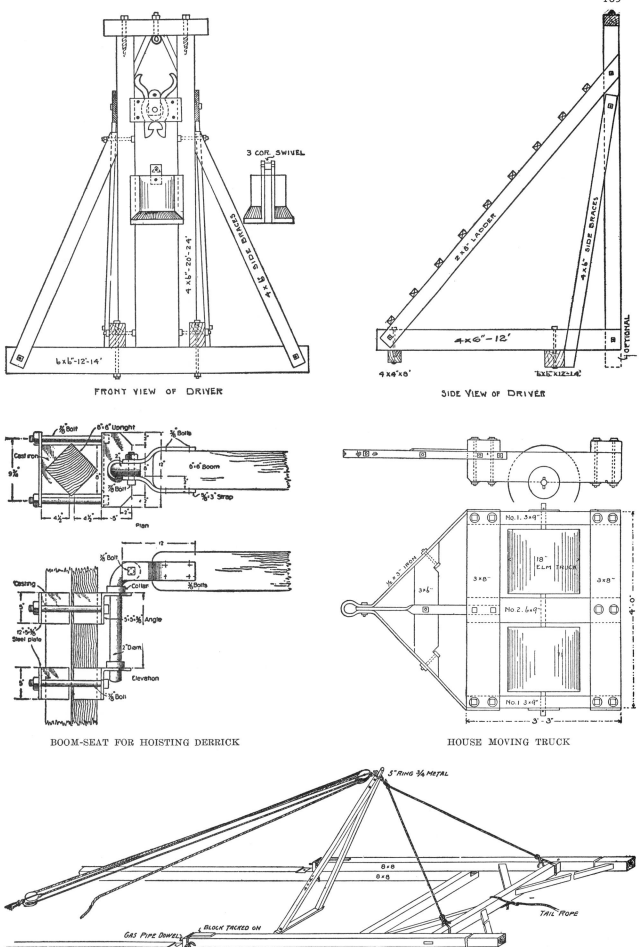

3 COR. SWIVEL

FRONT VIEW OF DRIVER

SIDE VIEW OF DRIVER

BOOM-SEAT FOR HOISTING DERRICK

HOUSE MOVING TRUCK

## PLATE 158—CONTRACTORS' EQUIPMENT

Barn-raising rig consisting of ring of one-inch iron and hook of three-quarter-inch iron. The ring is 6½ inches in diameter, made to slip over the end of two 4 by 4 inch poles. These poles should be long enough to raise the barn timbers to an angle of about 45 degrees before they slip out of the ring. The drawings show fully the construction of the boom seat for hoisting derricks; also a good house moving truck. The pile driver illustrated uses a hammer weighing 900 pounds.

170

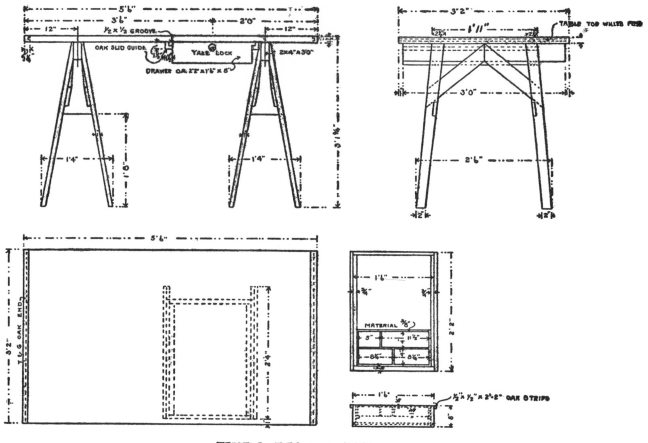

TRESTLE DRAWING TABLE.

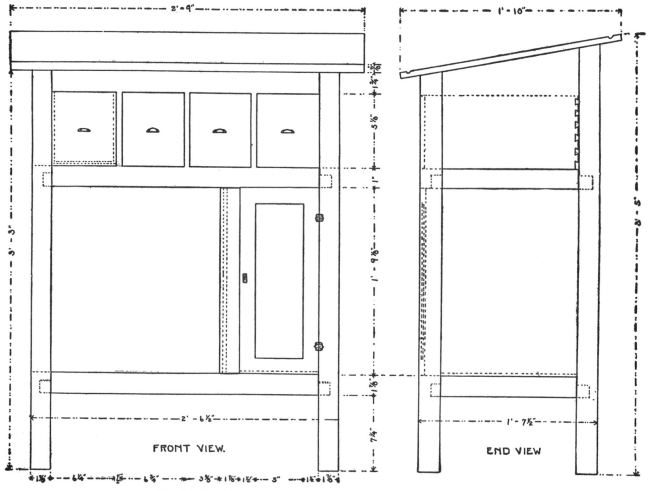

FRONT VIEW.

END VIEW.

**PLATE 159—TWO GOOD DRAWING TABLES**

Details for two convenient and serviceable drafting tables are presented herewith. The trestle table is light and easily made; the cabinet table provides very desirable drawer and locker space. Drawing table tops should be white pine or other soft wood, with hardwood strip ends.

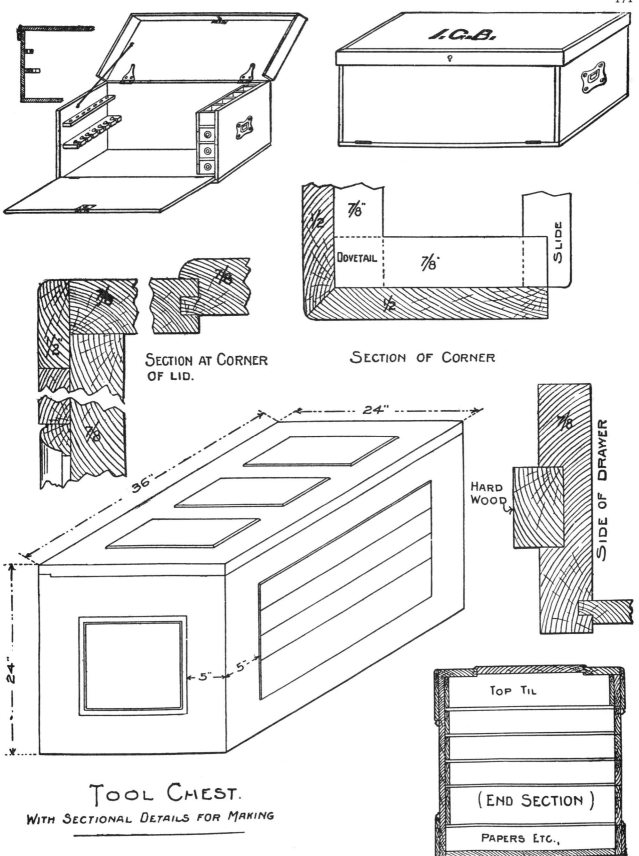

SECTION AT CORNER OF LID.

SECTION OF CORNER

TOOL CHEST.
WITH SECTIONAL DETAILS FOR MAKING

## PLATE 160—CHEST OF DRAWERS FOR TOOLS

A tool chest so arranged that any tool may be gotten at without moving any other tool is illustrated and detailed herewith. The lid of the chest gives access simply to the stationary top till, and to the two deep pockets, one at each end of the chest. The chest proper is a nest of drawers (the drawer pulls and locks are not shown in the drawing). These drawers will be of various depths to suit the special tools to be kept in them, and some of the drawers will be divided into smaller compartments. By making the top till the same length as the drawers there is a pocket at each end which can be utilized for special tools. Besides the outside lock which each drawer should have, there should be a locking device on the inside at the front end of the above mentioned pockets so that all the drawers can be locked at once. Another type of convenient tool chest is illustrated above in which the front lets down to give more easy access to the tools.

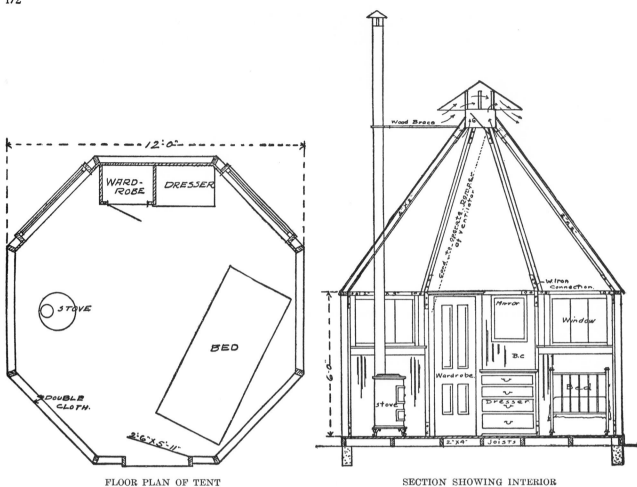

FLOOR PLAN OF TENT

SECTION SHOWING INTERIOR

## PLATE 161 B—TUBERCULOSIS CAMP TENT

Floor plan and cross section showing details of arrangement and construction for a sanitarium tent for the treatment of consumption, of the kind used in Colorado. This is an eight-sided tent with a wood floor and with roof and sides of double cloth over a light wood frame. The three sides of the tent containing the windows and built-in wardrobe and dresser are formed of beaded ceiling. It is stated that $250 is the total cost of one of these tents completely furnished.

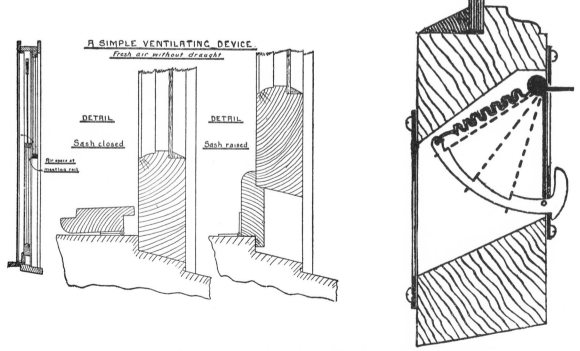

## PLATE 161 A—SIMPLE WINDOW VENTILATORS

An inexpensive ventilating device for schools, dwellings, etc., consisting of a rabbeted strip hinged to the window sill, which when in use causes an opening between the meeting rails of the sash for fresh air to come in. This provides for a change of air but does not allow direct draught. To the right, section of window bottom rail showing a patent ventilator.

# A SIMPLE SEPTIC TANK FOR A DWELLING HOUSE

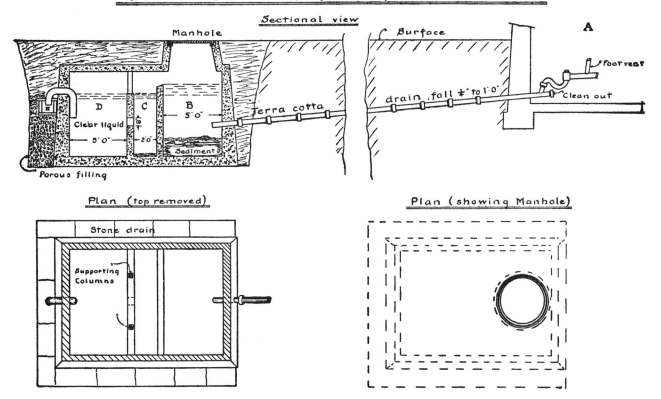

## PLATE 162 B—CONCRETE SEPTIC TANK

Arrangement and details for home-made septic sewage disposal system. "B" is the first chamber and receives the crude sewage which enters at a point half-way up from the bottom. Here, under the action of certain organic germs, all solid material is broken down into gas and clear harmless liquid which flows away intermittently through chambers "C" and "D" into the drain, "E." This may be a blind drain, or it may lead away to discharge on low land.

## PLATE 162 A—SEPTIC SEWAGE DISPOSAL

Sectional drawing showing arrangement of modern septic tank with filter bed, together with arrangement and proper connections for house plumbing fixtures where such a system is used. In country and suburban places away from regular sewage systems the septic tank method is the only sanitary arrangement for sewage disposal. It is broken down in the tanks and filter bed.

174

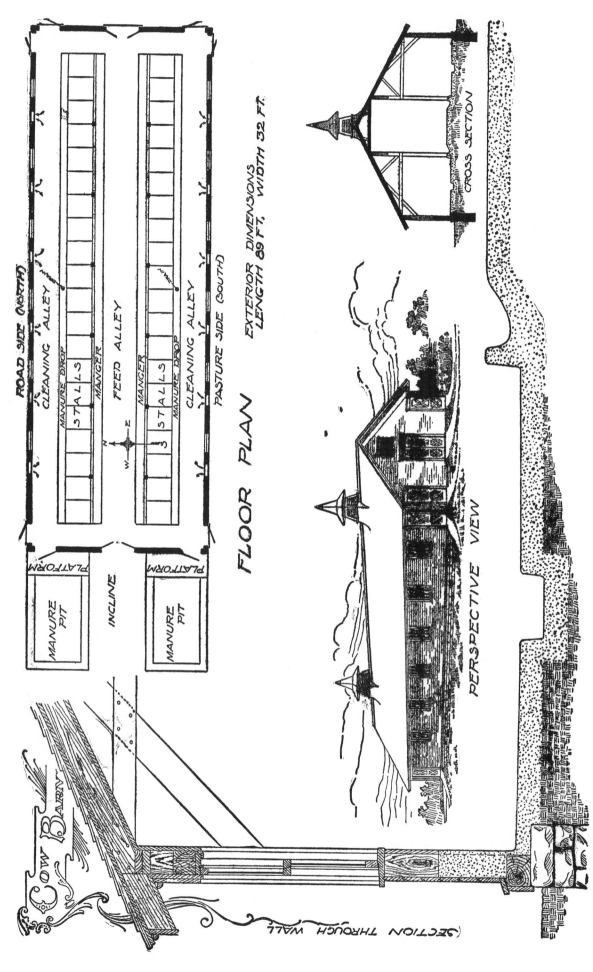

FLOOR PLAN

ROAD SIDE (NORTH)

CLEANING ALLEY

MANURE DROP

STALLS

MANGER

FEED ALLEY

MANGER

STALLS

MANURE DROP

CLEANING ALLEY

PASTURE SIDE (SOUTH)

EXTERIOR DIMENSIONS
LENGTH 89 FT. WIDTH 32 FT.

PLATFORM

PLATFORM

INCLINE

MANURE PIT

MANURE PIT

Cow Barn

(SECTION THROUGH WALL)

CROSS SECTION

PERSPECTIVE VIEW

**PLATE 163—ONE STORY DAIRY BARN**

Herewith is illustrated and detailed a cow barn for the accommodation of forty cows, having a feed alley of sufficient width to allow a wagon to be driven through from end to end to distribute the feed to the mangers along both sides. Mangers, as well as the whole floor surface, are built of concrete. Mangers and feeding alley are elevated three inches above the level of the stalls.

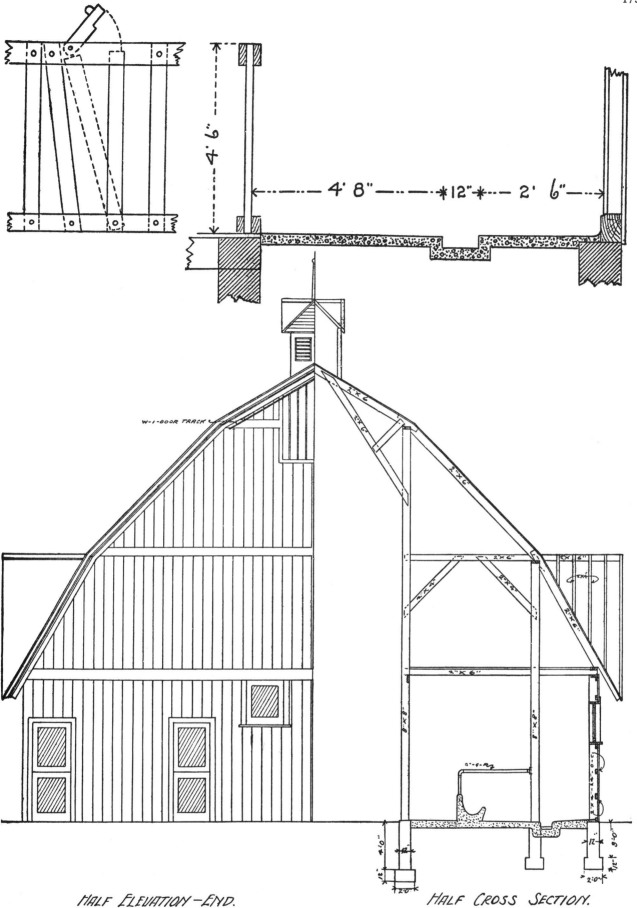

4' 6"

4' 8" — *12"* — 2' 6"

W-1-DOOR TRACK

HALF ELEVATION—END.                HALF CROSS SECTION.

## PLATE 164—LARGE BARN WITH DOUBLE GAMBREL ROOF

Cross section showing details of construction of barn 65 feet long, 48 feet wide, 13 feet high at the plate and 30 feet high at the ridge. The double gambrel roof gives the maximum amount of hay storage space with the minimum expense for roofing. Note method of heavy timber framing   In this barn there is a central driveway 15 feet wide for unloading and storage purposes. On the left are the horse stalls and across on the other side are the cattle. Stalls and passageways are ceiled over and the floors cemented. Siding is of inch boards set vertically, held in position by horizontal 2 by 4s, set 24 inches apart. Note also details for cow stanchions. The distance 4 feet 8 inches is for averaged size animals. An adjustment in the placing of the stanchions 4 inches either way may be required for small Jerseys or large Holsteins.

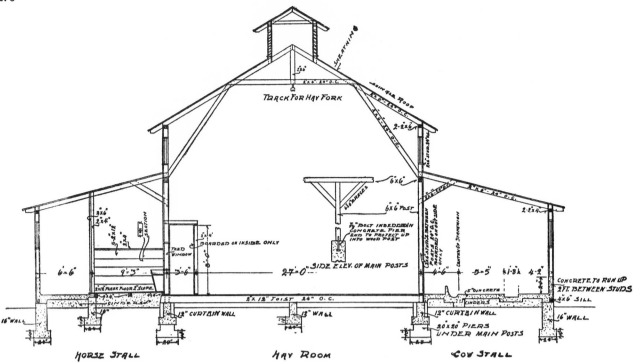

TRANSVERSE SECTION THROUGH BARN

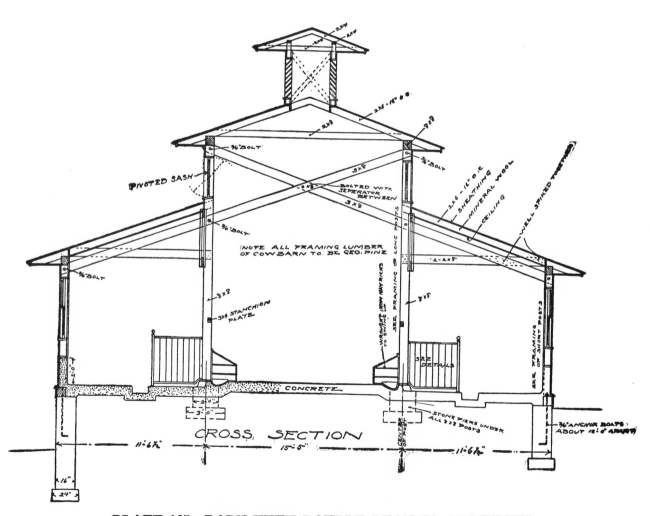

CROSS SECTION

## PLATE 165—BARN WITH DOUBLE LEAN-TO ADDITIONS

Cross sections showing details of construction and method of framing for a very useful type of farm building. The central portion is two stories in height and is lighted and ventilated with high windows in the second story. On each side are single story lean-to additions for stables. Two methods of roof framing are shown; upper detail allows clear space for hay fork.

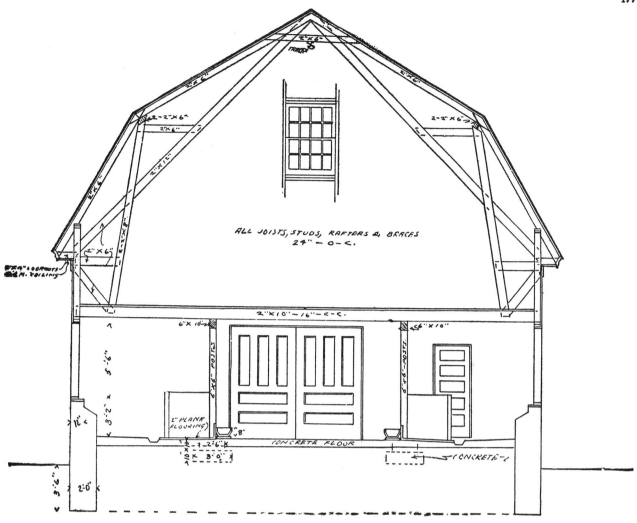

All joists, studs, rafters & braces 24" — O-C.

·SECTION·

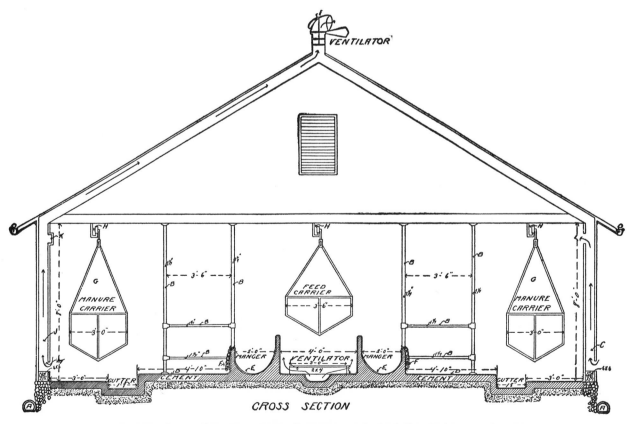

CROSS SECTION

## PLATE 166—SELF-SUPPORTING GAMBREL BARN ROOFS

Cross section showing details of construction and roof framing of a medium sized gambrel roof dairy barn with self-supporting roof so that the hay space is unobstructed by beams or posts.

Also cross section of one story cow stable equipped with feed and manure overhead track carriers. Note sanitary, continuous moulded cement floor for mangers, stalls, gutters, etc.

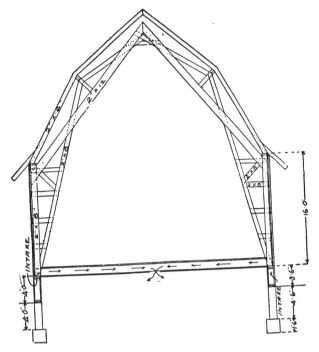

## SELF-SUPPORTING ROOF, CENTER BENT

Diagrams showing the construction of the model dairy barn recently erected at the Wisconsin State Fair Grounds. Note also fresh air intake and ventilating system for ventilating the basement.

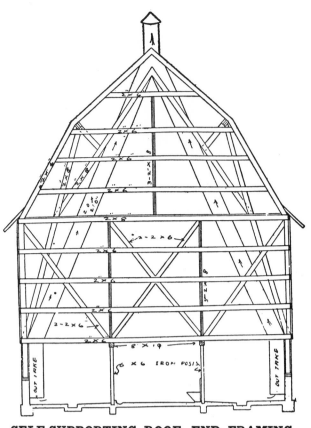

## SELF-SUPPORTING ROOF, END FRAMING

Diagrams showing the end construction together with improved method of ventilating used in the Wisconsin model dairy barn erected at the State Fair. This barn is thirty by eight feet in size.

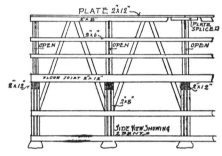

SIDE WALL FRAMING

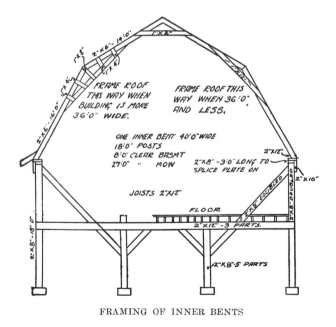

FRAMING OF INNER BENTS

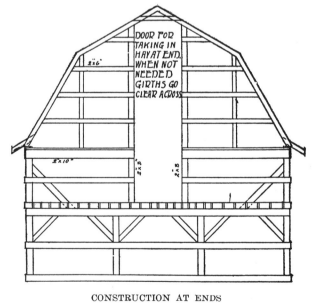

CONSTRUCTION AT ENDS

## PLATE 167—PLANK FRAMING AND SELF-SUPPORTING ROOFS FOR BARNS

Diagrams showing end framing, center bent construction and side wall framing for the "Wing" system of joist frame barn building. Side walls should be 18 to 20 feet high; and unless the barn is to be more than 50 feet wide no purlin posts are needed, the roof being safe when rightly framed with the supplemental truss beneath the gambrel roof angle.

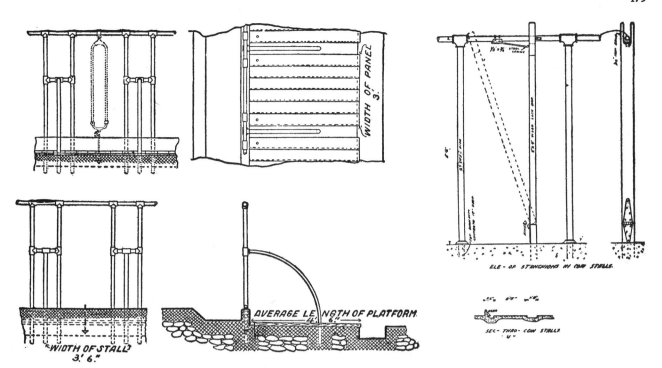

## PLATE 168 B—SANITARY AND HUMANE COW STALLS

Details of cow stall and stanchion arrangement recommended by the Dairy Division of the U. S. Department of Agriculture. The stalls are of concrete with iron pipe fittings. The dimensions are suitable for cows of average size. The stalls are provided with a movable wooden floor; the advantages of this will be appreciated by those who find the uncovered cement too cold for the best comfort of the cows during cold weather. The wooden platform is kept in place by two iron pins set in the cement floor near the front corners of the stall in such a way that the floor panel can easily be removed for cleaning. To the right another form of stanchion is detailed.

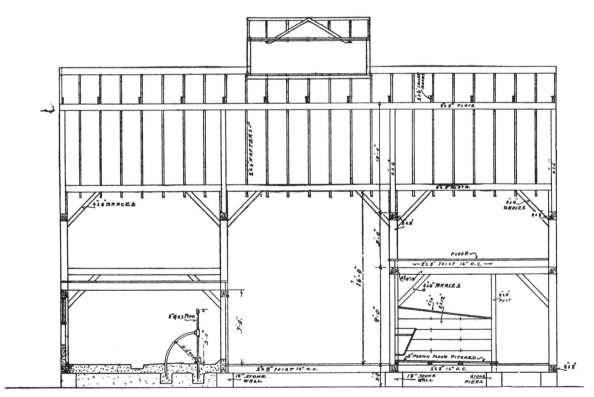

SECTION THROUGH RIDGE

## PLATE 168 A—HEAVY TIMBER BARN FRAMING

Section through ridge of barn showing typical heavy timber framing with all members mortised and tenoned. Sills and main posts are 8 by 8 inches, purlin posts and long braces 6 by 6 inches, short braces 4 by 4 inches, plate and purlins 6 by 8 inches, rafters and collar beams 2 by 6 inches and floor joists 2 by 8 inches, 16 inches on centers. Stalls are each side of central drive way.

180

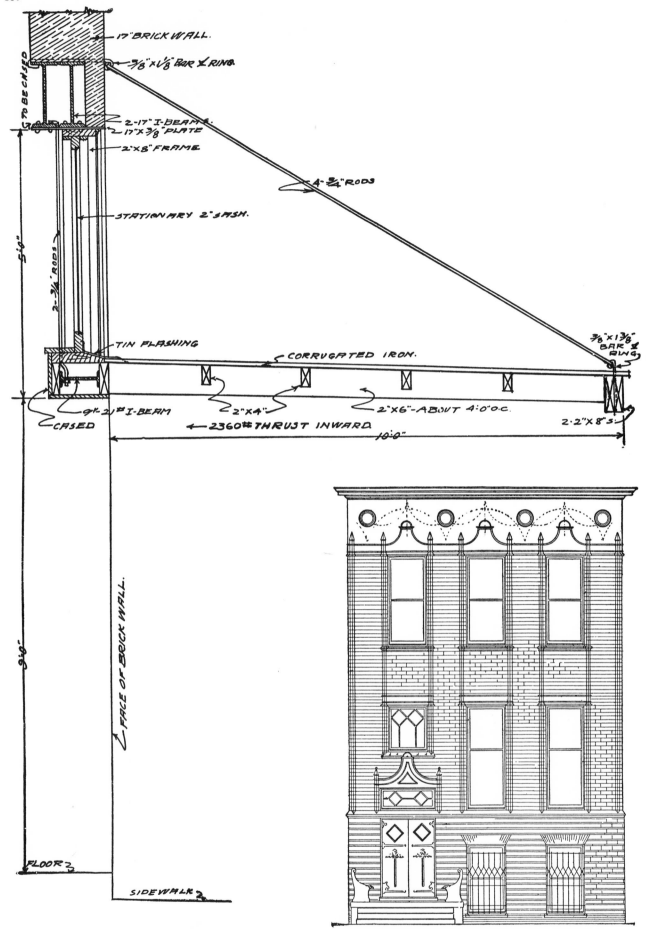

**PLATE 169—METAL AWNING FOR STORE FRONT**

Cross section of metal awning and of store front showing method of awning support. The awning is ten feet wide over the sidewalk and is supported by four iron rods. With the awning constructed of corrugated iron and for a store front 25 feet wide, a 9 inch, 21 lb. I-beam will be needed, built into the brick piers to take the thrust. Two three-quarter-inch rods connected to the main I-beams supporting the wall above would prevent sagging.

Note small sketch showing elevation of an old frame building remodeled by the use of tile veneering. For working details of this method, see Plate 170.

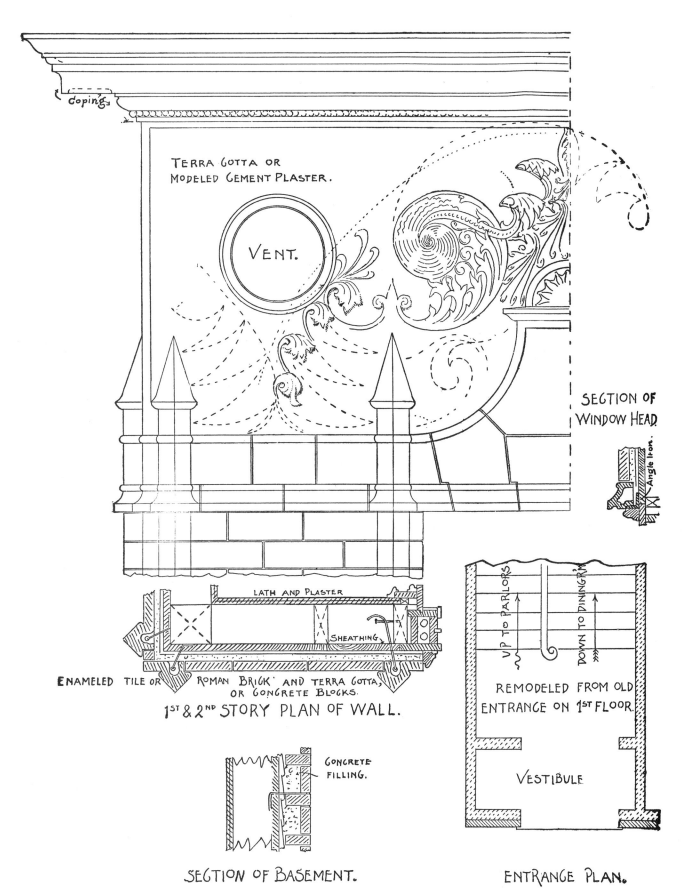

Coping.

TERRA COTTA OR
MODELED CEMENT PLASTER.

VENT.

SECTION OF
WINDOW HEAD

Angle Iron.

LATH AND PLASTER

SHEATHING

ENAMELED TILE OR ROMAN BRICK AND TERRA COTTA,
OR CONCRETE BLOCKS.

1ST & 2ND STORY PLAN OF WALL.

CONCRETE
FILLING.

UP TO PARLORS

DOWN TO DINING RM.

REMODELED FROM OLD
ENTRANCE ON 1ST FLOOR.

VESTIBULE

SECTION OF BASEMENT.

ENTRANCE PLAN.

## PLATE 170—REMODELING FRAME BUILDINGS WITH TILE VENEER

Details of construction of the remodeling job shown in front elevation in Plate 169. To remodel one of the typical, old style frame buildings in this manner, it is first necessary to do away with the old high steps, bringing the entrance down almost to grade and arranging for the stairway inside. The veneering is to be of enameled tile or brick or of concrete blocks, just as desired. The vertical projecting courses of the veneering are anchored to the sheathing boards, and the panel slabs are held by the cement plaster backing.

ELEVATION

SUGGESTED DESIGN FOR SIMPLE FRONT

CONSTRUCTION OF ELEVATED FLOOR

DETAIL OF FLOOR AT THE REAR AISLE

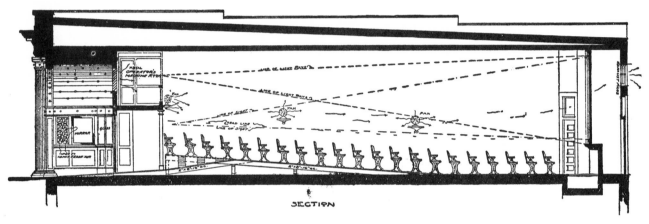

SECTION

SECTION SHOWING SLOPING FALSE FLOOR—NOTICE PICTURE AND SIGHT LINES

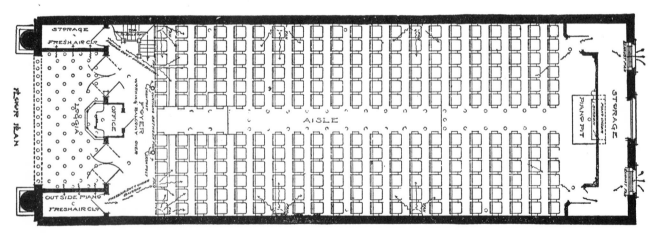

FLOOR PLAN SHOWING ALSO ARRANGEMENT OF LIGHTS AND OF VENTILATORS

## PLATE 171—REMODELING STORES INTO SMALL THEATRES

Almost all towns, no matter how small, now have or soon will have a moving picture theatre. The majority of these places find quarters in store rooms, which are required to be remodeled for this use. The room should be at least 18 or 20 feet wide and 60 feet long, the ideal size being 24 by 90 feet. The ceiling height is important on account of ventilation and should be 14 feet, though 16 or 18 feet is better. The room should have side or rear exits which must be marked and the doors hung so as to open out. The store front is always removed and the room closed in with a partition placed about 14 feet back from the front. This gives the wide vestibule which is so necessary in an attractive place. The floor plan shows a good arrangement for an up-to-date moving picture house. Note that each aisle is marked by a small red light placed under glass in the floor. The piano pit is placed below the level of the floor to keep the player out of the line of vision. The sectional view gives a good idea of the raised floor, balcony and ticket office. It will be noticed that the three rows of seats at the rear are above the level of the main aisle.

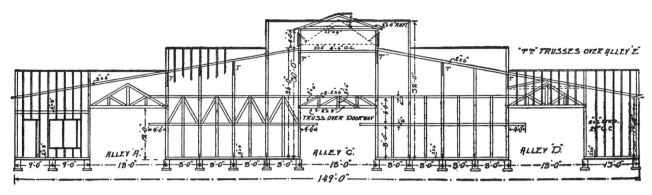

FRONT ELEVATION

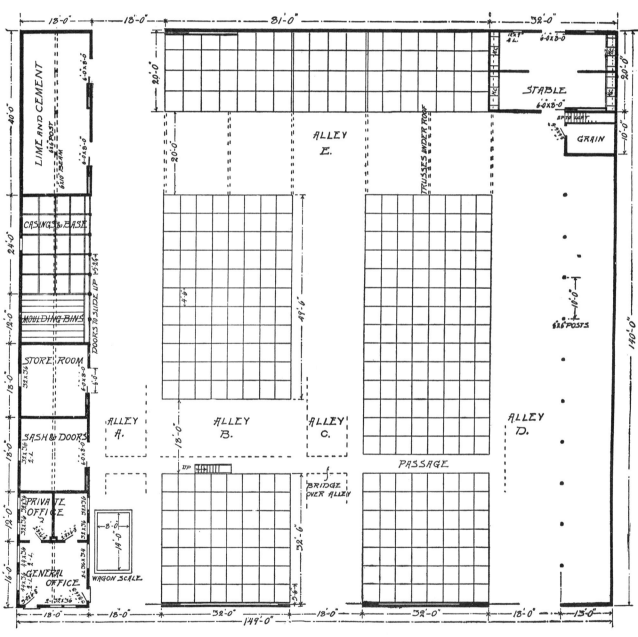

GROUND PLAN

## PLATE 172—PLANS FOR LUMBER AND SUPPLY BUILDING

Ground floor plan and front elevation showing arrangement and method of construction for a large, well-planned builders' supply depot. The stock accommodated includes a general lumber line, sash and doors, lime, cement, brick, etc. The moulding bins are provided with tight doors so that this stock is kept in the very best condition. The arrangement of this depot is ideal.

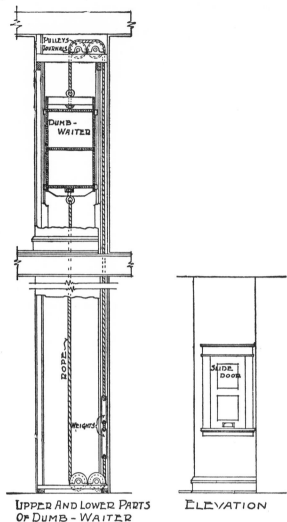

UPPER AND LOWER PARTS
OF DUMB-WAITER

ELEVATION

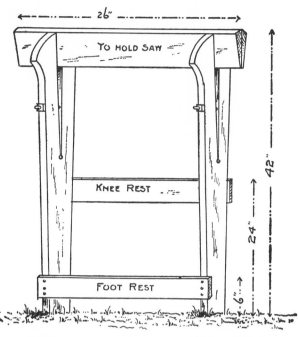

## HANDY CLAMP FOR SAW SHARPENING

The side pieces are of 2 by 4's about four feet long, ripped to form the shape. The jaws are 1 by 4 inches, 26 inches long, and are shaped to fit into the side pieces. The bolts adjust the opening in the side pieces so that the jaws will not clamp down too far. These jaws hold the saw securely while being sharpened.

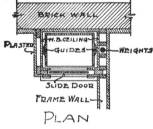

PLAN

## ARRANGEMENT FOR DUMB WAITERS

Hand elevators, or dumb waiters, are of various patterns or designs; yet, in general the idea is the same in all and the drawings herewith will show the methods of finishing the elevator shafting, arranging the sliding doors, etc.

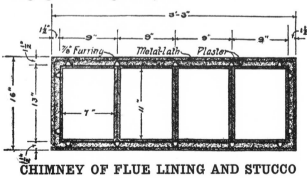

## CHIMNEY OF FLUE LINING AND STUCCO

Terra Cotta flue lining is laid in cement mortar and the outside surfaces covered with metal lath furred out with metal furring. To this lath is applied a heavy coat of cement mortar,—one part cement, one-half part lime, five parts sand. Two or three coats are applied until the total thickness of terra cotta and cement is 2½ inches.

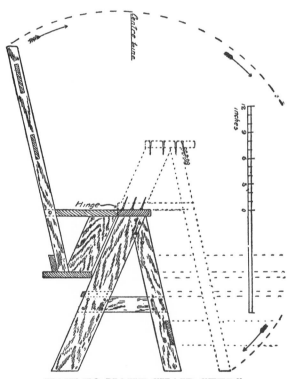

## HOW TO MAKE CHAIR STEPS

The step portion should be made first and after it is completed the seat portion can be marked out and made. The joints are of the simplest character, including the mortise and tenon, half lap and the housing joint. Screws are used to secure these. By the use of the graphic scale shown, the dimensions of all parts can be found.

## PLATE 173—WORTH-WHILE METHODS AND DEVICES

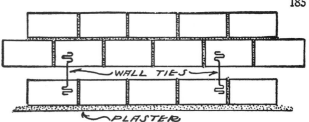

## BRICK WALL WITH AIR SPACE

Cross section of hollow brick wall, 8 inches outside and 4 inches inside with a 2 inch air space, bonded with metal wall ties every fifth course of brick. Since no moisture can penetrate through such a wall across this air space, the plaster can be applied direct to the inside face of the wall without the use of furring.

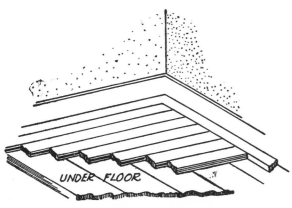

## THIN OAK FLOORING OVER OLD FLOORS

Frequently thin ⅜ inch oak flooring is desired to be put down over old soft wood floors. The sketch shows the method; the thin oak flooring runs in the opposite direction from the boards in the old floor. It is not necessary to disturb the interior trim in any way, except the shoe mould.

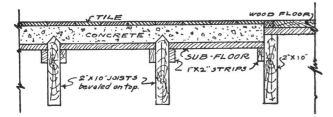

## FRAMING FOR TILE FLOOR

It is often necessary to lay a tile or mosaic floor in rooms where wood joists are used. This detail shows the best method of construction for this work. The tops of all the joists under the cement foundation are beveled to prevent the concrete from cracking.

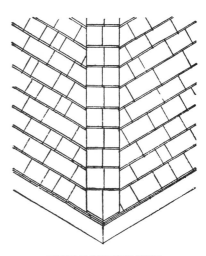

## THE BOSTON HIP

The sketch shows a shingled hip viewed from above. It is formed by laying a double row of shingles lengthwise along the hip, fitting them carefully so as to make a water tight job. These hip shingles are nailed on after all the rest of the shingling is done. The middle joint alternates from one side to the other along the hip.

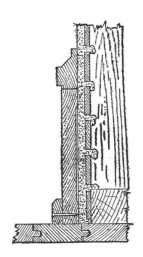
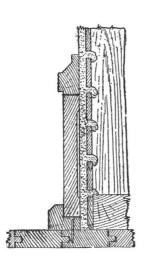
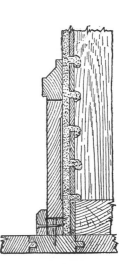

## PLATE 174—MOULD TO HIDE FLOOR LINE JOINT

Three methods for putting down base and shoe mould. The first arrangement shows the mould nailed to the base; when the floor joists shrink a crack shows between the bottom of the moulding and the floor. In the second arrangement the base is set into a shoe which is nailed to the floor; shrinkage of the floor joists does not in this case disclose a crack; yet, all the members should be painted and varnished before being nailed down, or a line of unfinished wood will show. The third arrangement accomplishes the same result in a slightly different manner.

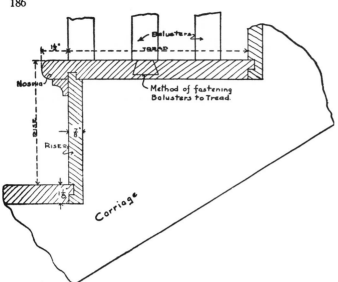

## JOINTS USED IN STAIR BUILDING

Details showing clearly the various parts of the stair, together with the joints used in fastening them together.

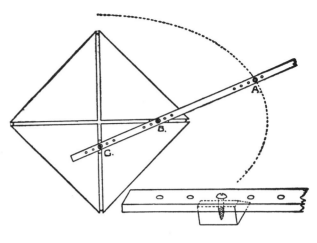

## TRAMMEL FOR STRIKING ELLIPSES

Grooves are made in a large square board from corner to corner. Small hardwood blocks travel in these grooves. The blocks are adjustable for various sizes of ellipses. The distance "A-C" represents one-half the long diameter and the distance "A-B" one-half the short diameter. A pencil point fixed at "A" scribes the ellipse.

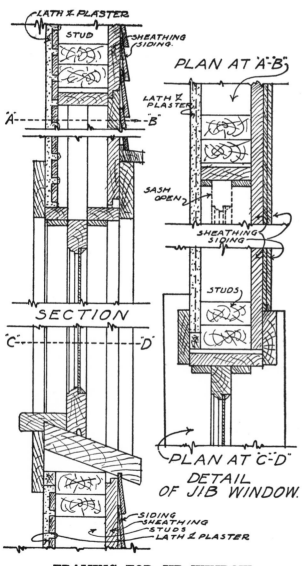

## FRAMING FOR JIB WINDOW

Details for a single sash window arranged to slide up out of sight. The side jambs run up past the head the length of the sash to keep it in place when raised.

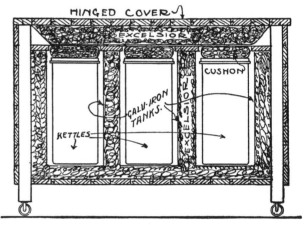

## HOME-MADE FIRELESS COOKER

The cross section shows the arrangement and method of construction for a fireless cooker. Dimensions will depend upon the size of the kettles to be used.

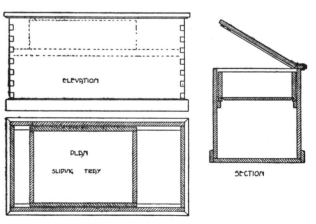

## MOTH-PROOF CEDAR CHEST

Elevation, plan and section of a well made cedar chest. The overlocking lid joint keeps out dust, and the aromatic odor of the wood will keep the moths away. The interior of the box should not be varnished or oiled.

**PLATE 175—USEFUL DETAILS FOR BUILDERS**

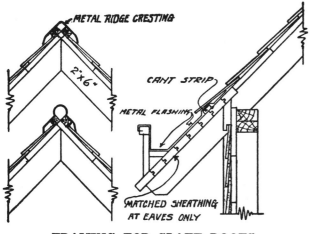

## FRAMING FOR SLATE ROOFS

Roofs to be covered with slate should be sheathed with surfaced boards from six to ten inches wide, the sheathing at the eaves to be matched lumber. For rafters 18 feet long, set 2 feet from centers, 2 by 6 pieces are strong enough for a slate roof. Three-penny galvanized or tinned nails with flat heads are usually used for slate, up to and including twenty inches in length.

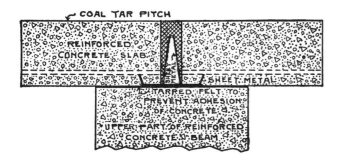

EXPANSION JOINT IN CONCRETE ROOFING.

## REINFORCED CONCRETE ROOFING

The detail for expansion joint for reinforced concrete roof construction shows a fold of sheet metal imbedded at each end into the concrete. This allows flexibility without giving a direct opening of any kind through the roof at the joint. The space above the metal is filled with coal tar pitch.

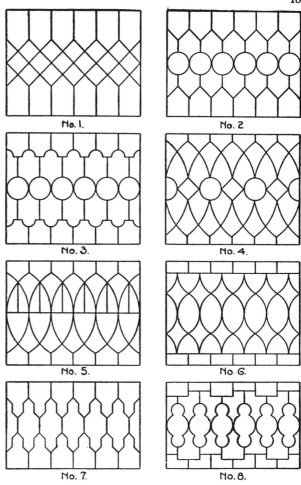

## ORNAMENTAL WOOD SHINGLING

Where ornamental shingling is desired one is apt to use simply the common hexagonal checker board style. These details show many other styles which will give a variety. In the ornamental schemes illustrated the number of different patterns required for each, counting the straight end butts as one, are as follows: No. 1, two; No. 2, four; No. 3, five; No. 4, eight; No. 5, six; No. 6, three; No. 7, three; and No. 8, three.

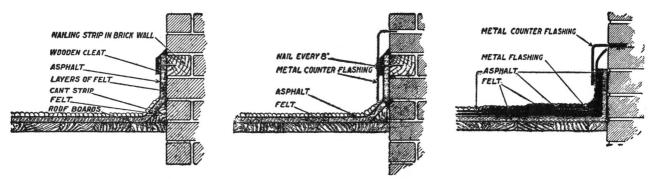

## PLATE 176—DETAILS OF ROOF CONSTRUCTION

Approved construction at the fire wall joint for tar and gravel flat roofs. The arrangements are detailed, ranging from the low-cost to the most expensive.

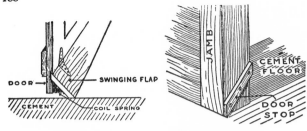

## SNOW-PROOF GARAGE DOOR

To make the wide swinging doors for garages snow-proof, the door is rabbeted out about two inches from the bottom to receive a swinging flap which is held tightly down, when the door is closed, by strips nailed to each jamb; when the door is opened the coil springs behind the flap raise it one-half inch from the floor, making it swing clear. When the door is closed the flap is forced down tight against the floor.

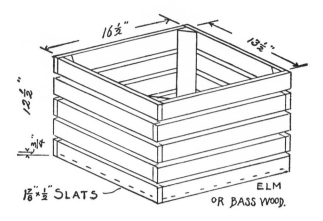

## A FARMER'S BUSHEL MEASURE

A bushel crate is a handy article; it should be made of strong light-weight wood. The dimensions given will make it an even bushel measure. The nails should be clinched so that it will be strong enough to be thrown about without coming to pieces.

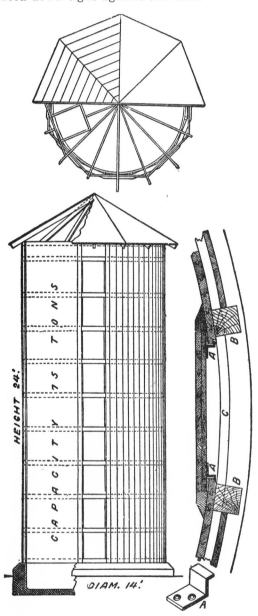

## INEXPENSIVE STAVE SILO

Design and details for a 75-ton stave silo with wooden hoops. Four thicknesses of tough one-half inch lumber are used in building up the three or four hoops nearest the bottom and three thicknesses for the rest of the hoops. The lining is of 7/8 inch matched lumber. Door detail is shown; A A A, clips bolted to door; B B, door posts; C, wooden hoop.

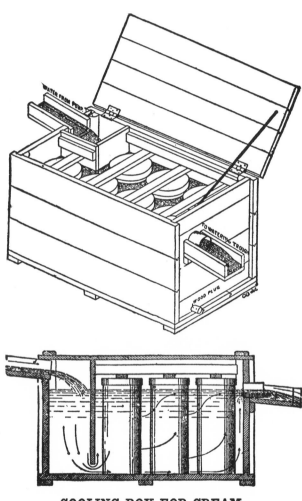

## COOLING BOX FOR CREAM

Perspective view and cross section showing arrangement and construction of a cooler to be installed between pump and watering trough. It is stated that by taking proper care of the separator cream during the period between shipments, much better cream is secured, commanding a higher price. The box should be constructed of tongued and grooved yellow pine, one inch and a half in thickness. A little cotton or white lead should be placed in all joints before the boards are fastened together so that there will be no leaking after the box has once become water soaked. The cans are the tall, narrow shotgun can, 8 inches in diameter, and 20 inches high.

## PLATE 177—DETAILS FOR THE COUNTRY CARPENTER

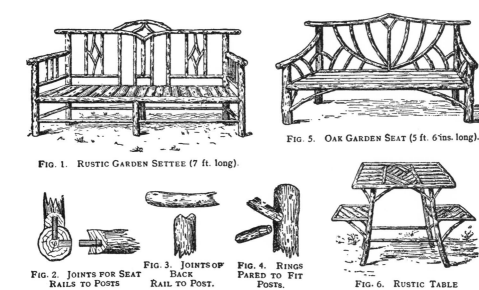

FIG. 1. RUSTIC GARDEN SETTEE (7 ft. long).

FIG. 5. OAK GARDEN SEAT (5 ft. 6 ins. long).

FIG. 2. JOINTS FOR SEAT RAILS TO POSTS

FIG. 3. JOINTS OF BACK RAIL TO POST.

FIG. 4. RINGS PARED TO FIT POSTS.

FIG. 6. RUSTIC TABLE

## PLATE 178 B—RUSTIC GARDEN FURNITURE

A branch of carpentry usually considered difficult and for the "specialist" only is rustic work. In reality, however, it is simple and the joints are easily made. Three good designs with details for their construction are shown. When nailing up rustic work, holes should be bored for all nails. This will prevent the wood from splitting. It is also wise to hold a weight against the portion to be nailed to relieve the jar of hammering on the parts already connected.

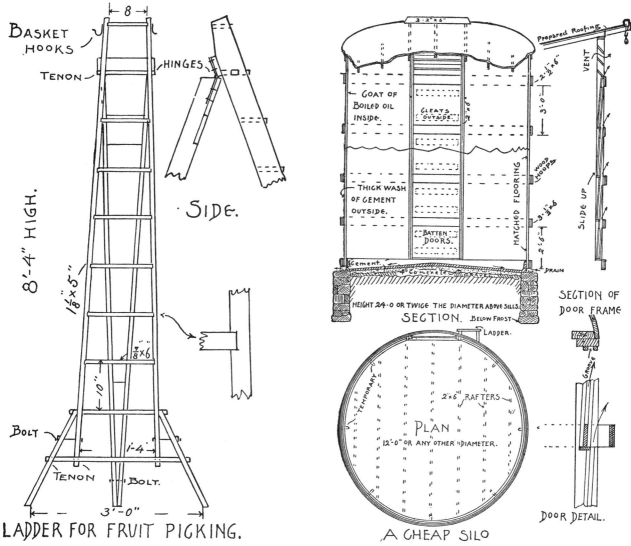

LADDER FOR FRUIT PICKING.

A CHEAP SILO

## PLATE 178 A—DETAILS FOR THE COUNTRY CARPENTER

Design and details of a special step ladder for picking fruit. The support behind is narrow so that it can be thrust in among the branches. This necessitates a wide front splayed out, as shown in the diagram. The farmer saves time by having special articles like this to work with and accomplishes more than where some temporary rig is improvised. Plan, elevation and details of construction of a cheap wood silo are shown. One-half by six inch wood strips are used for the hoops; and the staves are narrow matched flooring, or of special thicker material worked out on a curve for this particular purpose. Silo rests on a low foundation; floor is concrete.

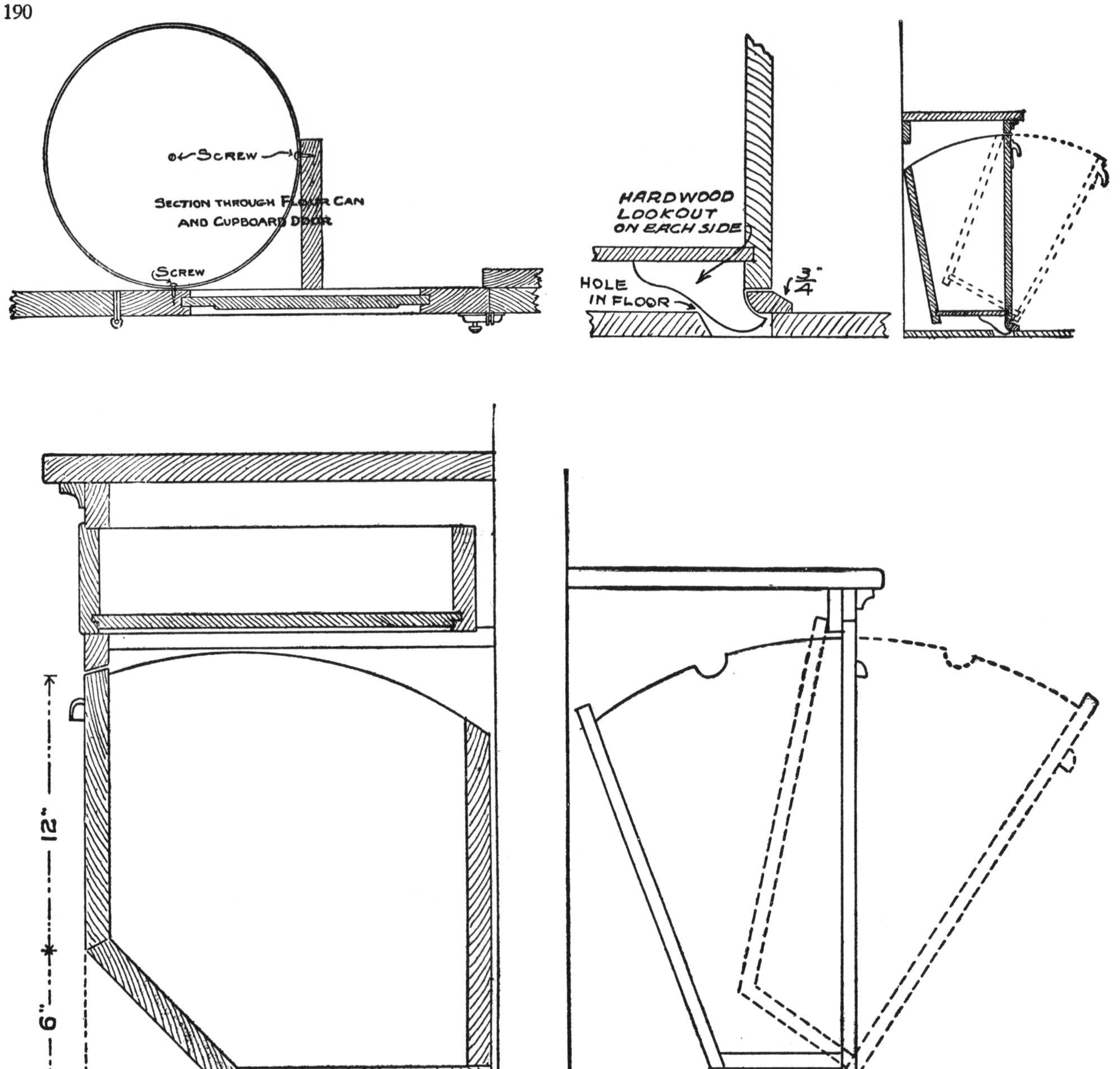

O screw

SECTION THROUGH FLOUR CAN
AND CUPBOARD DOOR

SCREW

HARDWOOD
LOOKOUT
ON EACH SIDE

HOLE
IN FLOOR

3/4"

12"

6"

6"     12"

A

**PLATE 179—FLOUR BINS**

Details showing the construction and arrangement of six tilting flour bins and of one flour can, to be
attached to the inside of a swinging cupboard door.

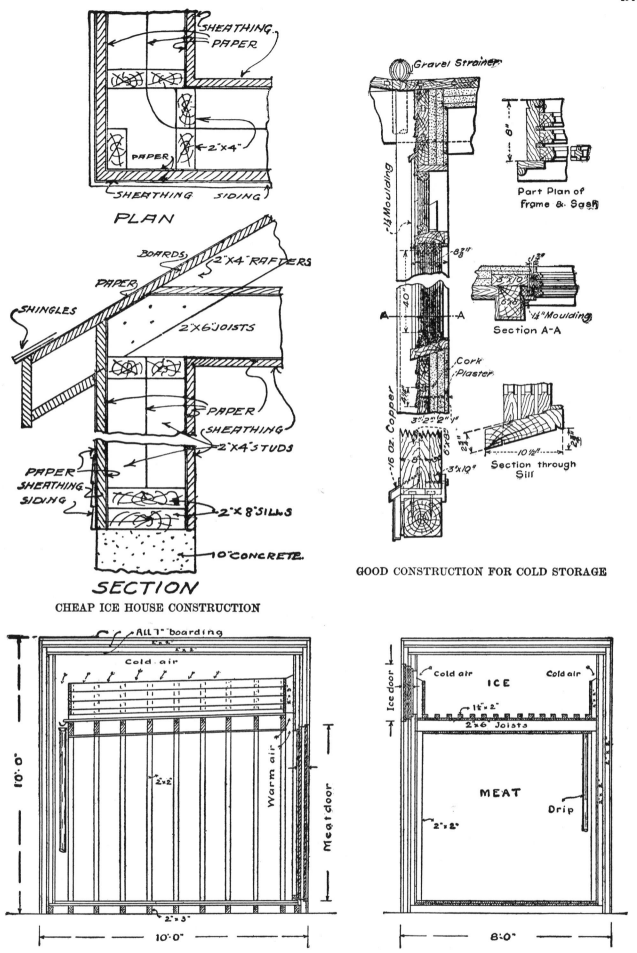

PLAN

SHEATHING
PAPER

PAPER

2"x4"

SHEATHING    SIDING

Gravel Strainer

Part Plan of
Frame & Sash

Section A-A

Cork
Plaster

Section through
Sill

GOOD CONSTRUCTION FOR COLD STORAGE

BOARDS
2"x4" RAFTERS
PAPER
SHINGLES
2"x6"JOISTS
PAPER
SHEATHING
2"x4"STUDS
PAPER
SHEATHING
SIDING
2"x8"SILLS
10"CONCRETE.

SECTION

CHEAP ICE HOUSE CONSTRUCTION

ALL 1" boarding
Cold air
Warm air
2"x2"
Meat door
2"x3"
10'-0"
10'-0"

Ice door
Cold air    ICE    Cold air
1½"x 2"
2x6 Joists
MEAT
Drip
2"x 2"
8'-0"

**PLATE 180—CONSTRUCTION FOR COLD STORAGE**

Sectional views showing arrangement and construction of a small refrigerator room for a meat market. The walls are built with three layers of one-inch boarding which provide two dead air spaces. The ice is put in the overhead compartment, while the meat or other food stuffs are placed below. Vents are arranged as shown to provide for a circulation of cold air. Windows should be triple glazed. Another type of good cold storage construction is also detailed; also wall sections of a small ice house, showing recommended construction at sill, plate and corner.

192

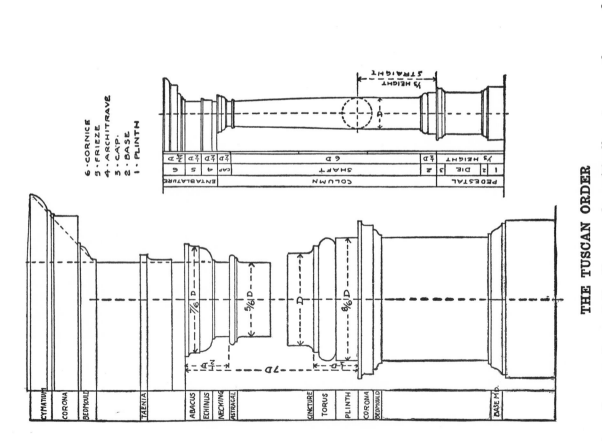

## THE TUSCAN ORDER

Parts and proportions of the Tuscan order, with all parts correctly named. In this as in all other of the classic orders, the diameter, "D," of the column at the base is used as the unit of measurement for all other parts of the column pedestal and entablature. Whatever the size of the column, proportions should be the same. The Tuscan is one of the Roman orders and is the simplest, being perfectly plain.

## THE DORIC ORDER

Parts and proportions of the Doric order. There are two types of cornices used with the Doric order, one with the mutules, or projecting flat blocks ornamented on the under surface; and the other with dentils, a course of small cubes in the bed moulding. The general profile of the cornice is different in the two types. In the Greek Doric the shaft is fluted and there is no pedestal.

## PLATE 181—ORDERS OF ARCHITECTURE

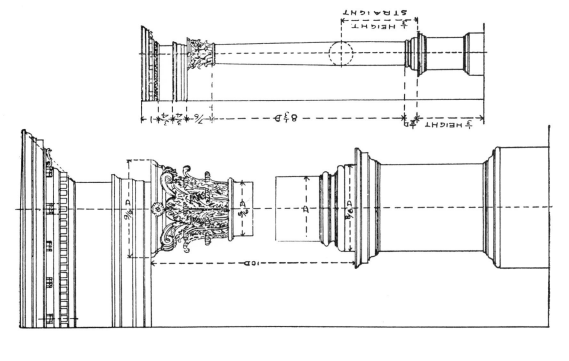

## THE CORINTHIAN ORDER

Parts and proportions for the Corinthian order. The main difference between this and the Ionic is the capital, which is highly ornamented by means of acanthus leaves. This order is considered the most dignified and is also the most expensive. Sometimes the shaft is fluted; the mouldings are all greatly ornamented, even more so than in the Ionic order.

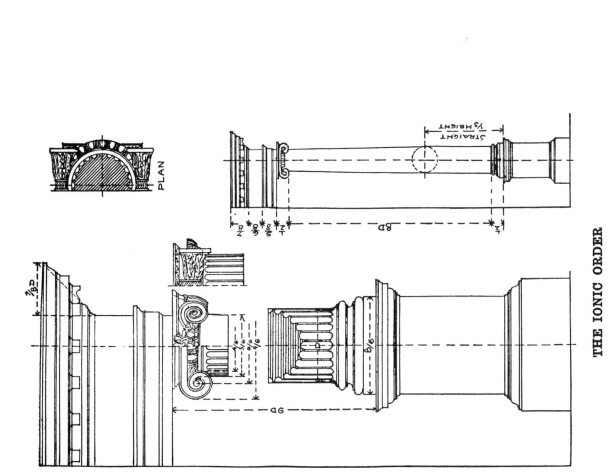

## THE IONIC ORDER

Parts and proportions of the Ionic order. The cornice may have brackets, called modillions, as illustrated; or it may have the dentils. The capital in this order is of two kinds; one is the cushion capital and is used on the inside pillars of a colonnade; the other has the volutes turned at an angle of 45 degrees, thus making all faces alike. These are for corner columns.

## PLATE 182—ORDERS OF ARCHITECTURE

194

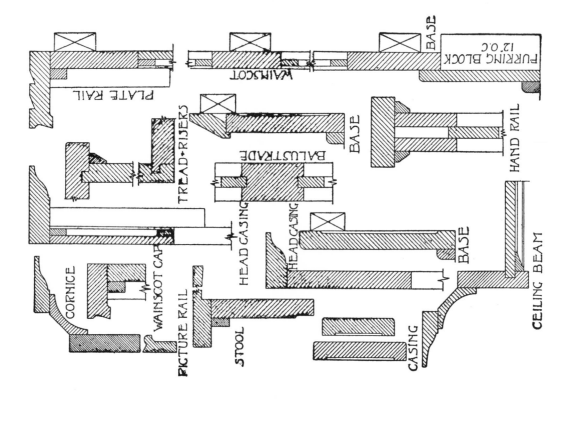

**PLATE 183 B—INTERIOR TRIM MEMBERS NAMED**

Reproduction of a sheet of full sized details giving the names and shapes of all the parts of regular inside trim.

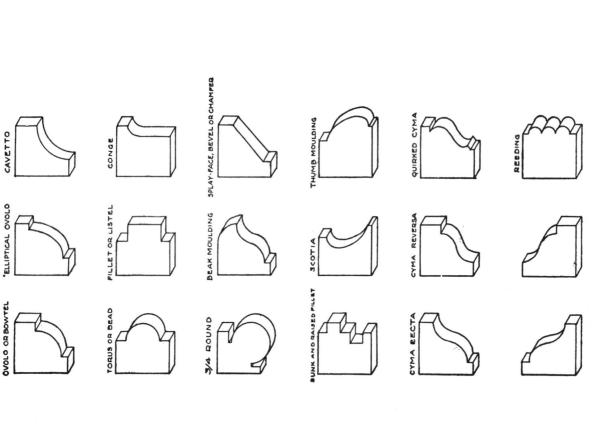

**PLATE 183 A—COMMON FORMS OF CLASSIC MOULDINGS**

Sketches showing the shapes and correct names of the well known classic mouldings. Various colloquial terms are in use for many of these.

# INDEX

196 INDEX